CONSCIENTIOUS OBJECTION IN HEALTH CARE

Historically associated with military service, conscientious objection has become a significant phenomenon in health care. Mark R. Wicclair offers a comprehensive ethical analysis of conscientious objection in three representative health care professions: medicine, nursing, and pharmacy. He critically examines two extreme positions: the "incompatibility thesis," which holds that it is contrary to the professional obligations of practitioners to refuse provision of any service within the scope of their professional competence; and "conscience absolutism," which holds that they should be exempted from performing any action contrary to their conscience. He argues for a compromise approach that accommodates conscience-based refusals within the limits of specified ethical constraints. He also explores conscientious objection by students in each of the three professions, discusses conscience protection legislation and conscience-based refusals by pharmacies and hospitals, and analyzes several cases. His book will be a valuable resource for scholars, professionals, trainees, students, and anyone interested in this increasingly important aspect of health care.

MARK R. WICCLAIR is Professor of Philosophy and Adjunct Professor of Community Medicine at West Virginia University and Adjunct Professor of Medicine, Center for Bioethics and Health Law, University of Pittsburgh. He is the author of *Ethics and the Elderly* (1993).

CONSCIENTIOUS OBJECTION IN HEALTH CARE

An Ethical Analysis

MARK R. WICCLAIR

CAMBRIDGE
UNIVERSITY PRESS

CAMBRIDGE UNIVERSITY PRESS
Cambridge, New York, Melbourne, Madrid, Cape Town,
Singapore, São Paulo, Delhi, Tokyo, Mexico City

Cambridge University Press
The Edinburgh Building, Cambridge CB2 8RU, UK

Published in the United States of America by Cambridge University Press, New York

www.cambridge.org
Information on this title: www.cambridge.org/9780521514316

© Mark R. Wicclair 2011

This publication is in copyright. Subject to statutory exception
and to the provisions of relevant collective licensing agreements,
no reproduction of any part may take place without the written
permission of Cambridge University Press.

First published 2011

Printed in the United Kingdom at the University Press, Cambridge

A catalogue record for this publication is available from the British Library

Library of Congress Cataloguing in Publication data
Wicclair, Mark R., 1944– author.
Conscientious objection in health care : an ethical analysis / Mark R. Wicclair.
p.   cm.
Includes bibliographical references and index.
ISBN 978-0-521-51431-6 (hardback) – ISBN 978-0-521-73543-8 (pbk.)   1. Medical
ethics.   2. Conscientious objection.   3. Refusal to treat.   I. Title.
[DNLM: 1. Ethics, Clinical.   2. Refusal to Treat – ethics.   3. Conscience.   4. Delivery
of Health Care – ethics. WB 60]
R725.5.W53   2011
174.2–dc22
2010048731

ISBN 978-0-521-51431-6 Hardback
ISBN 978-0-521-73543-8 Paperback

Cambridge University Press has no responsibility for the persistence or
accuracy of URLs for external or third-party internet websites referred to
in this publication, and does not guarantee that any content on such
websites is, or will remain, accurate or appropriate.

For Lucy and David

Contents

Preface

The subject of this book is conscientious objection in health care. Although conscientious objection historically has been associated with military service, it has become a significant phenomenon in health care. Some physicians, nurses, and pharmacists have refused to provide or assist in providing goods and services for reasons of conscience. Many of these conscience-based refusals are related to the perennial and sometimes controversial issues of sex/reproduction and death. Examples in the former category include abortion, sterilization, contraception, and assisted reproduction. Examples in the latter category include palliative sedation (the practice of sedating terminally ill patients to unconsciousness until death) and forgoing medically provided nutrition and hydration. Novel technologies, procedures, and therapeutic measures also have occasioned conscience-based refusals by health care professionals, and can be expected to do so in the future. Recent examples include conscience-based objections to participation in embryonic stem cell research, genetic testing and counseling, and donation after cardiac death (retrieving organs after life support has been withdrawn from patients who do not satisfy the neurological or whole brain criterion of death).

In this book, I offer an ethical analysis of conscientious objection in three representative health care professions: medicine, nursing, and pharmacy. There are several reasons for considering these three professions together. First, from the perspective of conscientious objection, the three professions are interdependent. On the one hand, physician conscience-based objections can affect the practice of pharmacists and nurses. On the other hand, conscience-based objections by pharmacists and nurses can affect physicians insofar as they rely on pharmacists to fill prescriptions and nurses to implement care plans. Second, many conceptual and ethical questions and issues related to conscientious objection are similar for each of the three professions. For example, no matter the profession, it is essential to understand what distinguishes refusals that are conscience-based from those that are not and to identify the ethical reasons for accommodating conscience-based refusals. These are among the topics that I explore in Chapter 1. Third, since there is considerable overlap in the core professional obligations of physicians, nurses, and pharmacists, similar ethical guidelines apply to conscience-based refusals by practitioners in each of the three health care professions.

This work is the culmination of a project that began about ten years ago when I wrote my first article on the subject of conscientious objection in health care (Wicclair 2000). My interest in the subject was stimulated by what struck me at the time as a paradox. Ethical guidelines on forgoing life-sustaining treatment issued by a number of recognized professional bodies such as the President's Commission for the Study of Ethical Problems in Medicine and Biomedical and Behavioral Research (President's Commission for the Study of Ethical Problems in Medicine and Biomedical and Behavioral Research 1983), The Hastings Center (Anonymous 1987), and the American Thoracic Society (American Thoracic Society 1991) stated that practitioners were not obligated to follow those guidelines if they did not accept them because of their personal ethical or religious beliefs. I observed a similar phenomenon in relation to hospital policies. When ethics committees on which I served formulated a policy, it was standard practice to grant an exemption to practitioners with conscience-based objections. At the time, I was puzzled by the seemingly inconsistent message about ethical standards and obligations. On the one hand, a guideline or policy might leave no doubt that option x (e.g. forgoing life-sustaining treatment) is the ethically right option in certain contexts. On the other hand, by allowing health care professionals to refuse to effect option x if they have conscience-based objections, the guidelines seemed to permit practitioners to refuse to do the right thing. If option x in a certain context is the ethically right option, then doesn't it follow that health care professionals are ethically obligated to bring it about? Shouldn't guidelines and policies insist that everyone – regardless of their personal ethical or religious beliefs – do the right thing?

I have come to recognize that this framing of the issue is overly simplistic. From an ethical perspective, option x may be the ethically right option for a patient. However, securing option x for the patient may not require that a particular health care professional effectuate it. For example, suppose the ethically right option for a patient is to withdraw medically provided nutrition and hydration (MPNH). Depending on the circumstances, however, effectuating that option and providing appropriate medical care may not require the attending physician to personally manage the withdrawal of MPNH and the subsequent care of the patient. All that may be required is for the attending physician to refrain from providing inappropriate care, withdraw from the case, and facilitate a transfer of the patient to a physician who is willing to withdraw MPNH and manage the patient's subsequent care. Accordingly, it may be possible to achieve the ethically right outcome for the patient without compromising a practitioner's conscience. A key question, then, is whether accommodating health care professionals' conscience-based refusals when it does not prevent a patient from receiving ethically appropriate medical care from another practitioner is compatible with the professional obligations of physicians and other health care providers.

Conceptions of professional obligations in relation to conscience-based refusals fall within a continuum. At one extreme, advocates of what I refer to as the "incompatibility thesis" maintain that it is contrary to the professional obligations of physicians, nurses, and pharmacists to refuse to provide any legal good or service within the scope of their professional competence. At the other extreme, advocates of what I refer to as "conscience absolutism" maintain that health care professionals should be exempted from performing any action that is contrary to their conscience, including providing information and referrals. I criticize both of these extremes and defend a compromise approach that provides some accommodation for conscience-based refusals but only within the limits of specified ethical constraints. According to the compromise approach I advocate, when a health care professional refuses to provide or assist in providing a legal good or service within the scope of her competence for reasons of conscience, the refusal is compatible with the practitioner's professional obligations only if it does not present an excessive impediment to a patient's timely and convenient access to the good or service. I now believe that this compromise approach satisfactorily addresses the aforementioned paradox.

I consider several possible accounts of the professional obligations of physicians, nurses, and pharmacists in Chapter 2, and I argue that conscience absolutism is incompatible with most, if not all, of those accounts; none unequivocally supports the incompatibility thesis; and most, if not all, favor a compromise approach. I present and defend a compromise approach in Chapter 3. Practitioners within each of the three professions have core professional obligations that provide the basis for constraints on the exercise of conscience. These include an obligation to respect patient dignity and refrain from discrimination, an obligation to promote patient health and well-being, and an obligation to respect patient autonomy. These core professional obligations justify limitations on the exercise of conscience in relation to discrimination, patient harms and burdens, disclosing options, referral and/or facilitating a transfer, and advance notification. Determining whether the corresponding ethical constraints are satisfied in particular cases is in part context-dependent. For example, whether or not a burden or harm is *excessive* depends in part on the seriousness and urgency of the medical condition and the timely availability of other providers. In Chapter 3, I illustrate the context-dependent nature of ethical constraints on the exercise of conscience by applying them to several cases.

Beyond their obligations to patients, health care professionals have obligations to colleagues, other professionals, and employers. I also examine these obligations in Chapter 3; they justify additional ethical constraints on the exercise of conscience by physicians, nurses, and pharmacists.

Conscience-based refusals have not been limited to individual practitioners. Pharmacies and health care institutions (e.g. hospitals) have also cited ethical and/or religious beliefs to justify refusing to provide a good or service. For example, pharmacies and hospitals have refused to stock and dispense emergency contraception (EC), and hospitals have refused to permit abortions, sterilization procedures, and forgoing MPNH. I examine refusals by pharmacy licensees and hospitals in Chapter 4, and I argue that such refusals also are subject to context-dependent ethical constraints.

Students of medicine, nursing, and pharmacy and residents can object to participating in educational activities for reasons of conscience. In Chapter 5, I present reasons for offering conscience-based exemptions to students and residents. I also identify several ethical constraints on such exemptions.

The primary focus of the book is on ethics. Accordingly, with the exception of the final chapter (Chapter 6), I do not address the legal rights and obligations of health care professionals in relation to conscientious objection. In that chapter, I consider so-called "conscience clauses," which offer legal protections to health care professionals who refuse to provide goods or services for reasons of conscience. Somewhat paradoxically, I argue, conscience clauses offer both too much and too little protection of conscience. They offer too much protection insofar as they do not apply the ethical constraints that I present in Chapter 3. They offer too little protection insofar as they protect only conscience-based *refusals* and do not accommodate health care professionals who believe that they have a conscience-based obligation to provide a good or service that is prohibited by legal and/or institutional rules.

Given the importance of the issue and the interest it has sparked, it is not surprising that there is a substantial amount of literature in each of the three professions on conscientious objection. However, my primary aim is to offer a sustained account of a justifiable approach to conscientious refusals by physicians, nurses, and pharmacists, and not to provide a comprehensive review of the conscientious objection literature in each profession. Accordingly, uncited works do not reflect a judgment that they are unimportant or without merit. Rather, their omission reflects my judgment only that citing them would not significantly advance the primary objective of the book.

Many people have given me valuable advice, assistance, and support. I am deeply grateful to the following persons for providing helpful comments on all or part of a draft of the book: Thomas Mappes, David Barnard, Pamela Grace, Mary Elizabeth Happ, Arthur Jacknowitz, Daniel Shapiro, Jessica Wolfendale, Matthew Talbert, Ralph W. Clark, Ernani Magalhaes, and Nathan Placencia. For their generous and helpful responses to my requests for references to pertinent literature and other information, I would like to thank David Brushwood, Kathy Cerminara, Gabriella Gosman, Pamela Grace, Mary Beth Happ, Arthur Jacknowitz, Anne Drapkin Lyerly, Alan Meisel, Valerie Satkoskie, Keith Voogd, and Douglas White. I also am grateful to Thomasine Kushner for giving me an opportunity to present preliminary drafts of sections of the book at several yearly International Bioethics Retreats.[1] Beyond these opportunities, she has been a consistent source of support and encouragement. I also appreciate Farr Curlin's invitation to participate in a conference on Conscience and Clinical Practice at the University of Chicago MacLean Center for Clinical Medical Ethics.[2] Chapter 2 grew out of my presentation for that conference. I am grateful to West Virginia University, and in particular, the Eberly College of Arts and Sciences, the Philosophy Department, and Sharon Ryan, the Department Chair, for a sabbatical leave to enable me to work on the book and for additional support. I also have benefitted from the support of the University of Pittsburgh Center for Bioethics and Health Law and its director, Alan Meisel. Finally, I want to thank Hilary Gaskin at Cambridge University Press for encouraging me to write this book.

---

[1] Revised versions of two presentations were published in the *Cambridge Quarterly of Healthcare Ethics*: (Wicclair 2009: 14–22), and (Wicclair 2010: 38–50).
[2] A revised version of my presentation was published in *Theoretical Medicine and Bioethics*: (Wicclair 2008: 171–85).

Introduction

WHAT IS CONSCIENTIOUS OBJECTION?

The subject of this book is conscientious objection in health care and the principal aim is to provide an ethical analysis of conscience-based refusals by physicians, nurses, and pharmacists. Before considering ethical issues, however, it is essential to understand what conscientious objection is, which calls for conceptual analysis.

A person engages in an act of conscientious objection when she refuses to perform an action, provide a service, and so forth, on the grounds that doing so is against her conscience. In the context of health care, physicians, nurses, and pharmacists engage in acts of conscientious objection when they: (1) refuse to provide legal and professionally accepted goods or services that fall within the scope of their professional competence, and (2) justify their refusal by claiming that it is an act of conscience or is conscience-based.[1] But what is "conscience?"

Conscience

There are several conceptions of conscience. Some are religious and others are secular. According to some conceptions, conscience has an epistemological function. Such conceptions typically identify conscience as a faculty that discerns moral truths, distinguishes between right and wrong, and/or makes ethical judgments. This, for example, is Joseph Butler's conception of conscience:

---

[1] As typically practiced by health care professionals and protected by so-called "conscience clauses" (i.e. laws and regulations that protect the exercise of conscience), conscientious objection has involved *refusals* to provide goods and services. However, providers can also have conscience-based objections to rules that prevent them from providing goods and services. I examine such conscience-based objections, "positive appeals to conscience," in Chapter 6.

[T]here is a superior principle of reflection or conscience in every man, which distinguishes between the internal principles of his heart, as well as his external actions; which passes judgment upon himself and them; pronounces determinately some actions to be in themselves, just, right, good; others to be in themselves evil, wrong, unjust: which without being consulted, without being advised with, magisterially exerts itself, and approves or condemns him, the doer of them, accordingly . . . (Butler 1827: 53)

A religious interpretation of the epistemological function identifies conscience as the source of knowledge of God's will (the "voice of God within"). Ryan Lawrence and Farr Curlin offer the following description of a religious-based view:

Within Christianity, Judaism and Islam, the conscience may be understood as enabling moral agents to know whether an act conforms to the divine law, that is, to God's standard of right and wrong . . . In each of the Abrahamic religions, right and wrong are divinely established categories, which the conscience enables a person to discern. (Lawrence and Curlin 2007: 10–11)

A broad conception identifies conscience with moral agency or capacity for moral choice. Martha Nussbaum attributes a conception of this type to "later followers of Stoicism" (Nussbaum 2008: 79). Following in this tradition and building on the views of Roger Williams, Nussbaum develops an expansive conception of conscience as "the faculty in human beings with which they search for life's ultimate meaning" (ibid.: 19). Conscience is said to be "that seat of imagination, emotion, thought, and will through which each person seeks meaning in his or her own way" (ibid.: 37). It "is identified in part by what it does – it reasons, searches, and experiences emotions of longing connected to that search – and in part by its subject matter – it deals with ultimate questions, questions of ultimate meaning" (ibid.: 169). This search for ultimate meaning can, but need not, be guided by religious beliefs.

In contrast to this expansive conception of conscience, it sometimes is identified as nothing more than an internalized set of social norms and conventions along the lines of the Freudian superego (Benjamin 2004; Sulmasy 2008). Yet another conception identifies conscience with a person's beliefs, but not specifically those that have the status of internalized social norms and conventions. Rather, conscience is said to refer to a person's secular or religion-based ethical beliefs. For example, according to the proposed Arkansas Health Care Rights of Conscience Act (SB 1141), which was introduced in 2005 but not enacted, "'Conscience' means the religious, moral, or ethical principles held by a health care provider or a health care institution."[2] A 2009 proposed Hawaii law, the Healthcare Providers Rights of Conscience Act (SB 257), provides a similar definition: "'Conscience' means the religious, moral, or ethical principles held by a healthcare provider, the healthcare institution, or healthcare payer."[3] The Illinois Health Care Right of Conscience Act identifies conscience with a specified subset of moral beliefs:[4]

'Conscience' means a sincerely held set of moral convictions arising from belief in and relation to God, or which, though not so derived, arises from a place in the life of its possessor parallel to that filled by God among adherents to religious faiths. (Ill Rev Stat ch 745, § 73-e (1998))

Several contemporary scholars have rejected the conception of conscience as a faculty with an epistemological function. Peter Fuss bluntly asserts, "whatever else conscience may be, it is not a faculty or source of moral knowledge" (Fuss 1964: 111). Agreeing with Fuss, Eric D'Arcy dismisses the notion that conscience is "a mysterious, suprarational faculty which can intuitively discern what is right or wrong, good or evil, in a given situation" (D'Arcy 1977: 98). Similarly, according to James Childress:

[C]onscience emerges *after* a moral judgment or after the application of moral standards . . . When a person consults his conscience, . . . he examines his moral convictions to determine what he really thinks and feels, even reconsidering his values, principles, and rules, their weight, and their relevance to the situation at hand. When he consults his conscience, it will only give him one answer: Do what you believe you ought to do. (1979: 319–20, emphasis added)

In place of the conception of conscience as a faculty that produces moral knowledge, Fuss identifies two features: a disposition to act in accordance with one's ethical beliefs and corresponding emotional responses:

[Conscience] establishes in the moral agent a felt need or disposition to act in accordance with his knowledge or belief, giving him a sense of personal integrity

---

[2] Available online at: www.arkleg.state.ar.us/assembly/2005/R/Bills/SB1141.pdf; accessed July 9, 2010.
[3] Available online at: www.capitol.hawaii.gov/session2009/bills/SB257_.pdf; accessed July 9, 2010.
[4] The language of this definition is similar to the test the US Supreme Court articulated in *United States v Seeger* (380 U.S. 163 (1965)) to determine whether a person qualifies for conscientious objection to military service. To qualify for conscientious objector status, the Selective Service Act at the time (1965) required opposition to all war based on "religious training and belief" which was defined in the Act as "an individual's belief in a relation to a Supreme Being involving duties superior to those arising from any human relation, but [not including] essentially political, sociological, or philosophical views or a merely personal moral code." In *Seeger*, the Supreme Court held that the test of whether a belief is "in a relation to a Supreme Being" is "whether a given belief that is sincere and meaningful occupies a place in the life of its possessor parallel to that filled by the orthodox belief in God of one who clearly qualifies for the exemption. Where such beliefs have parallel positions in the lives of their respective holders we cannot say that one is 'in a relation to a Supreme Being' and the other is not."

when he does so as best he can, and a corresponding sense of inner failure, frustration, or guilt when, through some fault of his own, he fails to do so. (Fuss 1964: 116)

Daniel Sulmasy, who also rejects the view that conscience is a faculty for discerning moral truths, associates it instead with a commitment to morality and one's core moral principles:

[Conscience] arises from a fundamental commitment or intention to be moral. It unifies the cognitive, conative, and emotional aspects of the moral life by a commitment to integrity or moral wholeness. It is a commitment to uphold one's deepest self-identifying moral beliefs; a commitment to discern the moral features of particular cases as best one can, and to reason morally to the best of one's ability; a commitment to emotional balance in one's moral decision making, to being neither too hard nor too soft; a commitment to make decisions according to the best of one's moral ability and to act upon what one discerns to be the morally right course of action. (Sulmasy 2008: 138)

Underscoring the connection between conscience and "self-identification," Jeffrey Blustein states: "conscience indicates a particular way of seeing moral and other normative demands, a mode of consciousness in which prospective actions are viewed in relation to one's *self* and *character*" (Blustein 1993: 294).

These differing conceptions of the nature and function of conscience give rise to several questions: What is the ontological status of conscience? Can it be said that (the) conscience *exists*? Does "conscience" refer to a faculty; a moral sense; a component of the will; a set of beliefs; an aspect/manifestation of consciousness, the subconscious, or the unconscious; or a set of dispositions? Is a person's conscience a source of moral knowledge, intuitions, and/or beliefs?

Fortunately, for the purposes of an ethical analysis of conscientious objection in health care, it is not necessary to address, let alone resolve, such thorny and complex ontological and epistemological questions about conscience. Such questions can be avoided by shifting the focus of conceptual analysis from characteristics of conscience to characteristics of *conscience-based refusals*, the primary subject of this book. Despite disagreement about ontological and epistemological issues, most of the foregoing conceptions of conscience incorporate the notion that matters of conscience involve a particularly important subset of an agent's ethical or religious beliefs – *core* moral beliefs.

Core moral beliefs are an agent's fundamental moral beliefs. They comprise the subset of an agent's moral beliefs that matter most to the agent.

They are integral to an agent's understanding of who she is (i.e. her self-conception or identity). Accordingly, acting contrary to core moral beliefs is perceived by the agent as an act of self-betrayal. As religious conversions indicate, core moral beliefs can develop suddenly and change over time. However, they tend to be persistent and subject to change only in response to significant life events, such as near death experiences, tragic events, and extreme changes in fortune (good or bad). Although core moral beliefs need not be blindly held, they tend to be resistant to influence by others. Agents may not be able to provide an eloquent articulation of their core moral beliefs. Nevertheless, agents generally are aware of their core moral beliefs and are disposed to explicitly endorse them.

The notion of core moral beliefs can be used to explicate the concept of *conscience-based* refusals and related concepts. An agent's refusal to provide a good or service is a conscience-based refusal if and only if: (1) the agent has a core set of moral (i.e. ethical or religious) beliefs; (2) providing the good or service is incompatible with the agent's core moral beliefs; and (3) the agent's refusal is based on her core moral beliefs. For example, a nurse's refusal to assist with an abortion is a conscience-based refusal if, and only if, assisting with an abortion is contrary to her core moral beliefs, and her refusal is based on them. Conscience-based refusals are instances of the *exercise of conscience*. Thus, the nurse's conscience-based refusal to assist with an abortion is an exercise of conscience. Her attempt to justify her refusal can be described as an *appeal to conscience* if and only if it is based on her core moral beliefs.

To be sure, a nurse, physician, or pharmacist might object to providing a good or service because she believes that it would be morally wrong to do so; and yet that belief may not be associated with her *core* moral beliefs. Accordingly, conscientious objection is to be understood as a subset of moral objection and conscience-based refusals are to be understood as a subset of refusals based on moral beliefs. As the foregoing discussion suggests, this conception of conscientious objection and conscience-based refusals is consistent with a common understanding of "conscience." This conception also helps to explain and support the belief that there are particularly compelling reasons for accommodating *conscience*-based refusals. I will present reasons for protecting the exercise of conscience in a subsequent section in this chapter.

Refusals which are not *conscience-based*

Conscience-based refusals to provide a health care good or service are based on the provider's core moral beliefs. Conscience-based refusals are distinguishable from those that derive from other reasons and do not involve conscientious objection. Refusals that are not conscience-based can include those that derive from self-interested reasons and considerations of professional integrity. Health care professionals can refuse to provide a good or service for more than one reason. However, insofar as a refusal is based exclusively on one or both of these reasons and not on a practitioner's core moral beliefs, it is not conscience-based.

Health care professionals can refuse to provide a good or service for a variety of self-interested reasons – broadly understood to include concern for one's own health and well-being as well as of persons one cares about. For example, in view of the protests and violence to which abortion providers have been subjected, obstetrician-gynecologists and family medicine doctors might refuse to perform abortions out of a concern for their safety and the safety of family members.[5] For similar reasons, nurses might refuse to assist with abortions. Physicians and nurses might also refuse to treat HIV+ patients and patients with other life-threatening infectious diseases, such as Ebola and Severe Acute Respiratory Syndrome (SARS), out a concern for their health and the health and well-being of family members. Obstetrician-gynecologists may decide to stop delivering babies due to a desire to have a more predictable schedule and/or to reduce the risk of lawsuits.[6] Pharmacy licensees might not dispense emergency contraception (EC) for financial reasons. None of these refusals is conscience-based.

Refusals based on considerations of professional integrity are grounded in professional norms and standards – or a provider's understanding of them. Insofar as refusals are based on a provider's understanding of professional norms and standards rather than her personal ethical or religious beliefs, they are distinguishable from conscience-based refusals. For example, an internist in Oregon, Washington, or Montana, the only US states in which physician-assisted suicide currently is legally permitted, may have no ethical or religious objection to suicide or suicide assistance.[7] Nevertheless, she

---

[5] According to NARAL Pro-Choice America, since 1993, 4 physicians, 2 abortion clinic employees, a clinic escort, and a clinic security guard were murdered in the United States by anti-abortion extremists. Additional acts of violence directed at abortion providers and clinics included attempted murders, bombings, arson, and chemical vandalism. Information available online at: www.prochoiceamerica.org/assets/files/Abortion-Access-to-Abortion-Violence.pdf; accessed July 9, 2010.

[6] A survey conducted by the American College of Obstetricians and Gynecologists (ACOG) reported that 8% of the ACOG Fellows and Junior Fellows who responded to the survey stopped delivering babies (obstetrics) during 2009 (Lumalcuri and Hale 2010: 223–8). About a third stopped delivering babies due to concerns about liability and/or litigation.

[7] The Oregon Death with Dignity Act (ORS 127.800–995) authorizes physicians to dispense or write prescriptions for medication to end life under specified conditions. It is available online at: www.oregon.gov/DHS/ph/pas/docs/statute.pdf; accessed July 3, 2010. The Washington Death with

might refuse to provide suicide assistance when patients request it because she believes that there are better options (e.g. palliative care) for terminally ill patients. Similarly, physicians may refuse to perform abortions and nurses may refuse to assist because they believe that having an abortion is not in a woman's best interests. Refusals to forgo medically provided nutrition and hydration (MPNH) and other life-sustaining treatments can be based on similar reasons. Of course, these beliefs may be false or unsubstantiated, and refusals based on them may be instances of unjustified paternalism. However, insofar as refusals are based on a practitioner's belief that providing a good or service that is contrary to a patient's best interests is contrary to professional norms and standards, they are distinguishable from conscience-based refusals.

Clinical norms are a common source of refusals based on considerations of professional integrity. For example, a pharmacist might refuse to fill a prescription for a patient because of a concern about drug interactions or adverse effects; a surgeon might refuse to perform surgery because she believes it is too risky and is not medically indicated; an obstetrician might refuse to perform a requested C-section because she believes it is not medically necessary; and a pediatrician might refuse to prescribe growth hormone for a patient because he believes it is not medically indicated. Insofar as refusals are based on such clinical considerations, they are distinguishable from conscience-based refusals.

Physicians' refusals to provide treatment that is variously referred to as "futile," "medically ineffective," "inappropriate," or "non-beneficial" sometimes can be understood as refusals based on professional integrity rather than personal conscience (Brody 1994). Insofar as the refusal is supported by citing *professional* norms and standards, the practitioner can at least expect a sympathetic response, if not agreement, from other professionals.[8] By contrast, conscience-based refusals involve appeals to a practitioner's *personal* ethical or religious beliefs. In relation to such refusals in a pluralistic society, a physician, nurse, or pharmacist can at most expect other professionals to respect, but not to share, the objection and the underlying beliefs.

Dignity Act (RCW 70.245.010–904) is identical to the Oregon law. It is available online at: http://apps.leg.wa.gov/RCW/default.aspx?cite=70.245&full=true#70.245.903; accessed July 3, 2010. On the last day of 2009, the Montana Supreme Court in a 4 to 3 decision held that physicians who provide suicide assistance to competent terminally ill patients who consent are not subject to prosecution for homicide (*Baxter* v *Montana* 2009 MT 449). In Montana, voluntary informed consent is a legal defense to a crime unless it is contrary to public policy, and the Montana Supreme Court held that "physician aid in dying" for competent terminally ill patients is not contrary to public policy. The decision is available online at the State Law Library of Montana website: http://fnweb1.isd.doa.state.mt.us/idmws/custom/sll/sll_fn_home.htm; accessed July 3, 2010.

[8] There can be disagreement about the interpretation of the relevant norms and standards.

Physicians can, however, appeal to *justice* as an alleged conscience-based reason for refusing to provide "futile," "medically ineffective," "inappropriate," or "non-beneficial" treatment.[9] For example, an Intensive Care Unit (ICU) physician might invoke considerations of justice to support refusing a request by family members to continue providing aggressive life-sustaining treatment for a patient who is not expected to survive to discharge (e.g. an obtunded terminally ill elderly patient with multiple organ failure). The physician might claim that it is unjust to allocate scarce and expensive health care resources (e.g. ICU beds and equipment, physician and nurse time, and Medicare funds) to a patient who is not expected to survive to discharge. Justice, he might claim, requires allocating those resources to meet the needs of patients who are expected to benefit.

Putting aside the plausibility of this physician's conception of justice, such justice-based refusals have at most a family resemblance to conscience-based refusals. According to the analysis provided earlier, a physician's justice-based refusal to provide requested treatment can be considered an act of conscientious objection only if: (1) the physician has a core set of moral beliefs; (2) the physician's conception of justice is among her core moral beliefs; and (3) providing the requested treatment is incompatible with the physician's conception of justice. Without questioning the sincerity of physicians with justice-based objections to providing medical treatment, it is unlikely that many will satisfy the second condition. If a person's conception of justice is among her core moral beliefs, she is likely to experience guilt, remorse, loss of self-respect, and/or shame if her actions are incompatible with her conception of justice. Regrettably, however, injustice is something that many physicians and non-physicians alike have learned to tolerate and live with. To be sure, perceived injustice may be a source of considerable moral distress for ICU physicians and other health care professionals. However, it is doubtful that promoting justice is essential to maintaining their moral integrity, and their sincere concerns about justice are unlikely to rise to the level of *conscience*-based objections.[10]

---

[9] I am indebted to Douglas White for informing me that some physicians equate such justice-based refusals with conscientious objection and seek legal protection under conscience clauses for refusing to provide life-sustaining treatment.

[10] I examine the connection between the exercise of conscience and maintaining moral integrity in the final section of this chapter. It is worth noting that even if such justice-based objections were to be recognized as appeals to conscience, at most they would warrant allowing an objecting health care professional to facilitate a transfer to another provider and withdraw from the case. An individual provider's justice-based objection would not justify a unilateral decision to withhold or withdraw care contrary to the wishes of patients or surrogates.

Conscientious objection and moral distress

Andrew Jameton has been credited with the initial identification and explication of the concept of moral distress (Pauly *et al.* 2009). As he defined it, moral distress occurs "when one knows the right thing to do, but institutional constraints make it nearly impossible to pursue the right course of action" (Jameton 1984: 6). Until recently, much of the literature on moral distress has focused on nurses (Hamric and Blackhall 2007; Pauly *et al.* 2009). However, as Ann Hamric has observed, "as physicians become employees of systems that erect obstacles . . . to ethically appropriate action, moral distress [among physicians] may become more frequent" (Hamric 2000: 200). According to Bernadette Pauly (Pauly *et al.* 2009: 562), "economic and political structures in health" are a major source of moral distress for nurses, and the effect of such economic and political factors is not limited to members of the nursing profession.[11]

There are several respects in which moral distress is distinguishable from conscientious objection.[12] First, moral distress is considerably more pervasive than conscientious objection. Typical acts of conscientious objection are limited to a few specific goods and services, such as EC, family planning, abortion, palliative sedation, and organ donation after cardiac death. By contrast, moral distress is a relatively pervasive, everyday phenomenon. According to Hamric, it is "a nearly universal phenomenon in the everyday ethics arena . . ." (2000: 199). Studies have identified a wide range of sources of moral distress, including: harm to patients (i.e. pain and suffering), treating patients as objects due to institutional requirements, health policy constraints, prolongation of dying without informing patients or family members of options, the definition of brain death, inadequate staffing, and cost containment (Corley 2002). Mary Corley and colleagues (Corley *et al.* 2001) designed a moral distress scale that measures moral distress in relation to 30 diverse items, which include:

- work with "unsafe" levels of nurse staffing;
- follow the family's request not to discuss death with a dying patient who asks about dying;
- carry out the physician's order for unnecessary tests and treatment;

---

[11] For a study of moral distress that includes pharmacists, see (Kälvemark *et al.* 2006: 416–27). For a study of moral distress among physicians, nurses, and pharmacists, see (Kälvemark *et al.* 2004: 1075–84).

[12] By distinguishing between conscientious objection and moral distress, I do *not* mean to minimize the importance of preventing situations that give rise to moral distress and implementing measures that will help health care professionals respond to moral distress when they experience it.

- observe without intervening when health care personnel do not respect the patient's dignity;
- follow the family's wishes to continue life support even though it is not in the best interest of the patient;
- let medical students perform painful procedures on patients solely to increase their skill;
- prepare a terminally ill elderly patient on a respirator for surgery to have a mass removed;
- carry out a work assignment in which I do not feel professionally competent; and
- avoid taking any action when I learn that a nurse colleague has made a medication error and does not report it.

When the instrument was tested on 214 nurses, the responses reportedly indicated that moral distress was experienced in relation to each of the 30 items.

Second, whereas moral distress often arises when a health care professional believes that generally recognized ethical and professional norms are violated, conscience-based objections arise when providing a good or service requires violating a health care professional's *personal* moral beliefs. With respect to most of the forementioned examples of situations that reportedly give rise to moral distress, it is arguable that there is an actual or potential lack of compliance with a generally recognized ethical and/or professional standard. Hence, an objection can be justified by those generally recognized standards. By contrast, when a health care professional has a conscience-based objection to procedures that do not violate professional standards, such as abortion or palliative sedation, the objection is based on her personal ethical or religious beliefs.

Third, acts of conscientious objection involve a *refusal* to provide a good or service. By contrast, moral distress typically arises when nurses and other health care professionals feel constrained to perform actions despite their belief that those actions are contrary to clinical, professional, and/or personal moral standards. Indeed, moral distress arises from *an inability to refrain from*: (1) acting inappropriately, (2) participating in inappropriate action, and/or (3) preventing others from acting inappropriately. Jameton's definition captures this characteristic of moral distress by referring to "institutional constraints [that] make it nearly impossible to pursue the right course of action."

Fourth, acts of conscientious objection are *conscience*-based. As such, they are associated with a person's core moral beliefs. Hence, to accept institutional constraints and act against one's conscience is nothing less than an act of self-betrayal. By contrast, moral distress can arise when a health care professional observes or participates in actions that are perceived to be morally *inappropriate*. Active or passive participation in actions that are perceived to be inappropriate undeniably can give rise to a variety of painful psychological and emotional responses (Hamric 2000; Jameton 1993). The frustration and anguish associated with moral distress should not be minimized. However, it is one thing to believe that one is acting inappropriately and quite another to believe that one is acting contrary to one's core moral beliefs and is engaging in an act of self-betrayal. Over time, cumulative moral distress can result in burn-out and a decision to resign (Corley 2002). By contrast, one instance of acting against one's conscience – an act of self-betrayal – can be devastating and unbearable. To be sure, it might be claimed that acting against one's conscience can give rise to extreme moral distress. However, such extreme instances should be distinguished from "everyday" moral distress.

The distinction between conscientious objection and civil disobedience

According to James Childress, "civil disobedience" refers to "public, non-violent, and submissive violations of law in protest based on moral-political principles and designed to effect or to prevent social, political, or legal change" (Childress 1985: 68). There are several important differences between acts of civil disobedience and conscience-based refusals.

First, there is a difference in their respective aims or goals. The primary aim of people who engage in civil disobedience is to bring about social change. For example, in the past people engaged in acts of civil disobedience to end racial discrimination and the Vietnam War. More recently, health care reform was the goal of people who engaged in acts of civil disobedience by participating in illegal demonstrations and sit-ins in the US Congress and insurance company offices. By contrast, the primary aim or goal of conscience-based refusals can be (and typically is) more personal. Rather than aiming to effect social change, the primary goal is to remain true to one's fundamental ethical or religious principles and to avoid complicity in perceived moral wrongdoing. This difference is illustrated in a documentary film entitled *An Act of Conscience* about a Massachusetts couple, Randy Kehler and Betsy Corner.[13] They are pacifists who, beginning in 1977, refused to pay federal taxes because they did not want to support war and

---

[13] The documentary's director is Robbie Leppzer. Information about the film is available at its website: www.turningtide.com/aoc.htm; accessed July 9, 2010.

military spending. They undoubtedly had no illusion that their conscience-based refusal to pay federal taxes would end war and military spending. To be sure, they may have believed that their action would serve as an example to others, but their primary aim was to avoid compromising their own core moral beliefs. However, after their house was seized by the federal government, the couple and several supporters engaged in acts of civil disobedience, which included illegally occupying the house after it was sold to another couple and participating in an illegal vigil outside the house. An aim of these protests was to enable Mr. Kehler and Ms. Corner to regain possession of the house that had been theirs. Thus what began as a conscience-based refusal to pay federal taxes transformed into acts of civil disobedience.

Second, related to the difference in goals, whereas acts of civil disobedience are essentially public acts of protest, acts of conscience can be more or less private. The actions of people who engage in civil disobedience are directed to the public. They want to be observed. They seek the attention of others (e.g. government officials, politicians, corporate executives, members of the general public) and want to affect their beliefs and actions. By contrast, acts of conscientious objection need not be directed to the public.[14] Conscientious objectors may have no interest in being observed by others or influencing them. Their interest may be limited to refraining from actions that will violate their core moral beliefs and avoiding complicity in perceived moral wrongdoing.

Third, in contrast to lawful protests, civil *disobedience*, by definition, involves engaging in unlawful activity (e.g. unlawful demonstrations, sit-ins, or occupations of buildings). People who engage in acts of civil disobedience deliberately violate the law as a means of protest and effecting change. By contrast, although conscientious objectors such as Mr. Kehler and Ms. Corner violated tax law, breaking the law was only incidental to their primary aim, which was to avoid contributing to war and military spending. Indeed, conscientious objectors often seek exemptions from laws, which, if granted, will enable them to avoid acting against their conscience

---

[14] Childress claims that both conscientious objection and civil disobedience are "open or public." To be sure, if actions are classified as either open/public or secret/concealed, then acts of conscientious objection, such as tax refusal, fall within the former category. For example, Mr. Kehler and Ms. Corner submitted tax forms and declared their refusal to pay taxes. If they had lied about their income or declared fraudulent deductions to avoid owing any taxes, their actions hardly would be classifiable as acts of conscientious objection. However, insofar as their aim was to avoid complicity in perceived moral wrongdoing, their tax refusal was not addressed to the public. In this respect, it was a (relatively) private act. By contrast, insofar as the aim of civil disobedience is "to effect or to prevent social, political, or legal change," it is directed to the public.

without violating the law.[15] When men burned their draft cards to protest the Vietnam War, they deliberately broke the law.[16] Such acts were instances of civil disobedience. By contrast, men who applied for conscientious objector status did not break the law. Quite the contrary, they sought a legally recognized exemption – either from any military service or only from combat service.[17]

It has been claimed that since people who engage in civil disobedience deliberately break the law, they should accept the specified legal penalty.[18] Similarly, it might be argued that people who cannot in good conscience comply with laws should be prepared to accept the legal consequences of refusal. Regardless of whether or not one accepts this line of argument in relation to civil disobedience, it fails in relation to conscientious objection. The argument in the case of conscientious objectors begs the question because it assumes, without providing any justification, that no exemptions or accommodations are warranted. But whether and when such exemptions or accommodations are warranted is a key ethical question in relation to conscientious objection.[19]

THE EMERGENCE AND EXPANSION OF CONSCIENTIOUS OBJECTION IN HEALTH CARE

In the context of military service, conscientious objection and some form of accommodation to conscientious objectors has a long history. According to the authors of a study of conscientious objection to military service during World War I and World War II, "there were probably conscientious objectors in Europe prior to the rise of Christianity. During the first two and a half centuries of the Christian era, Christians were almost without

---

[15] As Childress uses the term in the previously cited article, conscientious objection involves a violation of law. This condition derives from the subject of his article, which is announced in its title: *illegal* actions. Accordingly, it is unwarranted to infer that Childress mistakenly believes that a violation of law is a necessary condition of conscientious objection. A more plausible interpretation is that for the purpose of the article, he limited his analysis to a subclass of conscientious objection: *illegal* acts of conscience.

[16] During the Vietnam War, only men were subject to the military draft.

[17] In *An Act of Conscience*, it is stated that Mr. Kehler served two years in a federal prison for refusing to be drafted during the Vietnam War. No explanation is given of the circumstances, and it is not stated whether he applied for conscientious objector status.

[18] See, for example, (Hook 1971: 53–63). For an opposing view, see (Dworkin 1978: 206–22). Childress's "submission" condition does not prevent people who engage in civil disobedience from legal efforts to avoid prison or other penalties. It only excludes attempts "to evade arrest and punishment by flight, or concealment, or violence" (Childress 1985: 67).

[19] During the Vietnam War, conscience-based exemptions were granted in relation to military service, but, as illustrated by Randy Kehler and Betsy Corner, not in relation to paying taxes.

exception conscientious objectors ..." (Sibley and Jacob 1952: 1). In the United States, members of various pacifist Protestant sects, such as Quakers and Mennonites, objected to military service and were accommodated during the colonial period and, to some extent, also during the Civil War (Schlissel 1968; Sibley and Jacob 1952). In Great Britain, some accommodations were made to Quakers and other religious pacifists prior to World War I (P. Brock 2006) and both the United States and Great Britain exempted recognized conscientious objectors from combat during both world wars (Sibley and Jacob 1952).[20]

In contrast to conscientious objection to military service, until quite recently, conscientious objection by health care professionals does not appear to have been a familiar occurrence. Literature searches have not uncovered studies that attribute a significant place to it in the history of medicine or that apply the notion of "conscientious objector" to pre-twentieth-century practitioners.

In nineteenth-century Britain, the notion of "conscientious objection" was applied in the context of health care, but the objectors were not physicians or other health care professionals. Instead, they were parents who refused to comply with a compulsory smallpox vaccination requirement for children (Durbach 2005). These "anti-vaccinationists" were referred to at the time as "conscientious objectors," and an 1898 law enabled them to apply for "certificates of conscientious objection." However, in general, parents opposed vaccination because they believed that it was not safe or effective and not because vaccination was incompatible with their ethical or religious beliefs. To qualify for an exception under the Vaccination Act of 1898, a parent had to "conscientiously believe that vaccination would be prejudicial to the health of the child" (Durbach 2005: 180). In effect, then, parents were permitted to make risk/benefit judgments for their own children, and public health concerns did not trump parental decisions. Hence, it is doubtful that such parental refusals are appropriately characterized as instances of "conscientious objection."

An Ovid-Medline search identified no articles prior to the 1960s that specifically addressed the subject of conscientious objection in health care.

---

[20] During both world wars, the criteria to qualify as a "conscientious objector" were significantly more stringent in the United States than in Great Britain. Similarly, Great Britain imposed fewer obligations on individuals who qualified for conscientious objector status. To qualify as a conscientious objector in the United States during World War I, an individual had to belong to a "well recognized religious sect or organization" that prohibited participation "in war in any form." In World War II the opposition to participation in war in any form had to be "by reason of religious training and belief." No comparable requirements had to be satisfied to qualify for conscientious objector status in Great Britain during World War I or World War II: (Sibley and Jacob 1952).

It was not until the 1970s that a substantial literature began to develop on the subject of health care professionals' conscience-based refusals to provide legal and professionally accepted services. Most of the earlier articles dealt with abortion. In the United States this focus is likely due in part to several states eliminating or relaxing legal restrictions against abortion and the 1973 U.S. Supreme Court *Roe* v *Wade* decision (410 U.S. 113 (1973)) establishing a constitutional right to abortion. Indeed, the first US federal conscience clause law (legislation that protects health care professionals who refuse to provide a good or service for ethical or religious reasons),[21] the 1973 Church Amendment (42 U.S.C. § 300a–7(a–b)), was enacted in response to the *Roe* v *Wade* decision and a 1972 decision by a US District Court in Billings, Montana (369 F.Supp. 948).[22] The latter decision involved St. Vincent's, a private Catholic hospital, which refused to allow a physician to perform a requested tubal ligation (sterilization) while delivering the patient's baby. The court held that receiving funds under the Federal Hill-Burton Act subjected St. Vincent's to "state action" provisions. Accordingly the court issued a preliminary injunction enjoining St. Vincent's Hospital from prohibiting the physician from performing the sterilization procedure (Malpass 1976). This decision fueled a concern that physicians, nurses, and hospitals might be required to perform, assist in performing, or facilitate abortions and sterilizations despite their ethical or religious objections. The Church Amendment addressed this concern by stating that receipt of funds under three federal programs did not authorize any court, public official, or "other public authority" to require individuals or institutions with ethical or religious objections to provide or assist in the provision of abortions or sterilizations (42 U.S.C. § 300a–7(b)).

The endorsement by the American Medical Association (AMA) of refusals based on "personally held moral principles" illustrates how concerns about abortion contributed to the application of the notion of conscientious objection to health care. Shortly after the *Roe* v *Wade* decision, the AMA House of Delegates adopted a resolution about abortion that included the AMA's first explicit conscience clause provision. "Abortion" (House of Delegates Health Policy 5.995) includes the

---

[21] Although conscience clauses protect the exercise of conscience, their protection generally is not limited to refusals based on core moral beliefs. Instead, they often are broader in scope and protect refusals that are based on ethical or religious beliefs. I discuss conscience clauses in more detail in Chapter 6.

[22] *Congressional Record-Senate* (March 27, 1973, pp. 9595–604). See also, Jody Feder, "The History and Effect of Abortion Conscience Clause Laws," *Congressional Research Service Report for Congress* (January 14, 2005). Available online at: www.law.umaryland.edu/marshall/crsreports/crsdocuments/RS2142801142005.pdf; accessed July 9, 2010.

following conscience clause: "Neither physician, hospital, nor other hospital personnel shall be required to perform any act violative of personally held moral principles."[23]

The first AMA *Code of Ethics*, adopted when the organization was founded in 1847, had a brief section that addresses situations in which patients want to dismiss physicians, and it calls for patients to give their reasons.[24] However, with one exception, it is silent in relation to if and when physicians may withdraw from patient care. The exception is an admonition *not* to abandon patients with incurable illnesses.[25]

At first glance, the following passage from John Bell's *Introduction* to the 1847 Code may appear to sanction conscience-based refusals by physicians:

In thus deducing the rights of a physician from his duties, it is not meant to insist on such a correlative obligation, that the withholding of the right exonerates from the discharge of the duty. Short of the formal abandonment of the practice of his profession, no medical man can withhold his services from the requisition either of an individual or of the community, unless under the circumstances, of rare occurrence, in which his compliance would be not only unjust but degrading to himself, or to a professional brother, and so far diminish his future usefulness. (Bell 1995: 67)

The reference to "degrading *to himself*" may seem to suggest a violation of the physician's conscience or moral integrity. However, the references to "a professional brother" and "future usefulness" (presumably as a physician) seem to suggest that Bell's exception to a duty not to withhold services has more to do with maintaining a physician's standing *as a member of the medical profession* (or maintaining the status of the medical profession generally) than with enabling physicians to follow the dictates of their conscience and protect their personal moral integrity. That is, Bell's statement addresses refusals based on professional integrity rather than conscience-based refusals.

The "Principles of Medical Ethics," adopted by the AMA in 1912, and all subsequent revisions to date have included general statements granting

---

[23] House of Delegates Health Policy statements can be accessed online by means of "PolicyFinder," which can be downloaded at the AMA website: www.ama-assn.org/ama/no-index/about-ama/11760. shtml; accessed July 9, 2010.

[24] "When a patient wishes to dismiss his physician, justice and common courtesy require that he should declare his reasons for so doing" (Hays 1995: 75–87 at 78). An underlying assumption in the 1847 Code of Ethics is the principle of reciprocal obligations: the obligations of physicians generate reciprocal obligations on the part of patients. See (Baker 1995: 1–22). Accordingly, one section of the Code is entitled "Obligations of Patients to Their Physicians."

[25] "A physician ought not to abandon a patient because the case is deemed incurable; for his attendance may continue to be highly useful to the patient, and comforting to the relatives around him, even to the last period of a fatal malady, by alleviating pain and other symptoms, and by soothing mental anguish" (Hays 1995: 76).

physicians broad discretion in the choice of patients.[26] However, in contrast to the 1973 abortion conscience clause, none of these general statements specifically addresses refusals based on a physician's ethical or religious beliefs. It was not until 2000 that the AMA *Code of Medical Ethics* specifically stated that the "prerogative to choose whether to enter into a patient-physician relationship" includes the freedom to refuse patients who request services that are incompatible with the physician's "personal, religious, or moral beliefs" ("Potential Patients," Opinion 10.05).[27] Thus, it was not until 2000 that the *Code of Medical Ethics* left no doubt that, with some exceptions, physicians may decline to accept patients when a requested treatment is contrary to their ethical or religious beliefs.[28]

Although the focus of this book is on the United States, there are several noteworthy parallels between the United States and the United Kingdom. Conscientious objection to abortion is one of these parallels. In England, Wales, and Scotland, the Abortion Act of 1967 granted registered medical practitioners criminal immunity for terminating pregnancies under specified circumstances.[29] Anticipating ethical or religious objections to performing abortions, a conscience clause was incorporated directly into the legislation. The Abortion Act of 1967 included the following provision: "[N]o person shall be under any duty, whether by contract or by any statutory or other legal requirement, to participate in any treatment authorised by this Act to which he has a conscientious objection." However, objectors were not released from a "duty to participate in treatment which is necessary to save the life or to prevent grave permanent injury to the physical or mental health of a pregnant woman."

---

[26] When the AMA *Code of Ethics* was revised for the first time in 1903, the name was changed to "Principles of Medical Ethics." This name was retained for the 1912 revision. However, beginning in 1957, the Principles of Medical Ethics comprise only a small part of the AMA *Code of Medical Ethics*, the predominant components of which are Reports and Opinions of the Council on Ethical and Judicial Affairs (CEJA). The relevant statements in the various revisions of the Principles of Medical Ethics are: (1) "A physician is free to choose whom he will serve. He should, however, always respond to any request for his assistance in an emergency or whenever temperate public opinion expects the service" (1912). (2) "A physician may choose whom he will serve. In an emergency, however, he should render service to the best of his ability" (1957). (3) "A physician shall, in the provision of appropriate patient care, except in emergencies, be free to choose whom to serve" (1980 and 2001). All of these codes are reprinted in (Baker *et al.* 1999). There were no similar statements in the 1847 Code or the 1903 Principles.

[27] See (American Medical Association, Council on Ethical and Judicial Affairs 2010).

[28] There are three exceptions: (1) physicians may not refuse to accept patients in medical emergencies; (2) a decision to refuse to accept a patient may not be based on invidious discrimination; and (3) physicians may not decline to accept patients in violation of contractual obligations.

[29] Abortion Act of 1967 (c. 87). Available online at the UK Statute Law database: www.statutelaw.gov.uk/Home.aspx; accessed October 17, 2010.

Whereas abortion and sterilization were the primary initial targets of conscience-based refusals by US health care professionals, the scope of procedures and services subsequently widened significantly. One such area is end-of-life care. The case of Karen Quinlan, which began in 1975, was one of the earliest so-called "right to die" (right to refuse life-sustaining treatment) cases that attracted national attention in the United States.[30] Ms. Quinlan was 21 years old when she lost consciousness and stopped breathing on the night of April 15, 1975. A police officer was able to restore her breathing, and she was taken to a hospital, where she was admitted and placed on a respirator. She never regained consciousness, and after several months, her parents decided to have the ventilator withdrawn. The physicians refused, and the case eventually was heard by the New Jersey Supreme Court, which ruled in favor of the parents. The court held that the constitutional right to privacy includes within its scope the right of the family of an incompetent dying patient to decide to forgo life support. Although the court's decision had legal effect only in New Jersey, it helped to legitimate forgoing life-sustaining treatment throughout the United States. Subsequently, the President's Commission for the Study of Ethical Problems in Medicine and Biomedical and Behavioral Research (1983), the Hastings Center (Anonymous 1987) and several other organizations and professional associations issued ethical guidelines approving forgoing life-sustaining treatment under specified circumstances. Generally court decisions and legislation established a competent adult's right to refuse life-sustaining treatment contemporaneously or in advance and the right of next of kin and other surrogates to refuse for patients who lack decision-making capacity (Meisel and Cerminara 2009).

Despite such widespread legitimation of forgoing life-sustaining treatment, doing so was and still is incompatible with the ethical or religious beliefs of some physicians and nurses. Whereas some object generally to forgoing life-sustaining treatment, others object only to forgoing one or more specific types of life support. MPNH is a common target of such particularized objections. Although ethical or religious objections to forgoing MPNH are long-standing, a 2004 papal allocution may have intensified opposition to forgoing MPNH by Catholic health care professionals and institutions (Shannon and Walter 2004).[31]

Early influential ethical guidelines that recognized a right of patients and surrogates to refuse life-sustaining treatment also recommended

---

[30] The account of the Quinlan case presented here is based on (Pence 2004).
[31] Additional information related to the ongoing controversy generated by the papal allocution will be presented in Chapter 4.

accommodating practitioners' conscientious objections. For example, the President's Commission guidelines include the following statement: "Health care professionals or institutions may decline to provide a particular option because that choice would violate their conscience or professional judgment, though in doing so they may not abandon a patient" (President's Commission for the Study of Ethical Problems in Medicine and Biomedical and Behavioral Research 1983: 3). The Hastings Center guidelines state: "If a health care professional has serious objections to the decision of the patient or surrogate, so that carrying it out is impossible as a matter of conscience or commitment to principle, the professional is not obligated to do so" (Anonymous 1987: 32–3). Typically hospital policies on life-sustaining treatment include similar provisions. In addition, states enacted advance directive legislation, and those statutes typically allow providers with conscience-based objections to refuse to implement written instructions or surrogate decisions to forgo life-sustaining treatment (Meisel and Cerminara 2009).[32]

The legal situations in the United Kingdom and the United States in relation to decisions about forgoing life-sustaining treatment when patients lack decision-making capacity are somewhat different.[33] However, in both the United States and the United Kingdom, adult patients with decision-making capacity generally have a right to refuse life-sustaining treatment contemporaneously or by means of an advance directive. This view was unequivocally endorsed in a 1999 British Medical Association (BMA) report (British Medical Association 1999).[34] Yet, echoing the President's Commission and Hastings Center guidelines, in deference to practitioners who have an ethical or religious objection to forgoing life-sustaining treatment, the BMA calls for accommodation: "Where a member of the health care team has a conscientious objection to withholding or withdrawing life-prolonging treatment, he or she should, wherever possible, be permitted to hand over care of the patient to a colleague" (British Medical Association 1999: 62).[35]

---

[32] Most state statutes require transferring the care of the patient to a provider who will comply with the instruction directive or surrogate decision to forgo life-sustaining treatment.

[33] In England and Wales, the Mental Capacity Act 2005 provides a legal framework for decision-making on behalf of patients who lack decision-making capacity. The Act is available online at: www.opsi.gov. uk/acts/acts2005/ukpga_20050009_en_1; accessed July 11, 2010. It took effect in April 2007.

[34] The third edition of the report was published in 2007 (British Medical Association 2007). The third edition includes a discussion of the Mental Capacity Act and its implications.

[35] According to a UK Department for Constitutional Affairs (DCA) publication entitled "Mental Capacity Act 2005 Code of Practice," health care professionals who "disagree in principle with patients' [advance] decisions to refuse life-sustaining treatment ... do not have to act against their beliefs ... [provided they do] not simply abandon patients or act in a way that affects their care" (p. 159). Available online at: www.dca.gov.uk/legal-policy/mental-capacity/mca-cp.pdf; accessed July 11, 2010.

When Oregon became the first state in the United States to legalize physician-assisted suicide, health care providers (e.g. physicians, pharmacists, and nurses) were permitted to refuse to participate and were protected against a wide range of possible sanctions for such refusals.[36] Since Oregonians who took their own lives under the Death with Dignity Act often had to go to two or more physicians before finding one who was willing to prescribe medication to end life, it is evident that many Oregon physicians exercised their right of refusal.[37] In 2008, Washington became the second state to legalize physician-assisted suicide when voters approved Initiative Measure 1000, the Washington Death with Dignity Act. The two Death with Dignity acts are identical, and they include the following provision for conscientious objection:

> If a health care provider is unable or unwilling to carry out a patient's request under this chapter, and the patient transfers his or her care to a new health care provider, the prior health care provider shall transfer, upon request, a copy of the patient's relevant medical records to the new health care provider.[38]

Neither state requires objecting physicians to help the patient find a willing physician. An objecting physician's only obligation under both statutes is to transfer the patient's *medical records*.

Several bills have been introduced in the British Parliament to legalize assisted suicide, but none passed. The proposed Assisted Dying for the Terminally Ill Bill introduced in 2004 and the bill with the same title introduced in 2005 both included conscience clauses.[39] The earlier bill included a referral requirement. However, similar to the Oregon and Washington Death with Dignity laws, the later bill did not include this

---

[36] The Oregon "Death with Dignity Act" (ORS 127.800–127.995) was first approved by voter initiative in November 1994. Its implementation was delayed for three years due to legal appeals and an effort to repeal the Act. Oregon voters defeated the repeal effort in November 1997. For detailed information about the Death With Dignity Act, see (Task Force to Develop the Care of Terminally-Ill Oregonians 1998).

[37] During the first three years in which the Death with Dignity Act was in effect (1998–2000), only 41 percent of the patients who died after ingesting medication to end life obtained their prescriptions from the first physician they asked: Oregon Department of Human Services, *Oregon's Death with Dignity Act: Three Years of Legalized Physician-Assisted Suicide* (February 22, 2001). Available online at: www.oregon.gov/DHS/ph/pas/docs/year3.pdf; accessed July 9, 2010. This Oregon Department of Human Services yearly Death with Dignity Act report was the last to include information about how many physicians patients had to ask.

[38] Oregon Death with Dignity Act, ORS 127.885 §4.01(4); Washington Death with Dignity Act section 19(1)(d).

[39] The 2004 bill is available at: www.publications.parliament.uk/pa/ld200304/ldbills/017/2004017.htm; accessed July 9, 2010. The 2005 bill is available at: www.publications.parliament.uk/pa/ld200506/ldbills/036/2006036.htm; accessed July 9, 2010.

requirement. Instead, it explicitly states that an objecting physician has no obligation to assist patients by providing information or referrals.

Assisted reproduction and contraception, two areas in addition to abortion and sterilization that involve human reproduction, have given rise to a further expansion of the scope of conscientious objection in health care.[40] In a Committee Opinion that endorses a significantly limited right of conscientious objection, the American College of Obstetricians and Gynecologists (ACOG) Committee on Ethics observes, "Conscientious refusals have been particularly widespread in the arena of reproductive medicine" (American College of Obstetricians and Gynecologists Committee on Ethics 2007: 1203). In addition to abortion, fertility services are an area of reproductive medicine that has occasioned conscience-based refusals. A recurrent source of conscience-based refusals by health care professionals who provide fertility services has been requests by unmarried and/or lesbian women who request intrauterine insemination (IUI), *in vitro* fertilization (IVF), or other means of assisted reproduction.[41] Measures to prevent pregnancy have also repeatedly given rise to conscience-based refusals. For example, emergency department physicians have refused to offer EC to rape victims, and pharmacists have refused to dispense it.[42] Some pharmacists have refused to dispense any contraceptives.[43]

In August 2006, the US Food and Drug Administration (FDA) announced its approval of over-the-counter sales of an emergency contraceptive with the product name "Plan B" to women eighteen years and older

---

[40] In the UK, section 38 of the Human Fertilisation and Embryology Act 1990 (c. 37) includes the following provision: "No person who has a conscientious objection to participating in any activity governed by this Act shall be under any duty, however arising, to do so." Available online at: www.opsi.gov.uk/Acts/acts1990/ukpga_19900037_en_1; accessed July 9, 2010.

[41] For an illustrative example of a case of this type, see Greg Moran, 'Maternal Wish, Doctors' Faith at Odds in Court', *The San Diego Union-Tribune,* August 7, 2005, sec. News, p. A-1. I examine this case in Chapter 3.

[42] For an illustrative example of an emergency physician's refusal to dispense EC, see Tom Bowman and Diana Fishlock, 'Rape Victim Denied Morning-after Pill', *Patriot News,* July 25, 2006, p. A-1. For an illustrative example of a pharmacist's refusal to dispense EC, see Jim Ritter, 'Planned Parenthood Protests over Morning-after Pill; Downtown Pharmacist Wouldn't Sell Emergency Contraceptive', *Chicago Sun-Times,* March 23, 2005, sec. News, p. 10. I will present and analyze additional cases in Chapter 3.

[43] For an illustrative example of a pharmacist's refusal to dispense any contraceptives, see Anita Weier, 'Patient, Pharmacist Collide: Birth Control Pill Conflict Shows Dilemma', *Capital Times,* March 16, 2004, sec. Front, p. A-1. Additional examples of conscience-based refusals related to reproductive medicine are provided in ACLU Reproductive Freedom Project, "Religious Refusals and Reproductive Rights: Accessing Birth Control at the Pharmacy." Available online at: www.aclu.org/reproductive-freedom/religious-refusals-and-reproductive-rights-accessing-birth-control-pharmacy; accessed July 9, 2010. I will present and analyze more cases in Chapters 3 and 4.

(Stein 2006).[44] Plan B contains the hormone progestin and consists of two 0.75-mg doses of levonorgestrel to be taken 1 hour apart (Scolaro 2007). For maximum effectiveness, it should be taken within 72 hours of intercourse (Fine *et al.* 2010; Scolaro 2007).[45] In April 2009, following a judge's ruling invalidating the FDA's age requirement, the agency made Plan B available without a prescription to women 17 years and older (Stein 2009a). In July 2009, the FDA approved a one-dose 1.5-mg levonorgestrel tablet that is sold under the product name "Plan B One-Step," which is available without prescription to women 17 years and older.[46] Two-tablet, two-dosage levonorgestrel is now available as a generic under the product name "Next Choice," but a prescription still is required for women under 17 years of age.[47] The availability of levonorgestrel-based EC without a prescription to women who are at least 17 years old does not mean, however, that pharmacists no longer have an occasion for conscience-based refusals in relation to it. Women under the age of seventeen still need a prescription for Plan B One-Step and Next Choice; both forms of EC may be sold only in pharmacies and health clinics; and, to permit enforcement of the age requirements, they must be stocked behind the pharmacy counter and requested by consumers.[48] Moreover, ulipristal acetate-based EC (ella), which is effective up to 120 hours after intercourse, is available by prescription only.

---

[44] The FDA press release is available online at: www.fda.gov/NewsEvents/Newsroom/PressAnnouncements/ 2006/ucm108717.htm; accessed July 9, 2010.

[45] According to a recent study, "ulipristal acetate prevents pregnancies when used as emergency contraception up to 120 hours after intercourse, making it the first hormonal method of emergency contraception with solid evidence of efficacy for late intake" (Fine *et al.* 2010: 257–63). It has been approved for sale in the European Union under the product name "ellaOne." In August 2010, when this book was already in production, the FDA approved the longer-acting emergency contraceptive for sale in the United States: (Harris 2010). Its product name is "ella," and unlike Plan B, it will be available by prescription only.

[46] Information available at "Drugs@FDA": www.accessdata.fda.gov/scripts/cder/drugsatfda/index.cfm; accessed July 9, 2010.

[47] Information available at the product's website: www.mynextchoice.com/Consumer/whatis_Main. asp; accessed July 9, 2010.

[48] In December 2006, the FDA provided the following description of the restricted distribution of Plan B:

Plan B will only be sold in pharmacies/stores staffed by a licensed pharmacist. In order to purchase Plan B over-the-counter, personal identification showing proof of age (18) [now 17] is required. Plan B will be available behind the counter at the pharmacy in order to manage both prescription (17 years and under) [now under 17] and OTC (18 years and over) [now 17 years and over] dispensing. This means Plan B will not be sold at gas stations or convenience stores, where other OTC products are routinely available. (FDA, "Plan B: Questions and Answers August 24, 2006, updated December 14, 2006." Available online at: www.fda.gov/Drugs/DrugSafety/ PostmarketDrugSafetyInformationforPatientsandProviders/ucm109 783.htm; accessed July 9, 2010.)

Among areas other than reproductive medicine in which conscientious objection recently has become an issue are organ donation after cardiac death (DCD) and palliative sedation. DCD, or as it was referred to earlier, non-heartbeating organ donation (NHBOD), is the practice of retrieving organs for transplant after death has been determined according to the cardio-pulmonary rather than whole-brain criterion (Arnold and Youngner 1993). DCD has prompted several ethical concerns, including whether it satisfies the dead donor rule (i.e. the principle that vital organs may be removed only after the patient is dead), potential conflicts of interest, effects on patient care, and impact on family members (Arnold and Youngner 1993). Anticipating physicians' and nurses' objections to participating in DCD, the University of Pittsburgh, one of the first medical centers to implement a DCD protocol, provided for conscientious objection in its policy. It states: "Health care professionals shall not be required to participate in the procedures described below [in the policy] if such participation is against their personal, ethical or religious beliefs" (Anonymous 1993).

Palliative sedation, sometimes referred to as "terminal sedation," is the practice of sedating terminally ill patients to unconsciousness until death. An AMA Council on Ethical and Judicial Affairs (CEJA) report adopted by the AMA Council of Delegates in 2008 concluded that palliative sedation is:

an intervention of last resort to reduce severe, refractory pain or other distressing clinical symptoms that do not respond to aggressive symptom-specific palliation. It is an accepted and appropriate component of end-of-life care under specific, relatively rare circumstances.[49]

The report further states that under "specific, relatively rare circumstances," physicians have an *obligation* to *offer* palliative sedation: "When symptoms cannot be diminished through all other means of palliation, including symptom-specific treatments, it is the ethical obligation of a physician to offer palliative sedation to unconsciousness as an option for the relief of intractable symptoms."[50] It is noteworthy that the CEJA report acknowledges that a significant percentage of physicians have ethical objections to palliative sedation.[51] The report does not address conscientious objection,

---

[49] CEJA Report 5-A-08, "Sedation to Unconsciousness in End-of-Life Care." This Report, as well as most other CEJA reports, is available online at: www.ama-assn.org/ama/pub/about-ama/our-people/ ama-councils/council-ethical-judicial-affairs.shtml; accessed October 17, 2010.
[50] Ibid.
[51] The CEJA Report cites a study of Connecticut members of the American College of Physicians. That study reported the following responses to the statement, "If a terminally ill patient has intractable pain

but it is to be expected that palliative sedation and the AMA policy will provide fertile ground for conscientious objection by physicians as well as nurses. In Chapter 3, I consider whether physicians who are conscientiously opposed to palliative sedation have an obligation to disclose it as an option.

An action by the US FDA at the beginning of 2009 will undoubtedly further expand the scope and frequency of conscientious objection by health care professionals. In January of that year, it was announced that the FDA had given the green light to the first US government-approved human clinical trials using human embryonic stem cells (Stein 2009b). The FDA approved a relatively small clinical trial involving only 8 to 10 patients with severe spinal cord injuries. In view of the controversy surrounding the destruction of human embryos, such clinical trials are likely to occasion conscience-based refusals on the part of research staff. Moreover, if such clinical trials prove successful, conscience-based refusals on the part of practitioners are to be expected.

Subsequent to the passage of the Church Amendment by the US Congress in 1973, there has been a profusion of legislative action relating to conscientious objection in health care at both the federal and state levels in the United States. This legislative activity has produced numerous conscience clause statutes that accommodate and protect conscience-based refusals by health care professionals.[52] In addition, conscience clauses sometimes are included in legislation authorizing practices. In this context, a conscience clause protects health care professionals who have conscience-based objections to the practice authorized by the legislation. Examples include advance directive laws and the Oregon and Washington Death with Dignity statutes.[53]

Since the focus of this book is on ethics, I will not offer a comprehensive review of the patchwork of federal and local laws and regulations that accommodate and protect conscience-based refusals by health care

---

despite aggressive analgesia, 'terminal sedation' is ethically appropriate:" Strongly disagree: 3%; Disagree: 5%; Neutral: 9%; Unsure: 5%; Agree: 37%; Strongly agree: 41% (Kaldjian *et al.* 2004a: 499–503 at 500).

[52] Several websites post information about conscience clause legislation. The Protection of Conscience Project has a comprehensive list of conscience clause legislation in several countries, including the United States and the United Kingdom: www.consciencelaws.org/Protection-of-Conscience-Laws. html; accessed July 8, 2010. The National Conference of State Legislatures posts information about state conscience clause legislation in the United States: www.ncsl.org/Home/tabid/118/Default.aspx; accessed July 8, 2010. The Guttmacher Institute provides a summary of state conscience clause legislation in the United States relating to abortion, sterilization, and contraception: www.guttmacher.org/statecenter/spibs/spib_RPHS.pdf; accessed July 8, 2010.

[53] The Abortion Act 1967 and the Human Fertilisation and Embryology Act 1990 are examples of this type of conscience clause legislation in the United Kingdom.

professionals in the United States.[54] In the final chapter, however, I will briefly consider conscience clauses. Drawing on the ethical limitations to conscience-based refusals identified in Chapter 3, I will argue that some conscience clauses provide too much protection of health care professionals' exercise of conscience. I also will argue that insofar as conscience clauses typically protect only *refusals*, they offer too little protection.

WHY IS THE EXERCISE OF CONSCIENCE VALUABLE AND WORTH PROTECTING?

When the US Department of Health and Human Services (HHS) issued regulations in December 2008 that provided broad protection to conscience-based refusals by health care providers (45 CFR Part 88), Michael Leavitt, the HHS secretary at the time, stated: "Doctors and other health care providers should not be forced to choose between good professional standing and violating their conscience . . . This rule protects the right of medical providers to care for their patients in accord with their conscience."[55] The substance of the regulations will be discussed in Chapters 2 and 6, but Leavitt's statement gives rise to an important question. He clearly assumes that it is bad or undesirable to require health care professionals to act contrary to their conscience. His statement also assumes that it is good or desirable to give health care professionals "moral space" in which to exercise their conscience. Are these assumptions justified? Is the exercise of conscience by health care professionals valuable and worth protecting; and if so, why?

Moral integrity

For several reasons, the exercise of conscience by health care professionals is valuable and worth protecting. The first and foremost reason is the connection between the exercise of conscience and moral integrity. A person of moral integrity has: (1) a set of core moral (i.e. ethical or religious) beliefs and (2) a disposition to act in accordance with those core beliefs.[56]

---

[54] Conscience clause legislation is not the only legal basis for protecting conscience-based refusals by health care professionals in the United States. Additional legal grounds include the First Amendment of the US Constitution, similar provisions in state constitutions, and Title VII of the 1964 US Civil Rights Act. See (Wardle 1993: 177–230).

[55] Department of Health and Human Services News Release, Thursday, December 18, 2008. Available online at: www.hhs.gov/news/press/2008pres/12/20081218a.html; accessed July 11, 2010.

[56] This analysis of moral integrity is similar to Martin Benjamin's analysis of integrity. See (Benjamin 1990). He identifies three "elements of integrity," which "constitute the formal structure of one's identity as a person." Those three elements are said to be "(1) a reasonably coherent and relatively

To maintain one's moral integrity, a person must refrain from performing actions that are against her conscience (i.e. actions that violate her core moral beliefs). Thus, the exercise of conscience is essential to maintaining and protecting one's moral integrity. As Blustein rightly observes, when one acts against one's conscience, "one violates one's own fundamental moral or religious convictions, personal standards that one sees as an important part of oneself and by which one is prepared to judge oneself" (Blustein 1993: 295). By acting against one's conscience, then, one fails to maintain one's moral integrity.

Why maintain and protect moral integrity? There are several reasons. First, from the perspective of the conscientious objector, moral integrity can be an essential component of her conception of a good or meaningful life. In this respect, moral integrity has intrinsic worth or value to the objector.

Second, a loss of moral integrity can be devastating. It can result in strong feelings of guilt, remorse, and shame as well as loss of self-respect. Moral integrity can be of central importance to people whose core beliefs are secular as well as those whose core beliefs are religious. Nussbaum cites a powerful image that Roger Williams uses to defend liberty of conscience: "To impose an orthodoxy upon the conscience is nothing less than what Williams, in a memorable and oft-repeated image, called 'Soule rape'" (Nussbaum 2008: 37). The reference to rape of the *soul* suggests that this statement was meant primarily as a defense of religious tolerance. Nevertheless, when a failure to accommodate secular core beliefs results in a loss of moral integrity, it also can be experienced as an assault on one's self or identity.

Third, it might be claimed that when a failure to accommodate core moral beliefs gives rise to a loss of moral integrity, the result can be a general decline in a person's moral character, which is particularly undesirable in health care professionals.[57] Lynn Wardle presented a claim along these lines in Congressional testimony:

[James] Madison clearly understood that if men are not loyal to themselves, to their conscience, to their God and their moral duty as they see it, it is utterly irrational folly to expect them to be loyal to less compelling moral obligations of legal rules, statutes, judicial orders, or the claims of citizenship and civic virtue, much less professional duties. If you demand that a man betray his conscience, you have

---

stable set of highly cherished values and principles; (2) verbal behavior expressing these values and principles; and (3) conduct embodying one's values and principles and consistent with what one says" (ibid. 51).

[57] I consider a similar claim with respect to students in Chapter 5.

eliminated the only moral basis for his fidelity to the rule of law, and have destroyed the foundation for all civic virtue.[58]

Charles Hepler advances a similar claim in relation to members of his profession (pharmacy): "We would be naive to expect a pharmacist to forsake his or her ethics in one area (e.g. abortion) while applying them for the patient's welfare in every other area" (Hepler 2005: 434).

Finally, it can be claimed that moral integrity generally has intrinsic worth or value. That is, it might be asserted that, *having* core moral beliefs that are associated with one's self-conception and a *disposition* to act in accordance with them (to act conscientiously) are intrinsically valuable and worthy of respect. It is arguable that all other things being equal, a world with such people is a better place than one in which people with those characteristics are absent. To be sure, insofar as moral integrity can involve a commitment to any ethical or religious beliefs, it does not guarantee ethically acceptable behavior. For example, depending on the content of a person's core moral beliefs, maintaining moral integrity can require invidious discrimination, genocide, cruelty, and so forth. Nevertheless, similar to courage and honesty, admiration and respect for moral integrity is at least partially independent of an assessment of ends and consequences. That is, although we might justifiably withhold our admiration and respect if we judge the ends and consequences to be excessively bad, our admiration and respect is not always contingent on a favorable assessment of ends and consequences. Accordingly, it is not implausible to claim that similar to courage and honesty, which also can serve immoral ends and produce undesirable consequences, moral integrity is a moral virtue.[59]

Additional reasons

The exercise of conscience is valuable and worth protecting for several additional reasons, each of which also might apply to refusals based on a practitioner's ethical or religious beliefs that are *not* included within the scope of her *core* moral beliefs. The first derives from the value of autonomy and the principle of respect for autonomy. There is more than one conception of autonomy. However, according to Beauchamp and Childress,

---

[58] Testimony Re: Abortion Non-Discrimination Act, Committee on Energy and Commerce, Subcommittee on Health (July 11, 2002). Available online at: www.consciencelaws.org/Examining-Conscience-Legal/Legal06.htm; accessed July 9, 2010.

[59] Blustein claims that integrity is "an important virtue of a certain sort, one that, when combined with other valuable traits, provides an additional ground for admiration of the individual" (Blustein 1993: 289–314 at 290).

"[v]irtually all theories of autonomy agree that two conditions are essential for autonomy: (1) *liberty* (independence from controlling influences) and (2) *agency* (capacity for intentional action)" (2009: 58). The exercise of conscience (e.g. a conscience-based refusal to dispense EC) is an autonomous action, and constraints on the exercise of conscience also are constraints on autonomy. Accordingly, insofar as autonomy is valuable, so, too, is the exercise of conscience. Further, the principle of respect for autonomy provides a basis for protecting the exercise of conscience.[60] As Beauchamp and Childress explain the concept, "[t]o respect an autonomous agent is, at a minimum, to acknowledge that person's right to hold views, to make choices, and to take actions based on their personal values and beliefs" (ibid.: 63). Insofar as respect for autonomy requires permitting individuals to act on their personal values and beliefs, it provides a reason for not restricting the exercise of conscience by health care professionals.[61]

Second, the value of the exercise of conscience can be said to derive (in part) from the value of moral/cultural diversity, and protecting health care professionals' exercise of conscience can be defended as a requirement of tolerance of moral/cultural diversity. Wear, LaGaipa, and Logue cite toleration of moral diversity as a basis for recognizing conscientious objection in medicine (Wear *et al.* 1994). Toleration of moral diversity is said to be a "first principle" in "post-industrial, democratic societies" which lack "any common moral ground" for "the adjudication of our differences" (ibid.: 147). Citing H. Tristram Engelhardt (1986), they refer to the absence of any "common moral ground" as the "post-modern predicament" (ibid.: 47). The principle of toleration of moral diversity directs us to tolerate the moral views of others and not attempt to impose our ethical beliefs on them. On the basis of this principle, then, it might be claimed that the exercise of conscience by health care professionals should be permitted.[62]

Third, the notion of ethical epistemic modesty or humility can be cited as a basis for respecting and protecting the exercise of conscience. Ethical epistemic modesty is the view that although ethical beliefs can be correct or

---

[60] For justifications of the principle of respect for autonomy, see (Beauchamp and Childress 2009).

[61] Martin Benjamin bases respect for conscience on respect for persons, a principle that requires respect for autonomy: "Respect for conscience is a corollary of the principle of respect for persons. To respect another as a person is, insofar as possible, to respect the expression and exercise, if not the content, of a person's most fundamental convictions" (Benjamin vol. I 2004: 513–17). Judith Daar presents an autonomy-based defense of conscientious objection by physicians (Daar 1993: 1241–89). However, her focus is on cases in which physicians believe that continued life-extending treatments are "futile," and their refusals are based primarily on considerations of professional integrity.

[62] For a perceptive discussion of limits on toleration of cultural diversity in the context of health care, see (Macklin 1998: 1–22).

incorrect and justified or unjustified, we might be mistaken when we think that a particular ethical belief is correct or justified. This recognition suggests "modesty" or "humility" and a rejection of dogmatism in relation to beliefs that we do not accept. Sulmasy offers the following explanation of what he refers to as "epistemic moral humility" and its implications for tolerance:

> [W]e can declare a number of acts to be wrong with moral certainty (e.g., putting people in gas chambers to rid the world of "imperfect genes," such as those associated with mental retardation or certain ethnic groups, is morally wrong). But with respect to a wide range of other moral issues we have less certainty. As we approach the application of our moral principles and rules to particular cases, we also have less certainty. This is not to say that there are no correct answers to these questions. Rather, given the imperfections of our moral knowledge and reasoning, we must acknowledge that disagreements are inevitable. Call this moral realism tempered by epistemic moral humility. In the end, this is the true basis for tolerance. (Sulmasy 2008: 144)

Epistemic modesty or humility is not to be confused with metaphysical or epistemological ethical skepticism or ethical relativism. Metaphysical ethical skeptics deny that there are any ethical truths and epistemological ethical skeptics deny that ethical beliefs are justifiable. Ethical relativists believe that: (1) ethical statements have truth-value only in relation to some moral framework or other, and (2) there are several different moral frameworks, and when two or more clash, none is "privileged" (i.e. none is more valid than the others) (Harman 1996). Since these are metaethical positions (i.e. theories about ethics) rather than normative ethical theories, it is unclear how they can be cited to support a normative ethical position about the exercise of conscience. By contrast, advocates of ethical epistemic modesty might defend protecting the exercise of conscience as an expression of a lack of moral certitude.[63]

Fourth, a failure to accommodate health care professionals' conscience-based refusals may discourage people who value moral integrity from becoming physicians, nurses, or pharmacists. An unintended consequence might be to pre-select for individuals who are ethically insensitive. When the broad HHS conscience clause referred to above was published in the *Federal Register*, this concern was expressed in one of the cited written comments:

---

[63] Carolyn McLeod argues that an appeal to epistemic humility fails to support the claim that referral is an appropriate compromise that providers with a conscience-based objection to abortion should be willing to accept (Mcleod 2008).

[B]y insisting that those who are willing to violate their consciences in the delivery of health care are the only persons who should enter the health care field, one contributes to the creation of a health care delivery system of professionals who blindly follow directives rather than conscience, putting society at risk.[64]

An additional unintended consequence might be to significantly reduce the number of individuals who enter the health professions, which might have a detrimental impact on access to health care. When the HHS conscience clause was published in the *Federal Register*, this was another concern reportedly expressed in written comments:

Many Comments we received, including those of many health care providers, stated that forcing providers to perform or participate in procedures that violate their consciences discourages individuals from entering or remaining in careers in the health professions.[65]

Fifth, protecting health care professionals' exercise of conscience promotes diversity within the health care professions. This claim was included in the HHS defense of the federal conscience protection regulations when they were published in the *Federal Register*:

A health care system that is intolerant of individual conscience, certain religious beliefs, ethnic and cultural traditions, or moral convictions serves to discourage individuals with diverse backgrounds and perspectives from entering the health care professions, further exacerbating health care access shortages and reducing quality of care.[66]

Sixth, a broad defense of protecting the exercise of conscience can be based on political theory and a consideration of social stability. As Nussbaum presented the claim in relation to the early US colonial period: "[P]eople with different views of life's ultimate meaning and purpose really needed to learn to live together on decent terms if they were to survive at all" (Nussbaum 2008: 36).

For all these reasons, then, it can be maintained that the exercise of conscience is valuable and worth protecting. Some, such as respect for moral integrity, may be stronger and more convincing and compelling than others, but it is undeniable that there are good reasons for concluding that the exercise of conscience is valuable and worth protecting. These reasons acknowledge that physicians, nurses, and pharmacists are *moral agents*. However, they also are *professionals*. Accordingly, it remains to

---

[64] *Federal Register*, vol. 73, no. 245, Friday, December 19, 2008, 78081. Available online at: http://edocket.access.gpo.gov/2008/pdf/E8–30134.pdf; accessed July 9, 2010.
[65] Ibid.   [66] Ibid.

consider the limits and constraints that professional obligations impose on the exercise of conscience. This is the subject of the next two chapters.

CONCLUSION

Although conscientious objection has a long history in relation to military service, it is a relatively recent phenomenon in relation to health care. However, since 1973, the year in which the US Congress enacted legislation to protect conscience-based refusals in relation to abortion and sterilization, physicians, nurses, and pharmacists have refused to provide an increasingly wide range of goods and services. For reasons of conscience, some health care professionals have refused to: withhold or withdraw MPNH and other life-sustaining treatments; offer and provide palliative sedation; prescribe and dispense contraceptives and/or emergency contraception; provide fertility treatments, IVF, and other means of assisted reproduction; and participate in organ retrieval when performed according to a DCD protocol.

In response to these conscience-based refusals, numerous laws and regulations have been enacted to protect the exercise of conscience by health care professionals. Several reasons were presented in this chapter for concluding that the exercise of conscience is valuable and worth protecting. However, there also are reasons for limiting the exercise of conscience by health care professionals. Constraints on health care professionals' exercise of conscience are examined in the next two chapters.

CHAPTER 2

Three approaches to conscientious objection in health care: conscience absolutism, the incompatibility thesis, and compromise

Conscience-based refusals to provide legal and professionally accepted health care goods and services appear to present a conflict between health care professionals and patients.[1] On the one hand, patients seek goods and services to meet their health care needs and interests. On the other hand, health care professionals want to maintain their moral integrity, and doing so can prompt them to refuse to provide a good or service that will satisfy a patient's health needs and/or interests. Generally, an appropriate strategy for resolving such conflicts is to attempt to find a "reasonable compromise."

Addressing conscientious objection in pharmacy, Julie Cantor and Ken Baum endorse the search for a compromise: "most people can agree that we must find a workable and respectful balance between the needs of patients and the morals of pharmacists" (Cantor and Baum 2004: 2010). This approach is also recommended by the American Pharmacists Association (APhA). Its "Pharmacist Conscience Clause" states: "APhA recognizes the individual pharmacist's right to exercise conscientious refusal and supports the establishment of systems to ensure patient's [sic] access to legally prescribed therapy without compromising the pharmacist's right of conscientious refusal" (Winckler and Gans 2006: 12).

Dan Brock endorses what he refers to as "the conventional compromise," which permits physicians and pharmacists to refuse to provide a service or product that is against their conscience only if the following three conditions are satisfied:

The physician/pharmacist informs the patient/customer about the service/product if it is medically relevant to their medical condition;

---

[1] In addition to conflicts with patients, there can also be conflicts with colleagues, other professionals, employers, and institutions. Some of these additional conflicts will be explored in Chapter 3.

The physician/pharmacist refers the patient/customer to another professional willing and able to provide the service/product;
The referral does not impose an unreasonable burden on the patient/customer. (D. Brock 2008: 194)

The 2001 American Nurses Association (ANA) Code of Ethics for Nurses recommends a similar approach:

> The nurse who decides not to take part because of conscientious objection must communicate this decision in appropriate ways. Whenever possible, such a refusal should be made known in advance and in time for alternate arrangements to be made for patient care. The nurse is obliged to provide for the patient's safety, to avoid abandonment, and to withdraw only when assured that alternative sources of nursing care are available to the patient. (Fowler 2008: 160–1)

However, the search for a suitable compromise is not accepted by proponents of two extreme views. At one extreme, compromise is rejected by those who maintain that individuals who are not willing to provide any health care good or service that is legal and within the scope of a professional's competence should choose another profession. The following statement by Julian Savulescu, although he subsequently qualifies it, typifies this response: "If people are not prepared to offer legally permitted, efficient, and beneficial care to a patient because it conflicts with their values, they should not be doctors" (Savulescu 2006).[2] A *New York Times* editorial expressed a similar sentiment in relation to pharmacists: "Any pharmacist who cannot dispense medicines lawfully prescribed by a doctor should find another line of work" (Anonymous 2005). This view is seconded by the author of a syndicated op-ed piece who proclaimed:

> [N]o one has the right to refuse to perform some foreseeable aspect of their job . . . [A] candidate for a pharmacy job [should] understand that she might have to hand out contraceptive pills and devices. She should either resolve to mind her own business or keep searching the want ads . . . You don't like what the job requires? Fine. Get another job. (Pitts 2005: 13)

These responses assume that conscience-based refusals to provide legal and professionally permitted goods and services within the scope of a practitioner's competence are incompatible with the practitioner's professional obligations.[3] I will refer to this assumption as the "incompatibility thesis."

---

[2] Savulescu eventually qualifies this claim to permit conscientious refusals as long as they do not restrict patient access to health services. In addition, Savulescu's primary concern is with physicians who are government employees, such as physicians within the British National Health Service.
[3] This assumption underlies one of the five models for managing conscientious objection that Rebecca Dresser identifies (Dresser 2005: 9–10). That model, according to Dresser, "rules out the possibility of conscientious objection" (ibid.: 9).

At the other extreme, compromise is rejected by those who maintain that there are no ethical constraints on the exercise of conscience by health care professionals. This view will be referred to as "conscience absolutism." According to conscience absolutism, health care professionals generally do not have an obligation to perform *any action*, including disclosure and referral, contrary to their conscience.

In Chapter 3, I will explain and defend a compromise approach based on core professional obligations of physicians, nurses, and pharmacists. Contrary to conscience absolutism, I will argue that core professional obligations justify several constraints on the exercise of conscience by physicians, nurses, and pharmacists. Contrary to the incompatibility thesis, I will maintain that if health care professionals do not violate these constraints, the exercise of conscience can be compatible with fulfilling core professional obligations. In this chapter, I will explain conscience absolutism and critically analyze two challenges to it. Next, I will examine various accounts of the professional obligations of physicians, nurses, and pharmacists, and I will argue that with the possible exception of accounts based on general ethical theories: (1) conscience absolutism is incompatible with them; (2) they do not unequivocally support the incompatibility thesis; and (3) they favor a compromise approach.

CONSCIENCE ABSOLUTISM

According to conscience absolutism, in addition to not having an obligation to provide a good or service that violates a health care professional's conscience, the professional is not obligated directly or indirectly to participate in its provision or facilitate patient access to it. The claim that emergency department physicians with a conscience-based objection to emergency contraception (EC) are not obligated to inform rape victims of its availability as a means to prevent pregnancy or to provide referrals to other physicians or facilities is an instance of conscience absolutism.[4] Another example is the claim that a pharmacist with a conscience-based objection to contraceptives does not have an obligation to refer a patient to a pharmacist or pharmacy where she will be able to fill her prescription for birth control pills.[5]

---

[4] One telephone survey reports that only half of the staff in hospitals that do not provide EC stated that referrals are provided (Harrison 2005: 105–10).
[5] The National Women's Law Center reports that pharmacists in several states have refused to dispense contraceptives and provide referrals. Information is available online at: http://nwlc.org/details.cfm?id=2185&section=health; accessed July 9, 2010. Donald Herbe claims that pharmacists who object to

In the last few weeks of the Bush administration, the Department of Health and Human Services (HHS) issued a sweeping conscience protection regulation referred to in Chapter 1. The HHS Final Rule, entitled "Ensuring that Department of Health and Human Services Funds Do Not Support Coercive or Discriminatory Policies or Practices in Violation of Federal Law" (45 CFR § 88), exemplifies conscience absolutism.[6] It offered legal protections to health care professionals who refuse to perform or *assist in the performance* of specified activities that violate their ethical or religious beliefs. It provided a broad definition of "assist in the performance:" "to participate in any activity with a reasonable connection to a procedure, health service or health service program, or research activity, so long as the individual involved is a part of the workforce of a Department-funded entity" (45 CFR § 88.2). On the basis of this broad definition, "assist in the performance" was said to include "counseling, referral, training, and other arrangements for the procedure, health service, or research activity" (45 CFR § 88.2). Some state conscience clause statutes have similar broad protections that exemplify conscience absolutism.[7]

A model conscience protection statute and a model conscience protection policy for pharmacists also exemplify conscience absolutism. The Protection of Conscience Project Model Protection of Conscience Act prohibits compelled *direct* and *indirect* participation in specified activities if a health care professional has a conscience-based objection to such participation.[8] The Pharmacists for Life International Model Conscience Clause states:

The rights of conscience of any person being a duly licensed pharmacist, who shall object on personal, ethical, moral or religious grounds to the performance of *any act* in the normal course of professional performance or dispensing, shall be respected. Further, such a refusal to perform *any act* or the *omission of any act* based on such a

---

dispensing emergency contraception do not have an obligation to refer (Herbe 2002: 77–102). "For many pharmacists," he claims, "a referral would be no more [sic] than passive participation in the activity they initially refused to actively assist" (ibid. 89).

[6] *Federal Register* 73, 245 (December 19, 2008), 78072–101. The effective date of this regulation (hereinafter referred to as the "HHS Final Rule") was January 20, 2009 – the day Barack Obama, who had opposed the proposed regulation, became the 44th US president. The regulations were rescinded shortly after President Obama's inauguration: *Federal Register*, Vol. 74, No. 45, Tuesday, March 10, 2009, 10207–11. Available online at: http://edocket.access.gpo.gov/2009/pdf/E9–5067.pdf ; accessed July 9, 2010.

[7] I critically analyze the HHS Final Rule and other conscience clauses (i.e. laws and regulations that protect the exercise of conscience by health care professionals) in Chapter 6.

[8] Available online at: www.consciencelaws.org/Protection-of-Conscience-Model-Statute.html; accessed July 9, 2010. The model statute does not define "indirect participation." However, it explicitly protects health care professionals from being compelled to *counsel* or *educate* "persons in a manner which indicates that the activities [specified in the act] . . . are morally neutral or acceptable."

claim of conscience, shall not form the basis for any claim for damages or any recriminatory or discriminatory action against such a person (emphasis added).[9]

According to this broad policy, and contrary to the "conventional compromise" as well as the compromise approach that I will explain and support in Chapter 3, pharmacists who have conscience-based objections to dispensing a medication, such as oral contraceptives or Plan B (an emergency contraceptive) are not obligated to refer patients to pharmacists or pharmacies that will fill their prescriptions.

Moral complicity and conscience absolutism

In support of conscience absolutism, it can be argued that as moral agents who seek to preserve their moral integrity, health care professionals must be permitted to refuse directly or indirectly to participate in perceived ethical wrongdoing. Specifically, in defense of the claim that there is no obligation to disclose or refer when health care professionals have a conscience-based objection to a good or service (e.g. contraception, abortion, sterilization, or palliative sedation), it can be argued that even indirect participation in the perceived wrongdoing of others (i.e. other health care professionals and patients) involves *moral complicity*. For example, it can be claimed that a physician who has a conscience-based objection to palliative sedation but discloses the option and refers when it is requested, is morally complicit in the perceived wrongdoing of others and, therefore, morally culpable. Karen Brauer, president of Pharmacists for Life, appeals to this line of reasoning to defend the view that pharmacists with a conscience-based objection to filling prescriptions should not be expected to facilitate a transfer or provide referrals: "That's like saying, 'I don't kill people myself but let me tell you about the guy down the street who does.' What's that saying? 'I will not off your husband, but I know a buddy who will?' It's the same thing" (Stein 2005). Michael Bayles endorses a similar view in relation to abortion referral:[10]

---

[9] Available online at: www.pfli.org/main.php?pfli=modelpharmacistcc; accessed July 9, 2010.

[10] Bayles, however, argues that unless no other physician will perform an abortion, a physician who believes that abortion is morally wrong does not have a good ethical reason for refusing to provide it himself. His argument is based on two assumptions: (1) for physician *x* to have a good ethical reason to refuse to perform an abortion, his refusal must prevent a moral wrong; (2) if another physician performs the abortion, physician *x*'s refusal does not prevent a moral wrong. In response, it can be argued that an interest in maintaining moral integrity is a good ethical reason for refusing to provide a good or service that another health care professional will provide.

If a physician sincerely believes abortion in a particular case is morally wrong, he cannot consistently advise a patient where she may obtain one. To do so would be to assist someone in immoral conduct by knowingly providing a means to it. The physician would bear some responsibility for the wrongful deed. Believing the abortion to be morally wrong, he believes that it is wrong for anyone to perform it and for the woman to obtain it. If he directs her to a physician who will perform it, then he assists both of them in acting wrongfully. (1979: 167)

The foregoing argument for conscience absolutism is based on the assumption that *assisting* patients (e.g. by presenting options and providing referrals) establishes *moral complicity*. Accordingly, conscience absolutism might be challenged by questioning that assumption. An approach along these lines is based on a distinction between *direct* and *indirect* referral.

Direct and indirect referral

Frank Chervenak and Laurence McCullough (2008) distinguish between direct and indirect referral and claim that complicity is absent when referral is indirect. Direct referral involves communication between health care professionals: one who refers and one who receives the referral. The former contacts the latter and takes steps to assure that the patient will receive a medically indicated service that the former is unable or unwilling to provide. Chervenak and McCullough offer the following illustration of direct referral:

For example, an obstetrician suspects appendicitis in a pregnant patient. As the patient's fiduciary, the obstetrician has a beneficence-based obligation to see to it that this patient receives prompt surgical attention, which obligation is fulfilled by assuring that a surgeon does indeed see the patient promptly. (2008: 232.e2)

By contrast, indirect referrals are limited to providing patients with information (e.g. the names and contact information of providers from whom they can receive the service at issue). Indirect referral is said to be sufficient when a service is not medically indicated, for example, when a pregnant woman considers an elective abortion.[11]

Whereas it might be plausible to ascribe moral complicity in relation to direct referrals, Chervenak and McCullough maintain that a physician who provides an indirect referral "cannot reasonably be understood to be a party to, or complicit in, a subsequent decision that is the sole province of the patient's subsequent exercise of autonomy in consultation with a referral

---

[11] In cases of elective abortion, Chervenak and McCullough claim that obstetrician-gynecologists with conscience-based objections are at least obligated to provide indirect referral to an organization such as Planned Parenthood to protect patients from harm.

physician" (ibid.). Accordingly, they claim that although conscience-based objections to "direct referral for termination of pregnancy have merit; conscience-based objections to indirect referral do not" (ibid.: 232.e3).

In response to the claim that moral complicity is absent when referrals are indirect, it can be objected that there are obvious counter-examples. Indeed, Brauer provides one: A woman asks someone to kill her husband. The person responds that he cannot kill her husband, but he can tell her how to find someone who will. Giving the woman information that will enable her to enlist the services of a willing killer satisfies the criteria of "indirect referral." However, if the "referral" results in the spouse's murder, the person who provided the information is morally complicit. Surely, that person cannot avoid complicity by claiming that the decision to kill "is the sole province of the . . . [wife's] subsequent exercise of autonomy in consultation with a referral . . . [killer]." This analysis suggests that merely identifying a referral as indirect (i.e. limited to providing information) will not suffice to establish lack of moral complicity. Additional factors need to be considered to determine moral complicity or lack thereof.

Legal complicity as a model
Although the question at issue is the determination of moral complicity, legal criteria of complicity can provide a basis for corresponding ethical criteria. In a classic analysis of the legal doctrine of complicity, Sanford Kadish (1985) identifies three conditions that must be satisfied to attribute complicity to a secondary agent for the criminal conduct of a primary agent:[12]

(1) The secondary agent attempted to influence the primary agent's decision to commit the crime and/or provided assistance to the primary agent.
(2) The secondary agent's influence and/or assistance were intentional.
(3) The secondary agent's actions contributed to the criminal conduct of the primary agent.

These suggest the following corresponding conditions for ascribing moral complicity to a secondary agent (i.e. a health care professional with a conscience-based objection to a good or service) for the unethical conduct of a primary agent (i.e. another health care professional and/or a patient):

---

[12] Kadish also identifies various qualifications and exceptions. In a more recent article, he questions the intentionality condition and argues for an expanded conception of complicity that includes recklessness (Kadish 1997: 369–94).

(1*) The secondary agent attempted to influence the primary agent's decision to engage in unethical conduct and/or provided assistance to the primary agent.

(2*) The secondary agent's influence and/or assistance were intentional.

(3*) The secondary agent's actions contributed to the unethical conduct of the primary agent.

These three conditions can be applied to determine whether informing patients about clinical options and/or providing referrals can establish moral complicity. For the sake of this analysis, a health care professional's judgment that an intervention is unethical will not be questioned. Clearly, if a health care professional has a conscience-based objection to an intervention, she will not attempt to encourage a patient to decide to have it. However, disclosing the option and providing a referral both constitute assistance. Accordingly, the first condition is satisfied.

The intentionality condition is ambiguous and subject to differing interpretations. If it is understood to require only that the disclosure and/or referral are deliberate and voluntary actions, this condition is satisfied. However, if it is understood to mean that the health care professional shares the patient's goals or wants to help a patient receive the intervention, it is unlikely to be satisfied when health care professionals have conscience-based objections to the intervention. If they believe that they have a professional obligation to inform and/or refer, they may want only to satisfy that perceived obligation. Alternatively, their objective may be to respect the patient's autonomy, and they may not share the patient's goals. Finally, if the condition is understood to mean that the patient's receiving the intervention is a foreseeable or expected result, it will be satisfied in many, if not most, cases.[13]

Insofar as providing information about options and referrals facilitate patient access, which, after all, is the point of the corresponding requirements, the third condition is satisfied.[14] Since these three conditions appear

---

[13] Of the three conditions, the one that is most subject to dispute is the intentionality condition and its interpretation. The interpretation that requires the health care professional to want to help a patient receive the service at issue is associated with the controversial doctrine of double-effect. Accordingly, for health care providers who do not accept this interpretation of the intentionality condition, merely foreseeing that disclosure and/or referral will facilitate access can be sufficient to establish moral complicity. Below, I will argue that considerable deference should be given to a health care professional's conception of moral complicity.

[14] From a legal perspective, a person either is or is not guilty of complicity. However, from a moral perspective, there are degrees of complicity. A secondary agent's moral complicity is in part a function of the extent to which she contributes to the unethical conduct of the primary agent. I will examine the notion of degrees of moral complicity and its significance below.

to represent a credible conception of moral complicity, and the interpretation of the intentionality condition is the subject of ongoing controversy, it is not warranted to dismiss as baseless a health care professional's claim that to avoid moral complicity in a perceived moral wrong, she cannot disclose or refer.

Moral complicity and natural law

As Daniel Sulmasy observes, "the natural law tradition has developed a very complex and subtle set of principles" for determining whether one person is morally complicit in the wrongdoing of another (2008: 141).[15] Drawing on this tradition, he identifies several conditions. One, "formal cooperation," is a sufficient condition of moral complicity. According to this condition, if x shares in the intent (i.e. goal or purpose) of a wrongdoer y, x is morally complicit in y's wrongdoing. Accordingly, if a physician who has a conscience-based objection to palliative sedation refers a patient who requests it to another physician with the intent of helping the patient achieve her goal, the physician is morally complicit in a perceived wrongdoing.

However, a health care professional who has a conscience-based objection to providing a requested good or service can provide a referral without sharing the patient's purpose. The health care professional may intend only to respect the patient's autonomy and/or to fulfill a perceived professional obligation to refer. A similar point applies to disclosing options, including those which a health care professional is unwilling to provide due to conscience-based objections. According to Sulmasy, if formal cooperation is absent, it is necessary to assess "material cooperation," and he provides seven questions to guide an assessment of moral complicity:

(1) How necessary is one's cooperation to the carrying out of the act? Could it occur without one's cooperation? The more likely that it could occur without one's cooperation, the more justified is one's cooperation. (2) How proximate is one to the act, in space and time and in the causal chain? The further removed one is, the more justified is one's cooperation. (3) Is one under any degree of duress to perform the act? Is someone compelling the act at gunpoint? Does failure to cooperate mean loss of livelihood and ability to provide for a family? The more duress one is under, the more justifiable is one's cooperation. (4) How likely is one's cooperation to become habitual? The less likely, the more justifiable. (5) Is there a significant potential for scandal? I am using scandal here in the technical sense of leading others to believe that the one who is providing the material cooperation actually approves of the act so that observers might thereby be led to think it morally

---

[15] For an analysis informed by natural law of moral complicity in relation to voluntarily stopping eating and drinking, see (Jansen 2004: 61–74).

permissible. The less the potential for scandal, the more permissible the cooperation. (6) Does one have a special role that would be violated by this action? The less
one has special role responsibilities that potentially would be contravened by the
act, the more justifiable it is. (7) Does one have a proportionately important reason
for the cooperation? That is, is there some morally important good that will come
about because of one's indirect cooperation? If so, one has a better justification for
cooperation. (ibid.: 141)

None of these considerations is obviously indefensible as a criterion of
moral complicity, and together they suggest that determinations of moral
complicity are complex and context-dependent. According to these criteria,
then, it cannot be said categorically that health care professionals who
disclose options and/or refer are not morally complicit in the perceived
wrongdoing of others. For example, suppose a patient requests palliative
sedation from a physician with a conscience-based objection to it, and the
physician provides a referral to a physician who is willing and able to
administer it. Putting aside the last two criteria, which require potentially
contentious moral judgments, and applying the first five criteria, the
physician is (highly) complicit in a perceived wrongdoing if: (1) It is highly
unlikely that the patient would have received palliative sedation if the
physician had not provided the referral.[16] (2) The patient's care was transferred within a few hours of the referral and palliative sedation commenced
immediately. (3) The physician's decision to refer was voluntary. There was
no undue pressure, and the decision was not made under duress. (4) The
physician has a general policy of providing referrals for palliative sedation.
(5) Despite the physician's forceful denials, many of his professional colleagues believe that willingness to refer is inconsistent with genuine ethical
disapproval. Since they view him as a role model, they begin to question
whether palliative sedation is morally wrong.

Since the seven criteria support the proposition that moral complicity is a
matter of degree, it is necessary to determine whether in a particular case in
which there is *some* moral complicity, its extent is *acceptable* or *unacceptable*.
There may be some clear cases, such as the aforementioned palliative
sedation example. However, drawing the line between acceptable and
unacceptable may require contentious ethical judgments. The need for

---

[16] Below, I will argue that the obligation to refer is stronger when patient access to legal and
professionally accepted services is significantly diminished without referral. Accordingly, from the
perspective of the first condition, the obligation to refer is stronger when moral complicity is higher.
This conclusion is offset by the seventh criterion, according to which a stronger obligation to refer is
correlated with a lesser degree of moral complicity. If there is a professional obligation to refer, then,
absent a conflicting role-related obligation, the sixth criterion will not support diminished moral
complicity.

such judgments provides another reason for doubting that conscience absolutism can be convincingly refuted by arguing that health care professionals who disclose options and refer are not morally complicit in the perceived wrongdoing of others.

In addition, even if there are credible criteria that can unambiguously establish that a health care professional who refuses to provide a good or service due to a conscience-based objection is not morally complicit for informing a patient that it is an available option and/or providing a referral, the health care professional might not accept those criteria. Insofar as an important goal of accommodating conscientious objection is to respect moral integrity, considerable deference should be given to a health care professional's conception of moral complicity. Accommodating only credible or widely accepted metaethical beliefs about moral complicity is no less incompatible with respect for moral integrity than accommodating only credible or widely accepted normative ethical beliefs.

Conscientious objection to war and conscience absolutism

An alleged analogue to conscientious objection to wartime military service can provide the basis for another criticism of conscience absolutism. Specifically, it can be argued that conscience absolutism is no more acceptable in relation to health care than it is in relation to war. An argument along these lines is suggested by Eva and Hugh LaFollette (2007). Citing alternative service requirements for conscientious objectors to war, they claim that a similar requirement is appropriate in relation to pharmacists who seek conscience-based exemptions from filling valid prescriptions. They do not specify the "alternative service" that is appropriate for pharmacists and other health care professionals who are permitted to opt out of providing a good or service that is against their conscience.[17] However, it might be claimed that a suitable "alternative service" for health care professionals who are exempted from providing legal and professionally accepted health services against their conscience is to require them to disclose options and refer.[18]

---

[17] Although they focus on pharmacists, they intend their analysis to be generalizable to other professions.

[18] The LaFollettes criticize pharmacists who "want their conscience respected, but are unwilling to reciprocate by respecting the conscience of other members of their civil society, especially those who need these prescriptions" (LaFollette and LaFollette 2007: 249–54 at 252). It might be claimed that requiring pharmacists who are exempted from dispensing medications against their conscience to refer is an appropriate means of promoting "reciprocation." On the other hand, it might be objected that it is misleading to refer to "alternative service" for health care professionals who refuse to provide a

The alleged analogue with conscientious objection to war does not provide a sound basis for rejecting conscience absolutism. First, a key reason for requiring alternative service from conscientious objectors to war does not apply to health care professionals who are exempted from providing goods and services that are against their conscience. In view of the risk of death and injury and the other substantial sacrifices and burdens associated with military combat, it is arguable that fairness requires conscientious objectors to war to make some sacrifices and endure some burdens for the common good. Otherwise, they would be "free riders" who benefit from the sacrifices of others without making any comparable social contribution.[19] By contrast, disclosing information about a health care service and providing a referral do not place significant demands on health care professionals who are willing and able to do so. Hence, it is implausible to claim that health care professionals who receive conscience-based exemptions have a fairness-based obligation to provide information and referrals.

Second, conscientious objectors to war typically fall into two categories: individuals who are opposed only to combat roles and individuals who are opposed to any military service. Conscientious objectors in the former category are required to perform military service in non-combat roles (e.g. as medics), and conscientious objectors in the latter category are required to perform alternative non-military service (e.g. as hospital aids or public service volunteers). These requirements enable draft-eligible citizens to discharge a duty to serve their country during wartime without going against their conscience. However, depending on a health care professional's conception of moral complicity, disclosure and referral can be incompatible with her conscience. Accordingly, when that is the case, it cannot be claimed that requiring disclosure and referral is similar to requiring alternative service from conscientious objectors to war. Since the alternative

---

particular service but provide a wide range of services to which they have no conscience-based objections. By contrast, conscientious objectors to war refuse either to perform any military service or to participate in combat-related activity, a fundamental wartime military service.

[19] General Lewis Hershey, a Director of Selective Service, whose term spanned from World War II through the Vietnam War, appears to have endorsed a view along these lines. He was said to advocate that conscientious objectors "should be neither favored nor punished because of their beliefs, but as far as the law allowed, they should undergo the same inconveniences and receive the same benefits as the men in service" (Sibley and Jacob 1952: at 308). The LaFollettes provide two reasons for requiring alternative service from conscientious objectors to war: "One, it demonstrates the applicant's sincerity; two, it demonstrates his commitment to democracy, tolerance and the common good" (LaFollette and LaFollette 2007: at 251). It is doubtful that a requirement to disclose options and refer is an effective or suitable test of the sincerity of a health care professional who seeks a conscience-based exemption from providing a good or service. It also is questionable whether it is justified to require health care professionals to demonstrate their "commitment to democracy, tolerance and the common good" as a condition of receiving conscience-based exemptions.

service requirement for conscientious objectors to war does not require them to violate their conscience, it does not provide a suitable basis for rejecting conscience absolutism in relation to health care.[20]

CONSCIENTIOUS OBJECTION AND PROFESSIONAL OBLIGATIONS

It remains to consider whether conscience absolutism is compatible with a credible conception of the professional obligations of physicians, nurses, and pharmacists. May a physician, nurse, or pharmacist refuse any direct or indirect participation in a perceived wrongdoing without violating his or her professional obligations? On the one hand, for advocates of the incompatibility thesis, the answer is an unqualified "no." From their perspective, any refusal to provide legal and professionally permitted services within the scope of a practitioner's competence is incompatible with the professional obligations of physicians, nurses, and pharmacists, and the obligation to provide those services always trumps the exercise of conscience. Hence, there is no need even to ask whether conscience-based refusals to provide a service give rise to an obligation to inform or refer. On the other hand, for advocates of conscience absolutism, the answer to the foregoing question is an equally unqualified "yes." From their perspective, proponents of the incompatibility thesis view physicians, nurses, and pharmacists exclusively as professionals, and simply discount their status as *moral agents*.

If a middle ground or compromise approach is justified, neither of the two extreme positions in relation to professional obligations is defensible. If a compromise approach is acceptable, then: (1) contrary to the incompatibility thesis, there are situations in which a conscience-based refusal to provide a legal and professionally accepted good or service within the scope of a practitioner's competence does not violate the professional obligations of a physician, nurse, or pharmacist; and (2) contrary to conscience absolutism, there are situations in which refusing direct or indirect participation in a perceived moral wrong is incompatible with the professional obligations of a physician, nurse, or pharmacist. To assess the three views concerning

---

[20] The US government has not accepted conscience absolutism in relation to conscience-based objections to *any* indirect participation in war. During World War II, some conscientious objectors opposed civilian alternative service because of a perceived (indirect) connection with war-related activities, but they were not exempted from alternative service (Sibley and Jacob 1952). During the Vietnam War, some US citizens who were morally opposed to the war objected to paying taxes to support it. As in the case of the couple described in Chapter 1, individuals with conscience-based opposition to (indirect) participation in perceived wrongdoing did not receive an exemption from paying military- or war-related taxes.

conscientious objection and professional obligations, I will examine several accounts of the professional obligations of physicians, nurses, and pharmacists. I will argue that with the possible exception of accounts based on general ethical theories, they favor a compromise approach over conscience absolutism and the incompatibility thesis.

General ethical theories and professional obligations

One approach to professional obligations is to attempt to derive them from general ethical theories, such as contractarianism, rights-based theories, consequentialism, or an ethics of care. It is beyond the scope of this book to offer detailed explanations of these theories, and attempts to draw conclusions about practical issues, such as conscientious objection, from general ethical theories risk over-simplification and/or misinterpretation. Hence, it would be presumptuous to claim to be able to demonstrate conclusively that any general ethical theory provides a decisive basis for rejecting both extreme approaches and accepting a compromise approach. My aim is much more modest. I will attempt to show only that: (1) none of the general ethical theories considered unequivocally supports conscience absolutism or the incompatibility thesis; and (2) some general ethical theories can provide a basis for favoring a compromise approach.

From a contractarian perspective, one might imagine patients and health care professionals choosing a policy concerning conscientious objection from behind a "veil of ignorance" that prevents each from knowing whether he or she is a patient or a health care professional (a physician, nurse, or pharmacist).[21] In addition, although it might be stipulated that each appreciates the value of health and moral integrity, the veil of ignorance precludes knowledge of the individual's health status and distinctive moral beliefs. Now, suppose that the choice is among three principles specifying professional obligations of physicians, nurses and pharmacists: (1) principle P_1, based on the incompatibility thesis, requires health care professionals to

---

[21] In the real world, the same individual can be both a patient and a health care professional. However, for the purposes of this contractarian analysis the simplifying assumption will be made that the parties to the contract are either health care professionals or patients. Robert Veatch presents an approach along these lines (Veatch 1981). He proposes a "triple contract" account of medical ethics. The first provides a hypothetical contractarian basis for basic moral rules and principles. The second, a hypothetical social contract between society and a profession, establishes the obligations, responsibilities, privileges, and rights of the profession. The third involves an actual agreement between a health professional and a patient about practice styles, goals, and so forth. The contractarian approach presented here is similar to Veatch's second contract. I will consider an approach similar to the third contract later in the chapter.

provide all legal and professionally accepted goods and services within the scope of their competence; (2) principle P_2, based on conscience absolutism, permits health care professionals to refuse to perform any actions that are contrary to their conscience; (3) principle P_3, a middle ground approach, permits conscience-based refusals if, and only if, requirements designed to protect patients, such as those associated with the conventional compromise, are satisfied.[22] Insofar as P_1 does not protect moral integrity, it is a poor choice. P_2 is a poor choice insofar as it does not remove potential obstacles to satisfying health care needs and interests. P_3 has neither of these disadvantages. It is the only principle among the three that at least partially protects both values. Hence, it is at least arguable that from a contractarian perspective, P_3 is preferable to both P_1 and P_2.[23] In any event, however, contractarianism does not provide unequivocal support for conscience absolutism or the incompatibility thesis.

From a rights-based perspective, it might be claimed that there are two important rights at stake: health care professionals' rights of conscience and patients' right to informed health care decision-making. P_1 fails to protect rights of conscience, and P_2 fails to protect the right to informed health care decision-making. From a rights perspective, then, both principles are seriously flawed. To defend either principle, it would have to be argued that one set of rights has absolute priority over the other. Producing a convincing argument along these lines may well be an elusive task. On the other hand, P_3 can be defended by pointing out that it does not require a choice between two important rights, because it at least partially protects both. These sketchy remarks fall far short of a conclusive argument for P_3 from a rights perspective. However, at the very least, they identify serious problems with conscience absolutism and the incompatibility thesis from the perspective of a rights-based ethical theory. In addition, they may point toward a possible rights-based defense of a compromise approach. In any event, rights-based ethical theory does not provide unequivocal support for conscience absolutism or the incompatibility thesis.

From the perspective of consequentialism, the ethical assessment of conscientious objection in health care ultimately depends on empirical

---

[22] At this point, I am using the conventional compromise as an example of a middle ground alternative to the incompatibility thesis and conscience absolutism. In Chapter 3, I will propose a somewhat different compromise approach. For the purposes of this critical analysis of the two extremes, the specific features of a compromise approach are not at issue.

[23] This conclusion assumes that from behind a veil of ignorance, which deprives individuals of knowledge about their moral beliefs and social roles, if they have an opportunity to partially protect their moral integrity and health, they will not prefer to completely protect one at the expense of the other. Admittedly, this assumption is open to challenge.

data. For example, a rule consequentialist would ask: Which of the three principles, if accepted, will produce better outcomes? Suppose outcomes are assessed on the basis of well-being, and an outcome with more overall well-being is better than one with less overall well-being. There are several alternative conceptions of well-being, but for the purposes of illustration, let us assume a mental state criterion, according to which well-being is a function of how one feels.[24] A person's life is said to be going well insofar as he or she is happy or feels good; and a person's life is said to be going poorly insofar as he or she is unhappy or feels bad. Each of the following claims appears to be credible: (1) implementing P_1 can be expected to make some patients happy and some health care professionals unhappy; (2) implementing P_2 can be expected to make some patients unhappy and some health care professionals happy; (3) implementing P_3 can be expected to make some patients and health care professionals happy at a specified time t and other patients and health care professionals unhappy at t. P_1 might be criticized for promoting the happiness of patients at the expense of health care professionals, and P_2 might be criticized for promoting the happiness of health care professionals at the expense of patients. However, from a consequentialist perspective, the decisive criterion is overall happiness, and not whether its distribution satisfies a standard of fairness or justice. To show that either principle is unacceptable from a consequentialist perspective, it would be necessary to establish that, if implemented, it can be expected to fail to maximize overall happiness.[25] Although empirical evidence necessary to show that either principle is unacceptable is lacking, empirical evidence is also lacking to establish that either principle is acceptable. Hence, consequentialism fails to provide unequivocal support for either of the two extremes. However, for a similar reason (i.e. lack of required empirical evidence), consequentialism also fails to provide unequivocal support for a compromise approach. Accordingly, absent highly speculative assumptions, consequentialism cannot provide a definitive answer to the question: From an ethical perspective, which of the three views provides the best account of the professional obligations of physicians, nurses, and pharmacists?

A consideration of distinguishing characteristics of an ethics of care strongly suggests that it, too, does not support the incompatibility thesis

---

[24] For a discussion of alternate conceptions of well-being, see (Kagan 1998).

[25] To be more precise, to show that one of the three principles is ethically unacceptable, there would have to be empirical evidence establishing that, if implemented, it can be expected to promote less overall happiness than each of the other two principles.

or conscience absolutism.[26] The following propositions express several characteristics:[27] (1) The moral point of view does not require adopting an impersonal perspective and treating moral agents as abstract rational agents. Relationships matter and moral agents have concrete identities, based in part on their social roles and ties to others. (2) Morality is context-dependent and requires attention to particular situations and circumstances. (3) Due to differences among them, a decision or action that is ethically appropriate for one moral agent is not necessarily ethically appropriate for all moral agents in a similar situation. (4) Morality is not exclusively an intellectual activity. It involves emotion as well as cognition (understanding). (5) Morality is not primarily principle-based. As Lawrence Blum explains this characteristic, "morality is founded in a sense of concrete connection and direct response between persons, a direct sense of connection which exists prior to moral beliefs about what is right or wrong or which principles to accept" (1988: 476).

Insofar as an ethics of care is essentially contextual and places significant moral weight on particular relationships, it is an unlikely basis for either of the two unqualified blanket assertions: (1) conscience-based refusals to provide legal goods or services within the scope of a practitioner's competence are incompatible with professional obligations of physicians, nurses, or pharmacists; (2) health care professionals do not have an obligation to perform any actions contrary to their conscience. Instead, an ethics of care is more supportive of a nuanced view, such as a compromise approach, that takes seriously a health care professional's conscience-based refusal as well as the particular context and the relationships between the health care professional and his or her patients, colleagues/co-workers, employers, and so forth. From the perspective of an ethics of care such concrete factors, and not abstract principles, determine whether or not health care professionals have an obligation to provide a legal and professionally accepted service that is against their conscience.[28]

---

[26] In the following section, I will consider "caring" as the basis of an "internal morality" specific to nursing.

[27] This characterization of an ethics of care is suggested by Lawrence Blum (Blum 1988: 472–91). He distinguishes between the views of Lawrence Kohlberg and Carol Gilligan, and does not consider the views of those who have drawn on Gilligan's work to develop an ethics of care, such as Nel Noddings: see (Noddings 1984). Nevertheless, his exposition of Gilligan captures identifying characteristics of an ethics of care.

[28] Peter Allmark refers to an "unwillingness of 'caring' ethicists to acknowledge the importance of abstract ideals ..." (Allmark 1995: 19–24 at 20). According to Allmark, then, insofar as appeals to conscience are based on abstract moral principles, they might be viewed with some suspicion from the perspective of an ethics of care. Still, rejecting appeals to conscience out of hand would not be in keeping with the approach of an ethics of care.

Internal morality and professional obligations

Insofar as the foregoing accounts draw on *general* ethical theories, they might be said to base professional obligations on an "*external* morality." By contrast, an alternative account is based on an "*internal* morality." A morality is "internal" insofar as it is derived from a conception of a particular profession (e.g. its goals and/or distinctive character). Although the term "internal morality" is commonly associated with theories of medicine, there are corresponding conceptions of the ethical foundations of nursing and pharmacy. I will examine internal morality accounts of the professional obligations of physicians, nurses, and pharmacists with the aim of assessing the incompatibility thesis, conscience absolutism, and a compromise approach.

Internal morality of medicine

There are three conceptions of an "internal morality" of medicine: (1) an essentialist conception; (2) an evolutionary non-essentialist conception; and (3) a traditionalist non-essentialist conception.

An essentialist conception of the internal morality of medicine

According to an essentialist conception, the internal morality of medicine can be derived from an analysis of the nature of the profession (e.g. its ends or goals, and characteristics of the professional–patient relationship). Essentialism posits that medicine has an *inherent nature*, such that it is justified to refer to *the* (timeless) nature and goals of medicine and *the* (timeless) characteristics of the physician–patient relationship.

Edmund Pellegrino and David Thomasma are among the foremost exponents of an essentialist conception. There are some differences in the derivation and characterization of the internal morality of medicine in their numerous books and articles. However, these are all more or less variations on the same theme, which specifies the end of medicine as *healing* and which characterizes the physician–patient relationship as one between a professional committed to healing and a vulnerable patient who is ill and seeks help from the professional (Pellegrino and Thomasma 1981, 1993; Pellegrino 2001, 2002a, 2006). According to this account, insofar as the end or goal of medicine is healing, entering the profession requires a commitment to that end (i.e. healing patients). If an individual is not willing and able to make such a commitment, she should not become a doctor; and anyone with a medical license who does not make and consistently honor that commitment is not a virtuous physician. At first glance, this statement may appear to affirm the incompatibility thesis and deny conscience absolutism. However, a closer examination will reveal that while this conception of the end of medicine may rule out conscience absolutism, it does not support the incompatibility thesis, and it can be understood to favor a compromise approach.

Although it can be questioned whether healing is the *only* end of medicine, it is plausible to maintain that healing is associated with the concept of medicine (or any credible conception of it), and it is arguable that an individual who is not committed to that end fails to qualify as a *physician*, let alone a *virtuous* one. For example, suppose Dr. Brickstone becomes a Christian Scientist after completing a residency in obstetrics and gynecology. He now refuses to provide any medical intervention and promotes prayer as the only acceptable means of healing and pain control. We justifiably would be reluctant to say that he is promoting the goals of medicine, or even engaged in its practice. Accordingly, this interpretation of the internal morality of medicine provides a basis for rejecting conscience absolutism. However, it does not support the incompatibility thesis.

To understand why this interpretation of the internal morality of medicine fails to support the incompatibility thesis, suppose that due to conscience-based objections another obstetrician-gynecologist, Dr. Morrison, refuses only to prescribe emergency contraception (EC), perform abortions, and administer palliative sedation. There are at least two reasons for rejecting the claim that by refusing to provide these services, she fails to honor a commitment to promote healing.

First, the concept of "healing" is vague and ambiguous, and it is a contested concept. Healing can be interpreted narrowly, such that it is limited to curing and/or treating diseases; or, as Pellegrino proposes, it can be interpreted broadly: "To care, comfort, be present, help with coping, and to alleviate pain and suffering are healing acts as well as cure. In this sense, healing can occur when the patient is dying even when cure is impossible" (Pellegrino 2001: 568). As laudable as this more expansive conception of the end of medicine may be, the claim that it is derived from the *concept* of medicine as a profession is questionable. At most, it might be claimed that this conception is part of a time-honored (and commendable) tradition – that is, associated with a traditionalist conception of the internal morality of medicine.

Since the concept of "healing" is vague and ambiguous, it is subject to varying interpretations by individual physicians. Accordingly, Dr. Morrison can maintain that prescribing EC, performing abortions, and providing palliative sedation do not promote *healing*. This claim cannot be refuted by appealing to the "plain meaning" of "healing."

There is another reason for rejecting the claim that Dr. Morrison would fail to honor a commitment to promote healing if she refuses to prescribe EC, perform abortions, and administer palliative sedation. A physician can be committed to healing and still not provide *all* healing-related services. Specialists and subspecialists offer only a limited range of medical services that promote healing. For example, dermatologists treat skin cancer and acne, but they do not treat hernias and coronary artery disease. Even within specialties and subspecialties, physicians may limit the types of treatments that they offer. Yet, by virtue of limiting the healing-related services they offer, they cannot be accused of failing to honor a commitment to healing. Accordingly, if Dr. Morrison provides other healing-related services, it cannot be said that she fails to honor a commitment to healing whenever she refuses to prescribe EC, perform abortions, and provide palliative sedation.

In Chapter 3, I will argue that there are several ethical limitations on conscience-based refusals. For example, Dr. Morrison may not refuse to provide treatment for an emergency medical condition if no other physician is available to provide it without delay and without exposing the patient to excessive harms and burdens. Accordingly, it might be claimed that under certain circumstances, refusing to terminate a pregnancy would be incompatible with a commitment to healing. However, to support the incompatibility thesis, it would have to be asserted that refusing to provide a legal good or service within the scope of a practitioner's competence is *ipso facto* incompatible with a commitment to healing. Contrary to this assertion, whether or not a conscience-based refusal is incompatible with a commitment to healing is *context-dependent*. Moreover, it might be claimed that, depending on the circumstances, a willingness to refer to a provider who will provide a good or service is a sufficient commitment to the goal of healing. Thus, it can be claimed that in contrast to the two extreme approaches, a compromise approach can be supported by an essentialist conception of the internal morality of medicine.

There is another feature of the essentialist conception, however, that might be used to argue that it supports the incompatibility thesis and undermines both conscience absolutism and a compromise approach. This feature is the alleged nature of the physician–patient relationship and the corresponding professional obligation of physicians to give priority to patients' interests over their own. As Pellegrino puts it: a "suppression of self-interest" is mandatory "when the welfare of [patients] requires it" (Pellegrino 2002a: 378). This obligation is said to derive from the physician's commitment to healing combined with the vulnerability of patients, which is due to illness and the power and knowledge differential between them and physicians. The reasoning is as follows: In order to promote healing, physicians must not allow their own interests to interfere with their clinical judgment and recommendations. If physicians did not demonstrate a willingness to suppress their self-interest and, when healing requires it, place the interests of patients above their own, patients might be harmed. In addition, patients would be less inclined to trust physicians. Maintaining trust, however, is essential because it is a precondition of an effective and enduring physician–patient relationship (i.e. a relationship that enables the physician to practice her profession and pursue the goal of healing).

Insofar as physicians are said to be obligated to give priority to patients' interests when patient welfare is at stake, this interpretation of the internal morality of medicine clearly rules out conscience absolutism. It does not, however, support the incompatibility thesis. Indeed, Pellegrino himself endorses conscientious objection and therefore does not appeal to a professional obligation to give priority to patients' interests to maintain that conscientious objection is incompatible with the professional obligations of physicians.[29] However, Rosamond Rhodes criticizes Pellegrino for failing to draw that conclusion:

> When a physician chooses to act on his own values instead of honoring his patient's, the physician puts his own interests in ease of conscience above the altruism that Pellegrino otherwise recognizes as a defining feature of medicine … Someone who places his own interests above his patients' departs from medicine's standard of altruism and violates a crucial tenet of medical ethics that every physician is duty bound to observe. (Rhodes 2006: 78)

Granted that altruism is a professional obligation and physicians must be willing *in some contexts* to place the interests of patients above their own, it does not follow that physicians have an unqualified duty always to place patients' interests above their own.[30] Rhodes claims that a physician who

---

[29] The following statement is representative of Pellegrino's view:

Remember, however, that the physician too is a moral agent. Therefore, the patient cannot ask the physician to override his values. To respect the patient's moral agency does not mean submitting to whatever he wishes if it violates the physician's moral beliefs … We have in the medical relationship two interacting moral agents, each of whom most [*sic*] respect the dignity and values of the other. A logical consequence is that at times the physician is morally impelled to remove himself or herself from the relationship when he or she differs on a matter of moral principle with the values the patient expresses. (Pellegrino 2006: 65–71 at 68–9)

See also (Pellegrino 1994: 47–68), and (Pellegrino 2002b: 221–44).

[30] John Arras and Norman Daniels argue that a duty to treat patients with immunodeficiency virus (HIV) cannot be derived from an essentialist conception of the internal morality of medicine (Arras 1988: 10–20), (Daniels 1991: 36–46). In a later work, Daniels supports a similar claim in relation to a duty to treat during a severe acute respiratory syndrome (SARS) epidemic (Daniels 2008).

refuses to provide a service for reasons of conscience imposes "burdens of time, inconvenience, [and] financial costs" on patients (ibid.). To be sure, consistent with the compromise approach presented in Chapter 3, there are limits to the burdens that the exercise of conscience may impose on patients. However, if "medicine's standard of altruism" were to imply an unqualified obligation on the part of physicians to put patients' financial interests or interest in convenience above their own similar interests, let alone their arguably more significant interest in moral integrity, it would be a violation of a physician's professional obligations to charge patients who had financial problems, take vacations when it is not convenient for patients, limit time spent with patients, or refuse to make house calls or schedule night-time and weekend appointments for patients with day jobs.

When Pellegrino and Thomasma consider the nature and scope of physician altruism, they maintain that the "healing relationship" is the "moral fulcrum, the archimedian point at which the balance between self-interest and self-effacement must be struck" (Pellegrino and Thomasma 1993: 42). As this statement indicates, they reject the implausible interpretation of the physician's obligation to put her patients' interests above her own that would be required to support the incompatibility thesis (i.e. the claim that conscience-based refusals to provide a good or service within the scope of a physician's competence are contrary to the professional obligations of physicians). Consequently, although a reasonable interpretation of an obligation of physicians to put the interests of patients above their own rules out conscience absolutism, it does not support the incompatibility thesis. A reasonable interpretation of that obligation can support a compromise approach, which is characterized by ethical constraints on the exercise of conscience that may, *depending on the circumstances*, require physicians to act contrary to their conscience for the sake of patients. This is a reasonable interpretation of the obligation to put patients' interests above one's own insofar as it protects patients without unnecessarily restricting the exercise of conscience. Physicians are obligated to act contrary to their conscience if, but only if, a conscience-based refusal would unduly interfere with a patient's access to health care goods and services. I will present and explain specific constraints in Chapter 3.

An evolutionary non-essentialist conception of the internal morality of medicine
According to an evolutionary non-essentialist conception of the internal morality of medicine, which I will refer to as an "evolutionary conception," it is a mistake to think that the ends of medicine are timeless and unchanging.

There are alternative conceptions of the nature of medicine, its ends and goals, and the physician–patient relationship. Therefore, it is necessary to provide *reasons* for favoring one conception over another. Moreover, according to an evolutionary view, from the fact that a practice is contrary to entrenched goals of medicine, it does not follow that the practice is incompatible with the (proper) goals of medicine. Instead, it is necessary to ask "whether the proposed alteration would represent a possibly positive evolution in the nature of medicine" (Miller and Brody 2001: 585).

Franklin Miller and Howard Brody, two proponents of an evolutionary conception, identify multiple ends or goals of medicine: three in one article (Miller and Brody 1995); eight in a second article (Brody and Miller 1998); and four in a third (Miller *et al.* 2000) and fourth (Miller and Brody 2001). The four goals identified in the last two articles are:

(1) The prevention of disease and injury and promotion and maintenance of health.
(2) The relief of pain and suffering caused by maladies.
(3) The care and cure of those with a malady, and the care of those who cannot be cured.
(4) The avoidance of premature death and the pursuit of a peaceful death.

These are the goals that were endorsed in a report by an international group of scholars convened by the Hastings Center (Anonymous 1996). Neither Miller and Brody nor the Hastings Center panel claim that these goals are derivable from the concept of medicine or inherent features of the physician–patient relationship. Instead, they are to be understood as an *appropriate* conception of (scientific) medicine for contemporary society, and the Hastings Center panel presents several reasons in support of these four goals.

In addition to the four goals, Miller and Brody identify four duties along with the alleged derivation of each (1998: 388):[31]

(1) The physician must employ technical competence in practice. (This derives from medicine's nature as a skilled craft.)
(2) The physician must honestly portray medical knowledge and skill to the patient and to the general public, and avoid any sort of fraud or misrepresentation. (This derives from medicine's commitment to a scientific basis of knowledge.)

---

[31] There are variations in the formulation of these duties in two of the other three articles cited. With a few exceptions, however, these are minor differences. Notable exceptions include: adding competence in "humanistic skills" in the two most recent articles, and not including a duty "to minimize the indignity and the invasion of privacy involved in medical examinations and procedures" in any of the other articles. Variations in the number of ends and statements of the four duties in the four articles suggest that unambiguous criteria for their specification may be somewhat elusive.

(3) The physician must avoid harming the patient in any way that is out of proportion to expected benefit, and must seek to minimize the indignity and the invasion of privacy involved in medical examinations and procedures. (This derives from medicine's goal as a helping, beneficent practice.)

(4) The physician must maintain fidelity to the interests of the individual patient. (This derives from medicine's need to apply knowledge to individual cases and from its goal as a helping, beneficent practice.)

As the parenthetical statements indicate, Miller and Brody associate these duties with their conception of the nature and goals of modern, scientific medicine. It is in this respect that it is appropriate to classify those duties as components of an *internal* morality of medicine. In an earlier article, they offer the following explanation of the relation between the ends or goals of medicine and the four duties (which they also refer to as "means"):

As in the case of other skilled practices or arts, there is a conceptual and pragmatic fit between the goals and the means of medicine. The goals of medicine inform practitioners and theorists on the range of appropriate or inappropriate means of medical practice; and the understanding of the proper and improper means of medical practice elaborates the meaning of the goals of medicine. (Miller and Brody 1995: 11)

Since the aim of this examination of an evolutionary conception is only to assess conscience absolutism, the incompatibility thesis, and a compromise approach, there is no need to critically analyze Miller and Brody's interpretation of the ends of medicine or their reasoning for the four alleged duties. Instead, assuming that these goals and duties represent a reasonable and representative conception of an evolutionary inner morality of medicine, the question to ask is whether, from the perspective of professional obligations in relation to conscientious objection, there is a substantial difference between evolutionary and essentialist conceptions.

Let us begin by reconsidering Dr. Morrison. The claim that her refusal to prescribe EC, perform abortions, and provide palliative sedation is contrary to the goals of medicine is no more plausible when the goals of the evolutionary conception are at stake than when the goals of the essentialist conception are at stake. The reasons for challenging the claim that refusing to provide those services is incompatible with the single essentialist goal of healing apply as well to each of the evolutionary conception's goals. The stated evolutionary goals are no less vague than the essentialist goal of healing and include concepts that are subject to alternative theoretical constructions, such as "health," "disease," and "malady." Accordingly, the goals are subject to varying interpretations by individual physicians, and Dr. Morrison can maintain that an unwanted pregnancy is neither a disease nor a malady. In addition, an observation that applies to the essentialist conception applies as well to the evolutionary conception. Even if there are certain services that unequivocally promote a goal of medicine, physicians do not display a lack of commitment to that goal unless they provide *all* services within the scope of their competence that promote it. Accordingly, even if prescribing EC, performing abortions, and providing palliative sedation can promote the goals of medicine, Dr. Morrison's refusal to provide these specific services does not demonstrate her lack of commitment to those goals.[32]

Insofar as the evolutionary conception identifies multiple goals, there is an additional observation that applies to it and not the single-goal essentialist conception. Physicians who have conscience-based objections to providing a particular medical service might claim that refusing to provide it *promotes another goal*. For example, whereas it might be claimed that refusing to provide palliative sedation fails to promote the goal of facilitating a "peaceful death" (goal #4), it might also be claimed that such refusals promote the goal of avoiding a "premature death" (also goal #4).

The duty with the most relevance to conscientious objection is the obligation to "maintain fidelity to the interests of the individual patient." As long as this obligation remains general and unspecified, it might be deemed an undeniable truism. Even without further specification, however, it rules out conscience absolutism, which would never obligate physicians to act contrary to their conscience, no matter the impact on patients. Such a blank check to disregard patients' interests is hardly consistent with any credible conception of a duty of fidelity to patients.

Without further specification, a duty of fidelity to patients' interests fails to support the incompatibility thesis. To be sure, a duty to "maintain fidelity to the interests of the individual patient" might be specified to support the incompatibility thesis. That is, it might be specified to require physicians to put aside their conscience-based objections for the sake of patients and provide any good or service within the scope of their competence. However, it is arguable that this specification of the duty of fidelity to patients is overly demanding and unnecessarily hostile to the exercise of conscience because ethical constraints on its exercise can suffice to protect patients and assure that conscience-based refusals do not prevent them from

---

[32] To simply claim, without providing reasons, that such refusals demonstrate *insufficient* commitment to those goals begs the question.

having timely access to health care goods and services. Such ethical constraints are a distinguishing feature of a compromise approach. Accordingly, there is a good reason to accept a specification of the duty of fidelity to patients that favors a compromise approach.

A traditionalist non-essentialist conception of the internal morality of medicine

According to the traditionalist non-essentialist conception, which I will refer to as the "traditionalist conception," there is a distinctive moral tradition associated with the medical profession, and it provides an ongoing basis for determining the current professional obligations of physicians. For example, according to this conception of the internal morality of medicine, in order to determine whether physicians have a duty to treat during an influenza pandemic (e.g. an avian flu or SARS pandemic), it is necessary to review the historical record to ascertain whether there is a moral tradition within medicine that supports such a duty.[33]

A traditionalist account of the internal morality of medicine would support the incompatibility thesis only if there is a time-honored moral tradition within the medical profession that physicians have a duty to provide medical services that violate their moral or religious beliefs. Alternatively, that account would support conscience absolutism only if there is a time-honored tradition that physicians do not have an obligation to perform any action contrary to their conscience. However, it is doubtful that either tradition can be found within western medicine.

To begin with the incompatibility thesis, indirect evidence that it does not correspond to a time-honored tradition is provided by the medical profession's response to the Church Amendment (42 U.S.C. § 300a–7(a–b)), the first federal conscience clause legislation. As explained in Chapter 1, it was enacted by the US Congress in the wake of the 1973 *Roe* v *Wade* Supreme Court decision affirming a constitutional right to abortion and an earlier 1972 Federal District Court decision mandating a Catholic hospital to permit its facilities to be used for a sterilization procedure. The Church Amendment protects physicians who refuse to perform abortions and sterilizations for reasons of conscience. If permitting physicians to refuse to provide services that conflict with their religious and/or moral beliefs had

---

[33] The traditionalist conception is critically analyzed in relation to a duty to treat HIV patients by Arras and in relation to a duty to treat HIV and SARS patients by Daniels: (Arras 1988; Daniels 1991; 2008). According to Robert Baker, there is no consistent tradition within western medicine regarding physician behavior and expectations during epidemics such as the plague (Baker 2006: 93–133).

represented a significant break with a time-honored moral tradition within medicine, considerable opposition would have been expected. However, the medical profession did not engage in an organized effort to prevent the legislation or to repeal it after it was enacted. On the contrary, the American Medical Association (AMA) adopted a policy on abortion stating in part: "Neither physician, hospital, nor hospital personnel shall be required to perform any act violative of personally held moral principles" (Health Policies of the House of Delegates, "Abortion," 5.995).

As evidenced by numerous professional codes and guidelines enacted in ensuing years permitting physicians to refuse to provide services that violate their personal ethical or religious beliefs, it seems that the medical profession tended to embrace conscientious objection.[34] Thus, even if there once was a tradition within the medical profession that did not permit conscientious objection, it can be questioned whether the earlier tradition continues to be binding despite its rejection by the profession today. As slavery, racism, and sexism sadly demonstrate, some "moral traditions" are not worth preserving or restoring.[35]

To turn to conscience absolutism, there are several reasons for rejecting a claim that it is a time-honored tradition within the medical profession. First, it is only relatively recently that the notion of conscientious objection has been applied to medicine and health care generally. Second, when that notion was applied to medicine, and professional organizations and guidelines endorsed protections of conscience, typically conscience absolutism was rejected and a compromise approach was endorsed. For example, the AMA policy cited above that permits physicians to refuse to perform abortions includes the following qualification: "In these circumstances, good medical practice requires only that the physician or other professional withdraw from the case, *so long as the withdrawal is consistent with good medical practice*" (Health Policies of the House of Delegates, "Abortion," 5.99; emphasis added). Highly influential guidelines on decisions about life-sustaining treatment published by the Hastings Center (Anonymous 1987) and the President's Commission for the Study of Ethical Problems in Medicine and Biomedical and Behavioral Research (1983) permit conscience-based refusals but endorse a compromise approach rather than

---

[34] See, for example, (Anonymous 1987), (American Thoracic Society 1991: 478–85), (President's Commission for the Study of Ethical Problems in Medicine and Biomedical and Behavioral Research 1983) and (Anonymous 1996: S1–S27).

[35] According to the social contract model, discussed below, past professional norms retain their moral authority within a profession today only if they continue to be recognized and reaffirmed. See (Daniels 1991; 2008).

conscience absolutism. The former requires that "the responsible health care professional . . . assist in an orderly process [of transfer]" (Anonymous 1987: 32). The latter explicitly permits health care professionals only to "decline to *provide* a particular option" and includes the qualifier that "in so doing they may not abandon a patient" (emphasis added) (President's Commission for the Study of Ethical Problems in Medicine and Biomedical and Behavioral Research 1983: 3). The guidelines of some professional organizations explicitly reject conscience absolutism and endorse a compromise approach. For example, an American College of Gynecologists and Obstetricians (ACOG) Opinion states:[36]

[T]here are clearly limits to the degree to which appeals to conscience may justifiably guide decision making. Although respect for conscience is a value, it is only a prima facie value, which means it can and should be overridden in the interest of other moral obligations that outweigh it in a given circumstance. (2007: 1204–5)

Third, as indicated above, the HHS Final Rule included broad protections of conscience that exempted health care professionals from "counseling, referral, training, and other arrangements for the procedure, health service, or research activity" (45 CFR § 88.2). The expansive scope of exemptions for indirect participation is consistent with conscience absolutism. However, a major objection received by HHS during the comment period asserted that the broad scope of these exemptions implied by the proposed definition of "assist in the performance" substantially expanded previously recognized exemptions.[37]

Finally, although there may be no ancient tradition of a professional duty to treat in times of epidemics, the AMA Council on Ethical and Judicial Affairs in 1987 claimed that there had been such a tradition within the AMA since its inception: "The tradition of the American Medical Association, since its organization in 1847, is that 'when an epidemic prevails, a physician must continue his labors without regard to the risk to

---

[36] A critical response to the ACOG Opinion by the American Association of Pro-Life Obstetricians & Gynecologists (AAPLOG) is available online at: www.aaplog.org/physician-conscience-rights/february–6–2008–the–aaplog–response–to–opinion–385/; accessed July 9, 2010.

[37] *Federal Register*, Vol. 73, No. 245 (Friday, December 19, 2008), p. 78075; accessible online at: www. regulations.gov/search/Regs/home.html#documentDetail?R=09000064807e2d39; accessed July 9, 2010. One reported comment claimed that the proposed regulation "would require the American Medical Association to rewrite its code of ethics" (ibid.: 78089). A letter protesting the proposed regulation included the signatures of several national and state medical associations, including the AMA, the American Academy of Family Physicians, the American Academy of Pediatrics, the American College of Obstetricians and Gynecologists, the American College of Surgeons, the Society for Adolescent Medicine, and the Society of Gynecologic Oncologists. Among the objections expressed in the letter is the expansive protection of indirect participation implied by the broad definition of "assist in the performance." The letter is described in (Tanne 2008, 7673).

his own health' . . . That tradition must be maintained."[38] This statement does not directly address conscientious objection. Moreover, since it is unqualified, it may well overstate the duty of physicians to disregard risks to their own health. However, suppose it is assumed only that physicians have a tradition-based obligation to accept some unspecified risk of contracting an infectious disease. Consistency then would require affirming – contrary to both extremes and consistent with a compromise approach – that physicians are at least obligated to balance their interest in moral integrity with patients' health needs and interests.

   For the foregoing reasons, then, it is not credible to claim that time-honored traditions in medicine support either of the two extremes – the incompatibility thesis or conscience absolutism. Moreover, although there may not be a "time-honored tradition" with respect to conscientious objection in medicine, recent conventions typically support a compromise approach. Although the focus of this discussion of traditionalism has been the medical profession, corresponding reasons support a similar conclusion in relation to nursing and pharmacy.[39]

Internal morality of nursing
Although the term "internal morality" has been used mostly in relation to medicine, several theories of nursing provide a basis for conceptions of the ethical foundations of the profession, each of which bears at least some

---

[38] Cited in (Baker 2006: at 126). According to Baker, the 1847 Code was the first to address the issue of medical ethics during epidemics.

[39] Like the AMA, the American Nurses Association (ANA) opposed the HHS Final Rule. In a March 3, 2009 News Release, the ANA reiterated that opposition and expressed its approval of the Obama Administration's decision to suspend the Final Rule. It is available online at: www.nursingworld.org/ FunctionalMenuCategories/MediaResources/PressReleases/2009-PR/Provider-Conscience.aspx; accessed July 10, 2010. The News Release clearly expresses the ANA's support for a compromise approach and its rejection of the incompatibility thesis and conscience absolutism. In a March 2009 Government Affairs Issue Brief, although the American Pharmacists Association (APhA) did not take a position on the HHS Final Rule, it did reaffirm its commitment to a compromise approach:

> APhA recognizes the individual pharmacist's right to exercise conscientious refusal and supports the establishment of systems to ensure patient's [sic] access to legally prescribed therapy without compromising the pharmacist's right of conscientious refusal. When this policy is implemented correctly, and proactively, it is seamless to the patient, and the patient is not aware that the pharmacist is stepping away from the situation. In sum, APhA supports the ability of the pharmacist to step away, not in the way, and supports the establishment of an alternative system for delivery of patient care.

> The APhA Government Affairs Issue Brief is available online at: www.pharmacist.com/AM/Template.cfm? Section=Home2&TEMPLATE=/CM/ContentDisplay.cfm&CONTENTID=15688; accessed July 10, 2010. As noted earlier in this chapter, pharmacists for Life International (PFLI) advocates the adoption of a Pharmacist's Model Conscience Clause that supports conscience absolutism. Evidently, the PFLI believes that adopting conscience absolutism as a professional norm requires significant change.

family resemblance to an internal morality. Two illustrative examples are examined: the conception of nursing as caring and the conception of nursing as advocacy.[40] I will argue that conscience absolutism is compatible with neither and that both support a compromise approach over the incompatibility thesis.

Caring

Caring is commonly cited as a fundamental goal or value of nursing.[41] According to Sara Fry and Megan-Jane Johnstone, the concept of caring "has long been regarded as being foundational to the nurse–patient relationship and to the caring behaviours considered fundamental to the nursing role" (2008: 45).[42] It has been referred to as a "cornerstone" of nursing:[43]

A moral value that . . . is both a traditional and a contemporary one, and that serves as nursing's cornerstone, is that of caring. It is no doubt the most basic of all values in nursing and, in fact, serves as the springboard for the application of all the other values inherent in the nurse–client relationship. It enables another value, that of advocacy, to be operationalized, and encourages the nurse to take on a variety of roles, such as that of care giver, health educator, protector, surrogate, counselor, healer, and a variety of relationships with the patient, such as client and counselor, colleague and colleague, parent and child, and friend and friend. (Uustal 1987: 138)

There are several conceptions of caring.[44] According to one, "[n]urse caring is specifically directed toward the protection of the health and welfare of patients" (Fry and Johnstone 2008: 45). This conception of caring shares some of the characteristics of essentialist and evolutionary interpretations of the internal morality of medicine. Accordingly, it gives rise to similar challenges to conscience absolutism and the incompatibility thesis. Contrary to conscience absolutism, and consistent with a compromise approach, this conception of caring appears to require nurses to give

---

[40] According to Sara Fry, caring and advocacy are two of the "four moral concepts [that] provide a starting point for nursing ethics inquiry in the 21st century and help us understand the 'good' nurse and the nature of nurses' ethical practices" (Fry 2008: 45–55 at 51). The other two concepts Fry cites are cooperation and accountability.

[41] One of the general ethical theories considered above is an ethics of care. The subject of this section is the *concept of caring*. Advocates of a caring conception of nursing can also be committed to an ethics of care, and many are. However, utilitarians, Kantians, contractarians, and rights-based theorists can also accept a caring conception of nursing. Hence, there is no necessary connection between a caring conception of nursing and an ethics of care.

[42] In an earlier article, Fry maintains that "the value of caring ought to be central to any theory of nursing ethics," and caring is said to be "a foundational, rather than a derivative, value . . ." (Fry 1989: 9–22 at 20–1).

[43] It is noteworthy that Uustal posits caring as a foundational value and advocacy as a derivative value.

[44] Uustal observes that caring "is not easy to define or describe" (Uustal 1987: 136–53 at 138).

considerable weight to protecting the health and welfare of patients and to balance this obligation with their interest in maintaining moral integrity. Since conscience absolutism gives nurses what amounts to a blank check to refuse to provide or to assist in providing any service that is against their conscience no matter the impact on patient health or welfare, it is not compatible with this conception of caring.

The conception of caring as protecting patient health fails to support the incompatibility thesis with respect to some of the services that are a common target of nurses' conscientious refusals, such as abortion and maintaining brain dead organ donors prior to organ retrieval. Since health is a contested concept and abortion results in the death of a human fetus, as in the case of physicians with conscience-based objections to the procedure, nurses who refuse to assist in performing abortions can claim that the procedure does not protect health. Similarly, nurses who object to maintaining brain dead organ donors can assert that protecting health does not apply to dead patients. Moreover, a point made previously in relation to physicians also applies to nurses: Even when a particular service unequivocally promotes a goal of the discipline, a professional does not display a lack of commitment to that goal by failing to provide *all* services that promote it. Accordingly, even if a procedure such as abortion can protect the health and welfare of patients, as long as a particular nurse's conscience-based refusal to assist in providing the procedure does not jeopardize a patient's health or welfare – a constraint associated with a compromise approach – the nurse's refusal does not demonstrate a lack of commitment to the health and welfare of patients.[45]

Sally Gadow offers an account of caring in relation to nursing that is representative of conceptions that go beyond simply protecting patient health and well-being. She holds that caring is related to dignity:[46]

Caring as a moral ideal . . . entails a commitment to a particular end. That end . . . is the protection and enhancement of human dignity. Caring as the moral ideal of nursing is concern, above all, for the dignity of patients. (Gadow 1985: 32)

Gadow explicates dignity in terms of integrity: "Simply expressed, a being has dignity when it gives to itself its meaning and so creates for itself

---

[45] As noted above in relation to physicians, to simply claim, without providing reasons, that such refusals demonstrate *insufficient* commitment to those goals begs the question.

[46] In another essay, Gadow sketches a conception of caring in which the primary aim is the "alleviation of vulnerability" (Gadow 1988: 5–14). In that essay, she identifies care as "the moral end" of nursing. According to Gadow, "*care* is the ethical principle or standard by which interventions are measured" (ibid.: at 7). In both essays, she highlights the importance of the body in relation to care and caring.

integrity" (ibid.). The primary threat to patient integrity in a health care setting, according to Gadow, is to be treated exclusively as an "object." From a pure clinical perspective, patients are objects (i.e. diseased or unhealthy bodies). However, a caring approach avoids treating patients *exclusively* as objects: "caring is attending to the 'objectness' of persons without reducing them to the moral status of objects" (ibid.: 33–4). Accordingly, "the moral foundation of nursing" is said to be a "commitment to the dignity that distinguishes persons from objects" (ibid.: 43).

Gadow presents two "means of affirming the integrity of patients, one having to do with truth, the other with touch" (ibid.: 37). Truth, for Gadow, involves more than neither withholding information nor lying. Rather, from the perspective of caring, it includes nurses engaging in dialogue with patients, assisting patients with values-clarification, and, more controversially, sharing their own values with patients. Touch, according to Gadow, is a means for the nurse to avoid treating patients exclusively as objects. It facilitates intersubjectivity, thereby promoting an aim of caring:

> In the caring relationship, the body is regarded – and touched – by the nurse as the immediate, lived reality of the patient. This entails a breach of objectivity: empathic touch affirms, rather than ignores, the subjective significance of the body for the patient. Its purpose is not palpation or manipulation but expression – an expression of the nurse's participation in the patient's experience. (ibid.: 40–1)

Clearly, it is not compatible with Gadow's conception of caring for nurses always to put their interest in maintaining moral integrity above the values, interests, and needs of patients. For example, it is incompatible with that conception for nurses to refuse to provide information or facilitate referral whenever doing so is contrary to their conscience regardless of patients' goals, wishes, and needs. Such insensitivity to patients fails to express a concern for *patient* dignity and integrity. Accordingly, conscience absolutism is not compatible with this conception of caring.

Since providing specified nursing services is neither a necessary nor a sufficient condition of Gadow's conception of caring, her conception also provides no support for the incompatibility thesis. Providing specified nursing services is not a sufficient condition of caring because nurses can provide services in an uncaring manner. Caring involves an array of attitudes and behaviors that have to do with how nurses relate to patients, rather than which services they provide.[47] More importantly from the

---

[47] According to Chris Gastmans, caring involves a "moral attitude" and is the expression of a moral virtue (Gastmans 1999: 214–23). In the absence of this moral attitude, delivering nursing services cannot be characterized as *caring*.

perspective of implications for the incompatibility thesis, providing specified services is not a necessary condition of caring. To be sure, if a nurse who
refuses to provide a particular service, such as assisting in terminating
pregnancies or tubal ligations, also insults, badgers, or otherwise fails to
respect the dignity of a patient, she fails to treat the patient in a caring
manner. Moreover, if no other nurse is available to assist in an emergency
situation, a conscience-based refusal in that context is hardly consistent with
concern for patient dignity and integrity. In that context, a conscience-
based refusal also would not be permitted by a compromise approach.
However, if the nurse consistently interacts with patients in a caring manner
and does not jeopardize patient safety, refusing to provide or assist in
providing a particular service need not demonstrate a lack of caring.
Accordingly, it is implausible to claim that caring requires an unqualified
willingness to provide services against a nurse's conscience. Indeed, Gadow
explicitly cites sharing one's values with patients as a component of caring.

Advocacy
Advocacy is another commonly cited alleged fundamental goal or value of
nursing. According to Sara Fry and Megan-Jane Johnstone, it is "widely
recognized within the nursing ethics literature and nursing codes of ethics as
a professional ideal and as a 'moral imperative'" (2008: 39). Leah Curtin
proposes the concept of advocacy as "the philosophical foundation and ideal
of nursing" (1979: 2). According to Curtin:[48]

[Advocacy] involves the basic nature and purpose of the nurse–patient relationship.
It is proposed as a very simple foundation upon which the nurse and patient in any
given encounter can freely determine the form that relationship is to have, i.e.,
child and parent, client and counselor, friend and friend, colleague and colleague
and so forth through the range of possibilities. (ibid.: 3)

There are several different conceptions of advocacy (Fry and Johnstone
2008; Grace 2001). Fry and Johnstone identify three: (1) the patient rights-
protection model, (2) the values-based decision model, and (3) the respect-
for-persons model.

  According to the patient-rights protection model, nurses advocate for
patients by defending their health care rights:

---

[48] Sally Gadow's notion of "existential advocacy" provides a similar conceptualization of the foundation
   of nursing: "[Existential advocacy] is proposed as the philosophical foundation upon which the
   patient and the nurse can freely decide whether their relation shall be that of child and parent, client
   and counselor, friend and friend, colleague and colleague, and so on through the range of possibilities" (Gadow 1990: 40–51 at 42).

The nurse informs patients of their rights, makes sure that the patients understand these rights, reports any infringements and acts to prevent any further infringements of the patient's bona fide rights claims. In summary, this interpretation views the nurse as an arbitrator for the patient's human rights to and in healthcare. (Fry and Johnstone 2008: 40)

Clearly, conscience absolutism is not compatible with this conception of advocacy. For example, suppose a nurse who has a conscience-based objection to withholding or withdrawing life-sustaining treatment discovers that a physician refuses to honor a patient's request for a Do Not Resuscitate (DNR) order. According to the patient-rights protection model, the nurse has an obligation to report this infringement of the patient's rights and to act to prevent any further infringements. However, fulfilling this obligation requires the nurse to indirectly participate in a perceived moral wrong. Accordingly, conscience absolutism is not compatible with the patient rights protection model of advocacy.

Although this conception of advocacy is compatible with a compromise approach, there are several reasons for concluding that it does not support the incompatibility thesis. First, rights can be legal, ethical, or both. Insofar as nurses are said to be obligated to advocate for patients' *moral* rights, in the case of ethically contentious procedures such as abortion or palliative sedation, it may beg the question to reject a nurse's conscientious refusal on the grounds that he is neglecting his duty to advocate for patients' rights. Second, a nurse may be able to satisfactorily fulfill his responsibilities as an advocate in this sense without defending all health care rights. Since nurses have multiple responsibilities for numerous patients, it may not be practically feasible to defend all of the rights of all patients. Moreover, as Pamela Grace argues, it may be necessary in some situations for nurses to choose between advocating for the health needs of individual patients and the health needs of the general population (2001). If nurses cannot defend all of the health care rights of all patients, some prioritization is required, and it is arguable that prioritizing on the basis of their values is not unjustified or contrary to the patient-rights protection model. Third, this conception of the advocacy model does not require nurses to provide or assist in providing health care procedures or services. At most, it does not permit nurses to *impede* patients from receiving services to which they have a "bona fide rights claim," and it requires nurses to assure that patients receive information that will enable them to make informed choices and exercise their rights.

The values-based decision model pertains to a nurse's role in facilitating informed decision-making by patients:

[The values-based decision model] views the nurse as the person who helps the patient discuss his or her needs, interests and choices consistent with the patient's values and lifestyle. The nurse does not impose decisions or values on the patient but helps the patient examine the advantages and disadvantages of various health options in order to make decisions most consistent with his or her values and beliefs. (Fry and Johnstone 2008: 40)

Conscience absolutism is no more compatible with this conception of advocacy than with the patient-rights protection model. For example, it is not compatible with the values-based decision model for a nurse to with-hold information about an option that is morally objectionable to her if the likely result is depriving a patient of an opportunity to consider or assess that option. However, satisfying an obligation to disclose information about a perceived moral wrong requires the nurse to indirectly participate in that perceived moral wrong. Accordingly, conscience absolutism is not compat-ible with the values-based decision model of advocacy.

Although this conception of advocacy is consistent with a compromise approach, it does not support the incompatibility thesis. First, similar to the rights-protection model, the values-based decision model does not require nurses to provide or assist in providing health care procedures or services. Essentially, it requires nurses to facilitate informed decision-making. It may require counseling and assistance with values clarification, and it prohibits attempts to thwart patients' opportunities to make decisions in accordance with their values. However, it includes no requirement to actually partici-pate in providing medical services that patients choose. Second, it is unclear that a nurse who *generally* acts as an advocate in the relevant sense, but refuses to do so in relation to a procedure that is against her conscience, demonstrates an insufficient commitment to the values-based decision model of advocacy. Suppose a nurse has a conscience-based objection to a procedure that is within the range of options for one of her patients.[49] It is arguable that she can display a commitment to the values-based decision model by not abandoning the patient and by assuring that the patient has access to a member of the health care team who will perform the functions of an advocate in a timely fashion. This response to the situation is

---

[49] Nurses can reduce the number of occasions on which they will be confronted with a choice between fulfilling the functions of an advocate and not acting against their conscience by their selection of specializations and practice settings. For example, individuals who are morally opposed to maintain-ing brain dead organ donors can avoid working in an ICU in which a willingness to maintain such patients is an expectation; individuals with conscience-based objections to EC can avoid working in emergency departments; and individuals who believe that abortion and contraception are unethical can avoid serving as nurses in family planning clinics.

consistent with a compromise approach. It might be claimed that such referrals or transfers of care occasioned by conscientious objection are not significantly different from those that are due to considerations of clinical knowledge and expertise. Just as nurse A might defer to nurse B when nurse A believes that in view of nurse B's superior clinical experience and knowledge, nurse B is better qualified to care for a patient, so, too, nurse C might defer to nurse D when nurse C believes that in view of her (nurse C's) conscience-based objection to acting as an advocate with respect to a particular procedure, nurse D is more qualified to act as an advocate. Indeed, if a nurse is ethically opposed to a particular procedure, she is not likely to be the best source of accurate and unbiased information or a suitable decision-making partner for patients. Accordingly, depending on the circumstances, nurses who have a conscience-based objection to a procedure can demonstrate a commitment to the values-based decision model of advocacy by helping to facilitate patient access to nurses who do not have a conscience-based objection to the procedure.

The respect-for-persons model applies the corresponding ethical principle to nursing:

[The respect-for-persons model] views the patient as a fellow human being entitled to respect. As advocate, the nurse first considers the basic human values of the patient and then acts to uphold and protect the patient's human dignity, privacy and choices. (Fry and Johnstone 2008: 40–1)

Conscience absolutism is no more compatible with this conception of advocacy than with the other two models. For example, suppose a nurse fails to inform a patient of an option because he believes that it is morally objectionable. In addition, suppose the patient is likely to select this option if she is aware of it. Unless the nurse tells the patient that there is at least one available option that he cannot disclose due to his moral beliefs, thereby indirectly participating in a perceived moral wrong, she may not be aware of that option and may therefore not have an opportunity to choose it. Since the nurse would fail to "uphold and protect the patient's . . . choices" if he did not at least alert the patient to the availability of another option, conscience absolutism is incompatible with the respect-for-persons model of advocacy.

Moreover, that model is too general to support the incompatibility thesis. As long as a nurse respects patients whether or not they share her values, refusing to provide services to which a nurse is conscientiously opposed would not constitute a failure to act as an advocate according to the respect-for-persons model. To be sure, as already observed, protecting patient

choices may require providing information to patients and indirect participation in perceived wrongdoing, but participation in the delivery of health
care against a nurse's conscience is not required. Moreover, insofar as this
model is based on a general ethical principle of respect, that principle applies
as well to nurses and their values. Failing to reasonably accommodate
nurses' conscientious objections is hardly consistent with the principle of
respect for persons. Hence, this model of advocacy appears to favor a
compromise approach.

Grace argues for a broad notion of advocacy ("professional advocacy")
that includes measures to influence and change policies and practices within
health care institutions and society to promote the health needs of individual patients and the general population (Grace 2001).[50] Professional advocacy can require political action, such as active participation in institutional
policy-making and professional organizations and using the media to educate the public. She observes that professional advocacy can require "a
balancing of the health needs of individuals with the health needs of the
population" (ibid.: 159).

In view of its focus on patients, the notion of professional advocacy
hardly lends support to conscience absolutism. There are two reasons for
concluding that extending advocacy beyond practice-related activities for
individual patients does not support the incompatibility thesis. First, if it is
conceded that an obligation to act as a professional advocate is among the
professional obligations of nurses, it does not follow that they have an
obligation to discharge this function in relation to procedures and services
that are contrary to their ethical or religious beliefs. Nurses who are conscientiously opposed to a procedure may deny that there is a legitimate
"health need" for it. For example, a nurse who is conscientiously opposed to
abortion and contraception might believe that neither corresponds to
legitimate health needs. Since health is a contested concept, such claims
can resist conclusive refutation.[51] Second, a point made in relation to the
rights-protection model applies *mutatis mutandis* in this context as well.
Since nurses cannot advocate for all the health needs of their patients,
let alone the general population, some prioritization is required, and it is
arguable that prioritizing on the basis of their values is not unjustified or
contrary to the professional advocacy model.

---

[50] For Grace, the ethical basis of the professional obligation to serve as advocates is the goal of nursing.
      That goal, she claims, "is generally agreed to be that of promoting a 'good' which is health" (Grace
      2001: 151–62 at 155).
[51] Grace recognizes that "[h]ealth may be variously defined depending on philosophical and theoretical
      perspectives guiding practice." Ibid.

Internal morality of pharmacy

Somewhat akin to the situation in nursing ethics, the term "internal morality" is not as familiar in pharmacy as it is in medicine. However, as in the case of nursing, a theory of pharmacy can provide a basis for a conception of the ethical foundations of the profession which bears at least some family resemblance to an internal morality. Charles Hepler, who has written extensively about the foundations of pharmacy ethics, provides the basis for an illustrative analysis along these lines.

Hepler derives a type of non-essentialist internal morality from a conception of pharmacy that he refers to as "pharmaceutical care."[52] The primary goal of pharmaceutical care is to promote patients' quality of life. Health professionals provide a wide range of services that can enhance the quality of life of patients. However, drugs are the distinctive means of promoting patient quality of life associated with pharmaceutical care. As the concept is explained in an article Hepler co-wrote with Linda Strand, pharmaceutical care "is the responsible provision of drug therapy for the purpose of achieving definite outcomes that improve a patient's quality of life" (Hepler and Strand 1990: 539). They identify four outcomes: cure of disease, elimination or reduction of symptoms, arresting or slowing disease processes, and preventing diseases or symptoms. Insofar as achieving these outcomes requires designing, implementing, and monitoring therapeutic plans with the participation of patients and other professionals, the professional obligations of pharmacists are not restricted to filling prescriptions. In addition, the pharmaceutical care model requires pharmacists to assume an ongoing role in supervising and monitoring drug use. Hepler and Strand identify three specific responsibilities: "1) identifying potential and actual drug-related problems, 2) resolving actual drug-related problems, and 3) preventing potential drug-related problems" (Hepler and Strand 1990: 539).

Pharmaceutical care may be said to exemplify an internal morality of pharmacy insofar as general propositions about the nature and scope of the professional obligations of pharmacists are derived from its primary goal: promoting the quality of life of patients. The professional obligations associated with the pharmaceutical care model are far from trivial. Indeed,

---

[52] Hepler credits Brodie, Parish, and Poston for introducing the term "in its modern sense" (Hepler 1996: 19–47 at 23). They offer the following definition, which Hepler cites: "Pharmaceutical care includes the determination of the drug needs for a given individual and the provision not only of the drug required but also the necessary services (before, during or after treatment) to assure optimally safe and effective therapy. It includes a feedback mechanism as a means of facilitating continuity of care by those who provide it" (Brodie, Parish and Poston 1980: 276–8 at 277). Hepler adopts an evolutionary (non-essentialist) conception of pharmacy as pharmaceutical care (Hepler 1987: 369–85).

if anything, they are controversial insofar as it might be claimed that they are associated with a model of pharmacy that is too broad and largely inapplicable to the real world in which the opportunities for ongoing supervision and monitoring of drug use and coordination of care with other health professionals are limited.[53] However, the aim of this examination of the pharmaceutical care model is not to evaluate its suitability as a theory of pharmacy. Rather, the objective is to assess conscience absolutism, the incompatibility thesis, and a compromise approach from the perspective of a pharmaceutical care conception of an internal morality of pharmacy.[54]

Insofar as the primary goal of pharmaceutical care is to promote patients' quality of life, it undermines conscience absolutism. At the very least, pharmacists would have to weigh the impact of conscience-based refusals on patient quality of life. Depending on the circumstances, pharmacists might have an obligation to indirectly participate in perceived moral wrongdoing by providing information, transferring prescriptions, providing referrals, or even directly by filling prescriptions. Accordingly, conscience absolutism is incompatible with this conception of the internal morality of pharmacy.

According to the pharmaceutical care model, are conscience-based refusals to dispense a type of drug (e.g. contraceptives generally or only emergency contraceptives), as the incompatibility thesis implies, incompatible with the professional obligations of pharmacists?[55] It would be incompatible with the professional obligations of pharmacists according to that model if a pharmacist with a moral or religious objection were to dispense a contraceptive but express his objection by failing to discharge the duty to promote its effective and safe use. For example, suppose a pharmacist with a conscience-based objection to dispensing contraceptives reluctantly agrees to fill a patient's prescription. However, he does not provide any information about the contraceptive or invite the patient to ask questions. The pharmacist also makes no effort to determine whether there might be any contraindications, such as interactions with other drugs that the patient is taking. This pharmacist would fail to fulfill the professional obligations associated with the pharmaceutical care model. But suppose the pharmacist

---

[53] Pharmacists in retail pharmacies reportedly are playing an increasing role in facilitating medication compliance, managing chronic diseases, coordinating care, and promoting wellness. See Abelson and Singer (2010).

[54] Hepler also provides two alternative accounts of professional obligations. They will be discussed below in the sections on social contract- and covenant-based accounts of professional obligations.

[55] As explained in Chapter 1, although levonorgestrel-based EC is now available without a prescription to women who are at least 17 years old, it still must be kept behind the counter to enforce the age restriction. Accordingly, pharmacists and other pharmacy personnel (e.g. assistants and sales clerks) can still have conscience-based objections to providing it. Ulipristal-based EC requires a prescription.

were to inform the patient that he could not dispense a contraceptive due to his conscience-based objection and offer to refer the patient to either another pharmacist in the same pharmacy or another pharmacy that will fill the patient's prescription in a timely manner. Insofar as the pharmacist's refusal had no significant negative impact on the patient's health or quality of life, he has not failed to fulfill the professional obligations associated with the pharmaceutical care model. Since the impact on the patient is crucial, the mere fact that a pharmacist has refused to dispense a medication is not sufficient to establish that the pharmacist has failed to satisfy his professional obligations. Accordingly, the internal morality of pharmaceutical care does not support the incompatibility thesis. Instead, it appears to favor a compromise approach.

Indeed, the title of an essay on conscientious objection, "Balancing Pharmacists' Conscientious Objections with Their Duty to Serve" (Hepler 2005), indicates that Hepler himself rejects conscience absolutism as well as the incompatibility thesis and favors a compromise approach. In any event, insofar as the pharmaceutical care model is representative of internal morality accounts of the professional obligations of pharmacists, it is dubious that any such account of the basis of pharmacists' professional obligations favors conscience absolutism or the incompatibility thesis over a compromise approach.

Social contract and professional obligations

There are two explanations of professional obligations that can be designated "social contract" accounts. One utilizes an idealized hypothetical agreement associated with contractarian ethical theory, which is discussed in a previous section. The other, the social contract account that is the subject of this section, is based on an actual agreement or negotiation between a profession and society.

According to this version of the social contract account, professional obligations are based on an agreement between a society and a profession, according to which society grants certain rights, privileges, and benefits to a profession and its members in exchange for the profession's commitment to recognize and enforce certain professional obligations. Individuals acquire the specified obligations when they voluntarily enter a profession and either explicitly or implicitly promise to comply with the rules of their respective profession. A social contract account has been offered as a basis of the professional obligations of physicians, nurses, and pharmacists.

An example of a social contract account for medicine is presented by Rosamond Rhodes, whose critique of conscientious objection by physicians is based on it. According to Rhodes, it is "an agreement between society and the profession" that "empowers medicine" (2006: 77).[56] As its part of this agreement, society is said to grant the medical profession "the license to develop its distinctive knowledge and skills, the privileges to pry, to examine, to prescribe and to administer dangerous drugs, and the power to perform risky diagnostic interventions, treatments and therapies" (ibid.). For its part, the profession "publicly pledges to be trustworthy in its competence and use of its special knowledge, privileges and powers to help society and the individuals in it" (ibid.).

The notion of a social contract also has been used to provide a basis for the professional obligations of nurses and pharmacists. The second edition of *Nursing's Social Policy Statement* explicitly states that it "expresses the social contract between society and the profession of nursing" (American Nurses Association 2003: 1). A social contract is said to be the basis of the profession's authority: "The authority for the practice of professional nursing is based on a social contract that acknowledges professional rights and responsibilities as well as mechanisms for public accountability" (ibid.: 2). This statement is followed by a quote from the writing of Avedis Donabedian describing the social contract between a profession and society:[57]

Society grants the professions authority over functions vital to itself and permits them considerable autonomy in the conduct of their affairs. In return, the professions are expected to act responsibly, always mindful of the public trust. Self-regulation to assure quality in performance is at the heart of this relationship. It is the authentic hallmark of a mature profession. (ibid.)

Marcia Fowler, in her introduction to *Guide to the Code of Ethics for Nurses: Interpretation and Application*, states that a code of ethics "functions as a general guide for the profession's members and as a social contract with the public that it serves" (2008: xi).

---

[56] In December 2001, only a few months after the September 11 terrorist attacks in the United States, the American Medical Association adopted a "Declaration of Professional Responsibility: Medicine's Social Contract with Humanity" (Health Policies of the House of Delegates, 140.900). This document included, among other provisions, a pledge to "apply our knowledge and skills when needed, though doing so may put us at risk." At the time, bioterrorism was among the major contemplated risks. Unlike paradigm social contracts, this one was one-sided because it was limited to commitments by the medical profession.

[57] This statement is from Donabedian's *Foreword* in (Phaneuf 1972).

Charles Hepler offers a social contract account that applies to pharmacy as well as other professions:

Society asks a profession to obey certain rules in providing very valuable, complex, and personalized services. The effect of these rules is to ensure that the profession will serve society. For example, every profession accepts a duty to protect the long-term interest of its clients and never to take advantage of a client's dependency or weakness. Each profession promises to maintain its members in number, knowledge, skill, and attitude. In return, society promises to give the profession authority. This occurs through a long process of exchange in which the would-be profession demonstrates its value and commitment while society grants a bit of authority. (1985: 1301)

In an earlier essay, Hepler applies the social contact analysis at two levels – an agreement between a profession and society as well as an agreement between professionals and their clients:[58]

[T]he client (society) agrees to give the professional (profession) extraordinary autonomy and virtually exclusive loyalty, obedience, and trust for certain responsibilities. The professional (profession) agrees in return to give the client (society) expertise, diligence, and judgment, and, most importantly, to place the interests of the client (society) above the short-term selfish interests of the professional (profession). (1979: 104)

Since there is no literal agreement or contract between society and each of the health professions, it may be more apt to refer to a process of "social negotiation" (Daniels 1991; 2008).[59] Social negotiation is largely a political process that is carried out by representatives of professional groups (e.g. the AMA, the ANA, and the APhA), representatives of various interest groups (e.g. patient rights groups; disability rights groups; reproductive rights organizations; right to life groups; and lobbyists for insurance companies, pharmaceutical companies, health plans, and medical centers), legislators, and public officials. The outcome of this social negotiation is reflected in professional codes, laws, regulations, institutional policies, and so forth.

---

[58] In a third article, Hepler claims that "the professional promises competence and the client gives the professional authority. The relationship between society and a profession is analogous, except that the profession must also provide a sufficient number of competent practitioners" (Hepler 1987: at 375). The second sentence suggests that even if individual health professionals do not have an obligation to provide a legal and professionally accepted service that is contrary to their ethical or religious beliefs, each *profession* has an obligation to guarantee a sufficient supply of willing professionals to meet the demand. Holly Fernandez Lynch proposes an institutional resolution of "conflicts of conscience" that relies in part on licensing boards to ensure that there will be a sufficient supply of professionals to meet patient demand for legal health care services (Lynch 2008).

[59] According to Daniels, the social negotiation is subject to ethical assessment. Specifically, *justice* is an ethical constraint on social negotiation and corresponding professional obligations.

Any plausible general characterization of the outcome of this "social negotiation" is likely to be too vague and ambiguous to support the conclusion that conscientious objection is incompatible with the professional obligations of physicians, nurses, or pharmacists. Rhodes' statement of the alleged "public pledge" of the medical profession, cited above, illustrates this point. It is not readily apparent that conscience-based refusals to provide medical services are incompatible with a profession's pledge "to be trustworthy in its competence and use of its special knowledge, privileges and powers to help society and the individuals in it." As long as patients have access to health care professionals who are willing and able to provide services that meet their health care needs, it is implausible to claim that a profession that permits conscientious refusals *ipso facto* violates that pledge. It is no more plausible to claim that a health care professional violates an explicit or implicit promise to honor her profession's public pledge whenever she refuses to provide a particular service for reasons of conscience. Similar conclusions apply to Hepler's characterization of the social contract, which includes duties "to protect the long-term interest of its clients and never to take advantage of a client's dependency or weakness" as well as a profession's promise "to maintain its members in number, knowledge, skill, and attitude."[60]

In any event, the protection afforded to conscientious objection by physicians, nurses and pharmacists in laws, professional codes, and institutional policies appears to undermine the claim that the outcome of social negotiation between society and the health professions bars conscience-based refusals to provide legal and professionally approved services.[61] At most, laws, professional codes, and institutional policies provide some evidence for a socially negotiated constraint on conscientious objection that it not place an excessive burden on patients' access to health care. I will explain and defend such a constraint in Chapter 3.

Similarly, with a few exceptions, laws, professional codes, and institutional policies tend to undermine conscience absolutism. A few examples illustrate the widespread rejection of conscience absolutism: state advance directive legislation is one. Although most advance directive statutes permit health care providers to refuse to comply with instructions that would require them to participate in a perceived moral wrong, they typically require "reasonable efforts" by the provider to transfer the patient to a

---

[60] As noted above, Hepler does not accept the incompatibility thesis.
[61] Conscience clause legislation (i.e. legislation that protects health care professionals' exercise of conscience) will be examined in Chapter 6.

provider who is willing to carry out the directive (Meisel and Cerminara 2009: 11–77). A second example is AMA policy. An AMA Council on Ethical and Judicial Affairs (CEJA) report addresses conscientious objection and concludes that an obligation to refer is consistent with the *Code of Medical Ethics*:[62]

Principle VI makes clear that physicians may choose whom to serve. Accordingly, except in emergencies, they may refuse to provide a treatment to which they object on the basis of religious or moral beliefs. However, other Principles balance this prerogative with obligations to respect patients and their ability to access available medical care. Therefore, a conscientious objection should, under most circumstances, be accompanied by a referral to another physician or health care facility. (CEJA Report 6-A-07)

Policies of the ANA and the APhA provide additional examples. Although neither professional organization offers specific guidelines, both reject conscience absolutism.[63]

Contractual agreements and professional obligations

The core of the *social* contract model is a collective agreement between a health care profession and society. However, the notion of a contract can also be applied to agreements between individual professionals and patients. Robert Veatch's "triple contract" theory includes such individualized contracts (Veatch 1981). The initial contract provides a hypothetical contractarian account of basic ethical principles. The second provides a hypothetical contractarian account of professional obligations similar to one examined in a previous section of this chapter. The third and final contract is an actual negotiated agreement between individual professionals and patients. Within the parameters established by the prior contracts, it determines the specific terms of the relationship between the professional and the patient, such as their respective responsibilities and expectations. For example, a physician and a patient might agree that the former will: (1) accept the patient's preference for "watchful waiting" whenever it is a

---

[62] Principle VI states: "A physician shall, in the provision of appropriate patient care, except in emergencies, be free to choose whom to serve, with whom to associate, and the environment in which to provide medical care." The following are among the provisions cited: "A physician shall, while caring for a patient, regard responsibility to the patient as paramount" (Principle VIII). "A physician shall support access to medical care for all people" (Principle IX). "The physician may not discontinue treatment of a patient as long as further treatment is medically indicated, without giving the patient reasonable assistance and sufficient opportunity to make alternative arrangements for care" (*Code of Medical Ethics*, "Fundamental Elements of the Patient-Physician Relationship," 5).

[63] See n 39 above.

feasible option; (2) honor the patient's living will; and (3) accept the patient's use of alternative medicine as a supplement to conventional therapy unless it is clinically contraindicated.

Physicians and other health care professionals might attempt to negotiate contract-like agreements with (prospective) patients specifying that they will not provide services that violate their ethical or religious beliefs. These agreements could be general, or they could specify particular services (e.g. abortion, IVF, or palliative sedation). Consistent with conscience absolutism, they might even specify that the health care professional will not participate directly or indirectly in any perceived moral wrong. For example, the agreement might explicitly state that the health care professional will not provide information about all clinically acceptable options or referrals if doing so is against her conscience.

However, general professional obligations, which, according to Veatch, are determined by the second contract, set ethical constraints on such negotiated agreements between health care professionals and patients. Hence, if conscience absolutism is not consistent with independently established general professional obligations – and to assume it is consistent begs the question – it cannot be justified by appealing to agreements between health care professionals and patients. For similar reasons, negotiated agreements that permit conscientious objection do not refute the incompatibility thesis. Such agreements are ethically acceptable only if general professional obligations do not support the incompatibility thesis – and to assume that general professional obligations do not support the incompatibility thesis begs the question. Accordingly, negotiated contract-like agreements alone can neither justify conscience absolutism nor refute the incompatibility thesis.[64]

Alternatively, contract-like agreements between health care professionals and (prospective) patients might specify that providers will provide goods and services even when doing so is against their conscience. This type of agreement alone can neither justify the incompatibility thesis nor refute conscience absolutism. First, consistent with the incompatibility thesis, health care professionals who entered into such agreements would not be permitted to refuse to provide a good or service that is against their conscience. However, this account of the obligation to provide goods or services even if they violate a practitioner's ethical or religious beliefs does

---

[64] The power and knowledge differential between health care providers and patients provides another reason for questioning the justificatory authority of such agreements. For a perceptive critique of contractual agreements as a moral paradigm, see (Baier 1986: 231–60).

not justify the incompatibility thesis, for the basis of that obligation is the *agreement* between a provider and a patient, and not the former's professional obligations.[65] Second, although such contract-like agreements might require actions on the part of health care providers that are at odds with actions that are endorsed by conscience absolutism, those agreements do not refute conscience absolutism, for agreements of that type do not establish that conscience absolutism is incompatible with general professional obligations. They establish only that adhering to conscience absolutism is unacceptable if a health care professional has previously agreed not to.

Covenant, indebtedness, and professional obligations

In a classic and frequently cited article entitled "Code, Covenant, Contract, or Philanthropy," William May asserts that he "inclines to accept covenant as the most inclusive and satisfying model for framing questions of professional obligation" (May 1975: 38).[66] In that essay, May focuses on the medical profession, but his covenant account of professional obligations is generalizable and has been applied to both nursing and pharmacy. In an essay that was published four years after May's article, Marjorie Stenberg claims that his conclusion about professional obligation specifically applies to nursing: "Covenant emerges as an inclusive and satisfying model for nursing ethics" (Stenberg 1979: 21).[67] In its "Code of Ethics for Pharmacists," the APhA uses the concept of a covenant to explain the professional obligations of pharmacists:

Considering the patient–pharmacist relationship as a covenant means that a pharmacist has moral obligations in response to the gift of trust received from society. In return for this gift, a pharmacist promises to help individuals achieve optimum benefit from their medications, to be committed to their welfare, and to maintain their trust.[68]

As the title of his essay suggests, May offers a covenant-based model as an alternate to code-based, contract-based, and philanthropy-based models of the physician–patient relationship. Code-based models construe physicians' obligations in terms of technical rules. Although May does not deny their

---

[65] I critically examine a promise-based justification of the incompatibility thesis in the final section of this chapter.
[66] May's conception of a professional covenant is more fully developed in (May 1983).
[67] Stenberg's essay is entitled "The Search for a Conceptual Framework as a Philosophic Basis for Nursing Ethics: An Examination of Code, Contract, Context, and Covenant."
[68] Available online at: www.pharmacist.com(searchfor"codeofethics");AM/Template.cfm?Section=Practice_Resour; accessed July 10, 2010.

importance, he plausibly maintains that they do not exhaust physicians' obligations.

According to May, philanthropy-based conceptions portray physicians' commitments to their patients essentially as acts of generosity or selfless altruism. He criticizes this view and suggests that a more appropriate model is the covenantal relationship between student and teacher in the Hippocratic tradition. Students' duties to their teachers are said to have had an essential characteristic of covenant-based obligations insofar as they arose in response to a gift or service. By contrast, according to May:

> Duties to patients are not similarly interpreted in the medical codes as a responsive act for gifts or services received. This is the essential feature of covenant which is conspicuously missing in the interpretation of professional duties from the Hippocratic Oath to the modern codes of the A.M.A. . . . The A.M.A. thought of the patient and public as indebted to the profession for its services but the profession has accepted its duties to the patients and public out of noble conscience rather than a reciprocal sense of indebtedness. (1975: 31–2)

May claims that physicians are indebted to society for their education, training, and privileged economic status; and they are indebted to patients for providing opportunities to learn, practice, and conduct research. According to May, then, physicians' obligations are *duties of indebtedness* to society collectively as well as to individual patients. A similar analysis can be applied to nursing and pharmacy. For example, Hepler claims that physicians, pharmacists, and nurses have a "duty to serve," and he attributes this alleged duty in part to benefits that health care professionals enjoy, such as monopoly status; privileged income, educational status, and authority; government-subsidized education; and patients' willingness to provide opportunities for practice and training (Hepler 2005). Mary Carolyn Cooper applies May's account to nursing and claims that:

> [C]ovenantal relationships originate within the context of indebtedness, i.e., the nurse responds to a gift received from the patient. Such responsiveness acknowledges the caregiver's debt to the community for educational advantages and to the patient for the opportunity to practice. (Cooper 1988: 51)

In contrast to a social contract account of professional obligations, a covenant/indebtedness account does not postulate an agreement or process of negotiation between a profession and society. Rather, obligations are said to be generated by the voluntary acceptance or enjoyment of certain benefits, such as rights, privileges, and opportunities. Although both accounts might cite similar benefits, only the social contract model cites a negotiated agreement to accept duties and responsibilities in return for those benefits; and only the covenant account cites duties of indebtedness, which might include duties of gratitude and/or reciprocal justice. Nevertheless, the distinction between covenant/indebtedness and social contract accounts is sometimes blurred. The statement from the APhA Code cited above is an example. The reference to "moral obligations in response to the gift of trust received from society" suggests indebtedness-based obligations. By contrast, the statement, "in return . . . a pharmacist promises" can be understood to refer to an obligation based on a mutual agreement between society and pharmacists (a social contract).[69] Similarly, John Arras's description of "a social contract between society and the medical profession" includes features from both models:

In exchange for the performance of a vital public service – that is, ministering to the needs of the sick and vulnerable – physicians as a group are granted monopolistic privileges over the practice of medicine. By seeking and receiving such a benefit, physicians incur a corresponding obligation founded on the notion of reciprocity. (1988: 11)

The reference to "reciprocity" (reciprocal justice) in the second sentence is consistent with an indebtedness account. By contrast, the language of the first sentence suggests a social contract account, whereby privileges are *granted* by society to the medical profession *in exchange for* a commitment to provide certain services.

Although the terms "contract" and "covenant" are sometimes used interchangeably, May denies that "covenant simply [is] another name for a contract in which two parties calculate their own best interests and agree upon some joint project in which both derive roughly equivalent benefits for goods contributed by each . . ." (May 1975: 33). According to him:

[A] contractualist approach . . . reduces everything to tit-for-tat: do no more for your patients than what the contract calls for; perform specified services for certain fees and no more. The commercial contract is fitting instrument in the purchase of an appliance, a house, or certain services that can be specified fully in advance of delivery. The existence of a legally enforceable agreement in professional trans-actions may also be useful to protect the patient or client against the physician or

---

[69] According to May, "[k]ey ingredients in the notion of covenant are promise and fidelity to promise" (May 1975: 29–38 at 37). Strictly speaking, according to an indebtedness account, duties of indebted-ness, not promises, are the primary and direct ethical basis of professional obligations. Promises can express a practitioner's commitment to honor those obligations. An obligation to keep one's promises can generate a secondary set of ethical obligations. In addition, promises might serve to specify how a professional intends to fulfill unspecified and indeterminate duties of indebtedness. An attempt to base the incompatibility thesis on alleged promises by health care professionals to patients is discussed in the following section.

lawyer whose services fall below a minimal standard. But it would be wrong to reduce professional obligation to the specifics of a contract alone. (ibid.: 34)

In contrast to contractual relationships, obligations associated with covenantal relationships are indeterminate and open-ended and are not legally enforceable or based exclusively on mutual self-interest:

Contract and covenant, materially considered, seem like first cousins; they both include an exchange and an agreement between parties. But, in spirit, contract and covenant are quite different. Contracts are external; covenants are internal to the parties involved. Contracts are signed to be expediently discharged. Covenants have a gratuitous, growing edge to them that nourishes rather than limits relationships ... There is a donative element in the nourishing of covenant – whether it is the covenant of marriage, friendship, or professional relationship. Tit-for-tat characterizes a commercial transaction, but it does not exhaustively define the vitality of that relationship in which one must serve and draw upon the deeper reserves of another. (ibid.)

Some authors who endorse May's claim that professional–patient relationships are properly conceptualized as covenantal rather than contractual, focus on the distinctive characteristics of covenantal obligations (e.g. indeterminate and not legally enforceable) and pay little, if any, attention to May's claim that indebtedness is a distinctive ethical basis of professional obligations. For example, Hepler repeatedly invokes the distinction between contract and covenant and consistently maintains that the characteristics of the obligations associated with the latter (e.g. open-ended, indeterminate, and unenforceable by law) apply to pharmacy. However, as indicated in a previous section, Hepler provides what is essentially a social contract account of the ethical basis of pharmacists' professional obligations.[70] It is perfectly consistent to ascribe the characteristics of covenantal obligations to the obligations of pharmacists and also to provide a social contract account of the ethical basis of those obligations. Obligations based on mutual agreement or negotiation can be indeterminate and unenforceable by law. Thus, the social contract account is not committed to a contract conception of the character of the corresponding professional obligations.

As May suggests, duties of indebtedness are open-ended and indeterminate.[71] Accordingly, that account is best suited to provide an ethical basis for unspecified obligations, such as an obligation to promote the health interests

---

[70] Insofar as the "duty to serve" referred to above is attributed to the benefits and advantages enjoyed by professionals, Hepler also presents an indebtedness account of the ethical basis of professional obligations.

[71] In this respect, duties of indebtedness are similar to "imperfect" or "discretionary" obligations.

of patients. Duties of indebtedness may also at times require self-sacrifice. That is, depending on the circumstances, health care professionals may be obligated to give priority to their patients' interests over their own. However, it remains to specify how much self-sacrifice is required from professionals. For example, from the general principle that some self-sacrifice is required, it may follow that physicians and nurses are required to expose themselves to some increased risk of contracting an infectious disease for the sake of patients. However, in view of its indeterminacy, the principle fails to provide a criterion for distinguishing between obligatory and supererogatory risk-taking. Similarly, in relation to conscientious objection, even if it is assumed that duties of indebtedness need to be weighed with a professional's interest in moral integrity, as a result of the indeterminacy of those duties, they fail to provide a criterion for determining if and when professionals have an obligation to provide services that are contrary to their ethical and religious beliefs. Clearly, then, duties of indebtedness are too indeterminate to provide grounds for a blanket judgment against conscientious objection. Accordingly, although duties of indebtedness can support a compromise approach, they are not a promising source of support for the incompatibility thesis.[72]

Despite the indeterminacy of duties of indebtedness, it is reasonable to conclude that conscience absolutism is not compatible with the covenantal account of professional obligations. For, despite their indeterminacy, health professionals' duties of indebtedness are said to require them to promote the health interests of patients and to sometimes give higher priority to patients' interests than their own. At the very least, fulfilling these duties requires health professionals to adopt a case-by-case approach and to consider the potential impact on patients before refusing to provide a service, information, or a referral against their conscience. Since conscience absolutism rejects a context-dependent approach to conscientious objection, it is not compatible with a covenantal account of professional obligations.

PROMISES AND THE INCOMPATIBILITY THESIS

There is an argument in support of the incompatibility thesis that merits consideration even though it is not based on a general account of professional

---

[72] Hepler cites duties of indebtedness to argue that pharmacists and other health care professionals do not have an unqualified right to refuse to provide services that violate their ethical or religious beliefs (Hepler 2005: 434–6). However, he does not claim that these duties generate an overriding obligation to provide services regardless of the professional's ethical or religious beliefs. For Hepler, determining whether there is such an overriding obligation is context dependent. In effect, then, he rejects the incompatibility thesis as well as conscience absolutism and supports a compromise approach.

obligations. John Alexander argues that health care professionals are bound by a promise made to patients upon entering a particular specialty or subspecialty that precludes conscience-based refusals to provide services (Alexander 2005). This promise is not merely a general commitment to fulfill one's professional obligations (e.g. an explicit or implicit promise to honor the profession's social contract). Indeed, absent an argument demonstrating that conscience-based refusals violate professional obligations – an argument that has proven elusive – a promise to fulfill those obligations does not include a commitment to provide services regardless of one's ethical or religious beliefs. The promise that Alexander identifies is a commitment to provide all services that fall within the "normal" range for the corresponding specialty or subspecialty.[73] According to this promise-based account of professional obligations (the promise model), a commitment to provide a normal range of services is prior to and independent of specific professional–patient relationships, and it places ethical constraints on acceptable health care professional-initiated "ground rules."

Services are said to fall within a "normal" range if they are "a normal part of the services that the professionals would be called upon to provide in the normal course of their professional lives within the specific practice [i.e. specialty or subspecialty] with which they are associated" (Alexander 2005: 178). Accordingly, services can be classified as "normal" in relation to a specific specialty or subspecialty if they are routinely offered by professionals within that specialty or subspecialty and are not incompatible with the corresponding clinical and professional standards.

The health care professional's promise is said to generate an ethical obligation to provide all services within the normal range. According to the promise model, if an individual has a conscience-based objection to providing a particular health care service, and she cannot in good conscience promise to provide it when patients request it, she should refrain from entering any specialty or subspecialty that includes the service within its normal range. In other words, individuals have a choice: Become a member of a specialty or subspecialty, whereby one promises to provide the corresponding normal range of services; or, if providing any of those services is against one's conscience, select another specialty or subspecialty (i.e. one that is compatible with the individual's conscience).

---

[73] Alexander uses the term "practice," which is ambiguous. It could refer to a particular group or association of health professionals (e.g. pediatricians in a particular pediatric practice). However, as he uses the term, a practice is a specialty or subspecialty (e.g. pediatric pulmonology, labor and delivery nursing, or hospital pharmacy) within a profession (medicine, nursing, or pharmacy).

Alexander illustrates the promise model with an example from nursing. A pregnant patient is informed that "the fetus she is carrying has abnormalities that preclude the possibility of surviving the pregnancy" (2005: 178). The patient opts for labor induction. However, the labor and delivery nurses on duty believe that induced labor resulting in the premature death of a fetus is an abortion, and they refuse to participate on moral grounds. Applying the promise model to the case, Alexander maintains:

> ... [W]hen one becomes a professional nurse she promises to provide the necessary professional care as outlined by the standards and practices of the nursing profession of which she is an active member. The standard of care is defined by the various codes that define nursing practice as well as the norms, values and procedures that define specific practices [specialties and subspecialties] ... If she [the nurse] believes that abortion is wrong ... she ought not to join a specific professional practice [specialty or subspecialty] where having procedures that result in the death of the fetus is permissible as an alternative course of medical action that a client can choose to follow in a relationship with professions [professionals?] in that specific practice. If they [the nurses in the example] believed that an induction in this type of circumstance was tantamount to performing a morally unjustifiable abortion then they ought not to have joined that practice [labor and delivery nursing]. They should have found another practice that did not offer an induction as a legitimate alternative in this type of health care situation. (ibid.: 185)

There are several problems with this use of the promise model to demonstrate that conscience-based refusals are contrary to the professional obligations of individuals who have chosen to enter a particular health care specialty or subspecialty.

First, as observed earlier, within particular specialties and subspecialties, there can be further specialization. For example, even if it is assumed that assisting with labor inductions in situations similar to that described in Alexander's example is within the "normal" range of services provided by labor and delivery nurses, it does not follow that *all* labor and delivery nurses must do so. Ethical or religious beliefs aside, there can be a differentiation of work assignments within nursing specialties and subspecialties. Whereas some labor and delivery nurses might specialize in pre-delivery care of pregnant women or post-delivery care of newborns, others might specialize in delivery. Accordingly, it is questionable whether simply by virtue of choosing to enter labor and delivery nursing, a nurse can be understood to promise to assist with labor induction.

A similar point applies to physicians and pharmacists. For example, an orthopedic surgeon might specialize in foot surgery. She might even limit her practice to a particular type of foot surgery, such as bunion surgery.

Surely, if the surgeon who specializes in bunion surgery refers a patient with a traumatic foot injury to another orthopedic surgeon, the patient cannot legitimately claim that she has broken a promise to treat the patient's injury. To cite two additional examples, performing colonoscopies is a "normal" (standard) procedure within gastroenterology, but not all gastroenterologists perform colonoscopies; and delivering babies is a "normal" (standard) practice within obstetrics-gynecology, but not all obstetrician-gynecologists deliver babies. In neither case does a physician's failure to provide the service at issue constitute the breaking of a promise to provide it. For similar reasons, patients cannot have a legitimate expectation to receive all services within the scope of a health care professional's specialty or subspecialty (i.e. all services within the relevant "normal range"). At most, they might have a legitimate expectation to receive a referral.

This is not to deny, as acknowledged earlier, that there may be certain "core" services associated with a particular specialty or subspecialty that set limits to such specialization and division of labor. For example, as Savulescu observes, performing pelvic examinations may be a core service for obstetrician-gynecologists (Savulescu 2006), and administering, monitoring, and/or dispensing pain medication may well be a core service for palliative care physicians and nurses and hospital pharmacists.

Second, due to laws and professional norms that recognize and protect conscientious objection by health care professionals, they may have a legitimate expectation that efforts will be made to accommodate ethical or religious objections. Hence, it cannot be assumed that an individual who enters a health care specialty or subspecialty understands, or should understand, that: (1) no accommodation will be made for conscientious objection; and (2) entering a specialty or subspecialty requires and/or expresses a promise to provide all services that are routinely offered by professionals within that specialty or subspecialty and are not incompatible with legal and professional standards.

Third, according to Alexander's interpretation of the promise model, if an individual cannot in good conscience promise to provide all services that are routinely offered by professionals within a specialty or subspecialty and are not incompatible with the corresponding clinical and professional standards, he/she should find another specialty, subspecialty, or profession. However, no justification is provided for this version of the incompatibility thesis, which fails to consider whether a compromise approach can accommodate health care professionals' exercise of conscience while adequately protecting the health and well-being of patients. For example, it is not explained why, in non-emergency situations, it would be insufficient to require a promise either to: (1) provide a good or service within the relevant "normal range," or (2) offer to provide a referral and/or facilitate a transfer. Such a promise amounts to a commitment that a health care professional's conscience-based refusal to provide a good or service for reasons of conscience will not deny her patients timely and convenient access to it. In Chapter 3, I present and explain ethical constraints on the exercise of conscience that are designed to preserve timely and convenient access.

Finally, the promise is said to be made to patients. However, when individuals enter a health care profession, they have few, if any, patients. It strains the notion of a promise to hold that a health care professional makes a promise today to unidentified individuals who will become patients 5, 10, or 15 years in the future. Accordingly, if a pharmacist refuses to fill a woman's prescription for EC, it would not be plausible for her to claim that the pharmacist has broken a promise that he made *to her*. In response, it might be claimed that all professionals upon entering a particular specialty or subspecialty are *obligated to make a commitment* to provide all services that are routinely offered by professionals within that specialty or subspecialty and are not incompatible with the corresponding clinical and professional standards.[74] However, then the foundation of the duty to provide the normal range of services would be an alleged *obligation* to make a commitment, and not the commitment. On the one hand, to simply assume that there is such an obligation would beg the question. On the other hand, the most likely justification would appeal to one of the accounts of professional obligations considered in this chapter (i.e. general ethical theory, internal morality, social contract, and covenant/indebtedness), and each fails to unequivocally support the incompatibility thesis.

CONCLUSION

Three approaches to conscientious objection in health care were critically examined: conscience absolutism, the incompatibility thesis, and a compromise approach. Conscience absolutism is the extreme view that there are no ethical constraints on the exercise of conscience by health care

---

[74] Savulescu presents a commitment-based critique of conscientious objection: "[P]eople have to take on certain commitments in order to become a doctor. They are a part of being a doctor ... To be a doctor is to be willing and able to offer appropriate medical interventions that are legal, beneficial, desired by the patient, and a part of a just healthcare system" (Savulescu 2006: 294–7 at 295). Pellegrino refers to a "promise, commitment and dedication to an ideal" as an "act of profession" (Pellegrino 2002a: 378–84 at 378). He identifies two ways in which the alleged commitment is expressed: (1) a public proclamation by means of the oath medical students take at graduation, and (2) a private (explicit or implicit) promise or commitment to individual patients.

professionals. The incompatibility thesis is an extreme view at the opposite end of the continuum. According to it, conscience-based refusals to provide legal goods or services within the scope of a practitioner's competence are contrary to the practitioner's professional obligations. According to a compromise approach, conscience-based refusals can be compatible with professional obligations if specified ethical constraints are satisfied.

Defenders of conscience absolutism generally appeal to an interest in avoiding moral complicity in perceived wrongdoing. It is claimed that a health care professional is morally complicit if she discloses options, provides referrals, or facilitates transfers in relation to goods or services that are contrary to her conscience. There are no uncontroversial standards of moral complicity that can be used to decisively refute this claim. However, with the possible exception of general ethical theories, conscience absolutism is incompatible with each of the following accounts of the professional obligations of health care professionals: general ethical theories, internal morality, social contract, and covenant/indebtedness.

The other extreme approach (the incompatibility thesis) is not unequivocally supported by any of the accounts of professional obligations. In addition, the promise model fails to support it. Finally, with the possible exception of general ethical theories, each account of the professional obligations of physicians, nurses, and pharmacists favors a compromise approach.

Accordingly, both extreme approaches to conscientious objection in health care should be rejected in favor of a more nuanced compromise approach. I will propose and explain an ethically acceptable compromise approach in Chapter 3. The core of this compromise approach is a set of ethical constraints on the exercise of conscience.

Ethical limitations on the exercise of conscience

A compromise approach to conscience-based refusals by health care professionals seeks to strike a reasonable balance between the integrity interests of health care professionals and the health care needs and interests of patients. In Chapter 2, I considered and rejected two extreme alternatives to a compromise approach: the incompatibility thesis and conscience absolutism. On the one hand, I argued that none of the common accounts of the professional obligations of physicians, nurses, and pharmacists unequivocally supports the incompatibility thesis – the claim that conscientious objection is incompatible with those obligations. On the other hand, with the possible exception of accounts of professional obligations based on general ethical theories, I argued that conscience absolutism – the view that there are no ethical constraints on the exercise of conscience – is incompatible with the accounts of professional obligations considered in Chapter 2. With the possible exception of accounts based on general ethical theories, all favor a compromise approach.

In this chapter, I explain and defend a compromise approach, according to which the justifiability of conscience-based refusals is context-dependent. I will argue that core professional obligations to patients justify ethical constraints on the exercise of conscience. I will also explain and defend ethical constraints in relation to employers and supervisors, colleagues, and members of other health care professions.

The focus of this chapter is on ethical limitations on conscience-based refusals (i.e. those based on a practitioner's *core* moral beliefs). To be sure, as I observed in Chapter 1, there may be reasons to accommodate ethical or religious objections that are *not* based on a health care professional's core moral beliefs. However, if a conscience-based refusal in a particular situation is unjustified, then a refusal based on ethical or religious beliefs that are not among the practitioner's core moral beliefs also would not be justified.

OBLIGATIONS TO PATIENTS

Core professional obligations

A survey of professional codes for physicians, nurses, and pharmacists reveals considerable overlap among them. In particular, each profession recognizes three core professional obligations – i.e. obligations to patients which are central to its self-definition or identity and provide a basis for more specific obligations. These are an obligation to respect patient dignity and refrain from discrimination, an obligation to promote patient health and well-being, and an obligation to respect patient autonomy.[1] Several possible accounts of these recognized core professional obligations were presented in Chapter 2.

Medicine

The first of nine principles in the American Medical Association (AMA), "Principles of Medical Ethics," requires respect for human dignity: "A physician shall be dedicated to providing competent medical care, with compassion and respect for human dignity and rights." The requirement to respect human dignity and rights can be understood to prohibit invidious discrimination. The AMA "Declaration of Professional Responsibility: Medicine's Social Contract with Humanity" proclaims a commitment to "[t]reat the sick and injured with competence and compassion and *without prejudice*" (Council on Ethical and Judicial Affairs (CEJA) Report 5-I-01; emphasis added).[2] An interpretive statement explains that prejudice is to be understood as "racial, ethnic, and other forms of bias." The AMA *Code of Medical Ethics* explicitly prohibits invidious discrimination when physicians decide whether or not to accept a patient: "physicians who offer their services to the public may not decline to accept patients because of race, color, religion, national origin, sexual orientation, gender identity, or any other

---

[1] Obligations to promote patient health and well-being in professional codes are reflected in model practice acts for each of the three professions which proclaim that licensing board regulations and enforcement measures aim to promote "public health, safety, and welfare." Federation of State Medical Boards, "A Guide to the Essentials of a Modern Medical and Osteopathic Practice Act" (2010). Available at: www.fsmb.org/pdf/GRPOL_essentials.pdf; accessed July 10, 2010. National Council of State Boards of Nursing, "Model Nursing Practice Act" (2004). Available at: www.aanp.org/NR/rdonlyres/4A2E6B99-EDB0–4EA7-A1E2–8A51A6DDA7C5/0/Model_Nursing_Act_and_Rules.pdf; accessed July 10, 2010. National Association of Boards of Pharmacy, "Model State Pharmacy Act and Model Rules of National Association of Boards of Pharmacy" (2009). Available online at: www.nabp.net/publications/model-act/; accessed July 10, 2010.

[2] Available online at: www.ama-assn.org/ama/upload/mm/369/decofprofessional.pdf; accessed July 10, 2010.

basis that would constitute invidious discrimination" (Patient–Physician Relationship: Respect for Law and Human Rights, Opinion 9.12).[3] The proscription of invidious discrimination is reiterated in relation to the care of patients: "Physicians cannot refuse to care for patients based on race, gender, sexual orientation, gender identity, or any other criteria that would constitute invidious discrimination" (Potential Patients, Opinion 10.05).

The following statements from the *Code of Medical Ethics* express a strong commitment to patient well-being:[4]

The medical profession has long subscribed to a body of ethical statements developed primarily for the benefit of the patient. As a member of this profession, a physician must recognize responsibility to patients first and foremost ... (Preamble, Principles of Medical Ethics).

A physician shall, while caring for a patient, regard responsibility to the patient as paramount (Principle VIII, Principles of Medical Ethics).

The relationship between patient and physician is based on trust and gives rise to physicians' ethical obligations to place patients' welfare above their own self-interest and above obligations to other groups, and to advocate for their patients' welfare (The Patient–Physician Relationship, Opinion 10.015).[5]

In a section on informed consent, the *Code of Medical Ethics* includes the following implicit recognition of the value of patient autonomy: "The

---

[3] (American Medical Association 2010). This volume includes 3 of the 4 components of the *Code of Medical Ethics*: Principles of Medical Ethics, Fundamental Elements of the Patient–Physician Relationship, and Current Opinions with Annotations of the Council on Ethical and Judicial Affairs. The fourth component is Reports of the Council on Ethical and Judicial Affairs. The Principles, Fundamental Elements, and Opinions (without annotations) are available online at: www.ama-assn.org/ama/pub/physician-resources/medical-ethics/code-medical-ethics.shtml; accessed July 10, 2010.

[4] In the United Kingdom, the following are among the "duties of a doctor registered with the General Medical Council:" a duty to "[m]ake the care of your patient your first concern" and a duty to "[p]rotect and promote the health of patients and the public" (General Medical Council 2006). Available online at: www.gmc-uk.org/static/documents/content/GMC_GMP_0911.pdf; accessed July 10, 2010.

[5] The obligation of physicians to place patients' welfare above their own self-interest is a characteristic of a fiduciary relationship. In Chapter 2, I argued that no plausible conception of the fiduciary relationship would require physicians to put *every* patient interest above *any* interest of their own. In other words, the actual obligation depends on the circumstances and is not unqualified. Each of the three professions conceptualizes the professional–patient relationship as a fiduciary relationship. Various accounts of the professional obligations of health care professionals examined in Chapter 2 can provide a justification of the fiduciary model. For example, an internal morality account can claim that there is an inherent connection between the fiduciary model and the vulnerability and dependence of patients, which are due to illness, lack of knowledge, and relative lack of power and authority. From a contractarian perspective, it can be claimed that the fiduciary model represents a reasonable agreement between members of a profession and society. A social contract account can claim that the fiduciary model is part of the agreement between the professions and society. A reciprocity account can claim that adopting the fiduciary model is an appropriate means for health professionals to express their gratitude for the benefits and privileges that they enjoy as professionals.

patient should make his or her own determination about treatment" (Informed Consent, Opinion 8.08). An opinion on "therapeutic privilege" (the practice of withholding medical information from patients "in the belief that disclosure is medically contraindicated") recognizes an obligation to respect patient autonomy: "It [therapeutic privilege] creates a conflict between the physician's obligations to promote patients' welfare and respect for their autonomy by communicating truthfully ... Withholding medical information from patients without their knowledge or consent is ethically unacceptable" (Withholding Information from Patients, Opinion 8.082). In addition, a House of Delegates Health Policy statement calls on physicians to respect patient autonomy in the context of decisions to forgo life-sustaining measures: "The principle of patient autonomy requires that physicians must respect the decision to forgo life-sustaining treatment of a patient who possesses decision-making capacity" (Decisions Near the End of Life, House of Delegates Health Policy 140.966).[6]

Nursing

Three provisions of the American Nurses Association (ANA) *Code of Ethics for Nurses* are characterized as "the most fundamental values and commitments of the nurse" (Fowler 2008: 146). Together these provisions require respect for dignity, prohibit discrimination, and require commitments to patient health, well-being, and autonomy. The first provision requires "respect for the inherent dignity, worth, and uniqueness of every individual," and thereby also prohibits discrimination:

The nurse, in all professional relationships, practices with compassion and respect for the inherent dignity, worth, and uniqueness of every individual, unrestricted by considerations of social or economic status, personal attributes, or the nature of health problems. (ibid.: 147)

An interpretive statement explains that the first provision does not permit "prejudice:"

The need for health care is universal, transcending all individual differences. The nurse establishes relationships and delivers nursing services with respect for human needs and values, and without prejudice. (ibid.)

Another interpretive statement explicitly links the first provision to patient self-determination: "Respect for human dignity requires the recognition of

---

[6] As noted in Chapter 1, HOD Health Policy statements can be accessed online by means of "PolicyFinder," which can be downloaded at the AMA website: www.ama-assn.org/ama/no-index/about-ama/11760.shtml; accessed July 9, 2010.

specific patient rights, particularly, the right of self-determination" (ibid.: 148). Two provisions of the *Code of Ethics for Nurses* express a commitment to patient health and well-being. Provision 2 states: "The nurse's primary commitment is to the patient ..." (ibid.: 150). The third provision states: "the nurse promotes, advocates for, and strives to protect the health, safety, and rights of the patient" (ibid.: 152).

Pharmacy

Principle III of the American Pharmacist Association (APhA) *Code of Ethics for Pharmacists* requires respect for dignity and autonomy: "A pharmacist respects the autonomy and dignity of each patient ... In all cases, a pharmacist respects personal and cultural differences among patients."[7] An explanatory statement adds: "A pharmacist promotes the right of self-determination and recognizes individual self-worth by encouraging patients to participate in decisions about their health." Although Principle III does not explicitly prohibit discrimination, it arguably is contrary to that principle. In any event, Principle IV explicitly prohibits discrimination: "A pharmacist avoids discriminatory practices ..."

Principle II requires commitments to patient health and well-being: "A pharmacist promotes the good of every patient in a caring, compassionate, and confidential manner." An explanatory statement adds: "A pharmacist places concern for the well-being of the patient at the center of professional practice. In doing so, a pharmacist considers needs stated by the patient as well as those defined by health science."

Constraints on the exercise of conscience

The critical examination of the incompatibility thesis in Chapter 2 revealed that it is unwarranted to maintain generally that individuals are not suited for a health care profession if they can foresee having a conscience-based objection to providing a legal good or service that falls within that profession's accepted scope of practice. Nevertheless, core professional obligations set limits to the exercise of conscience. Since no one is required to enter or remain in a particular health care profession, core professional obligations do not require anyone to act against his or her conscience. On the contrary, they provide guidelines for choices of profession, specializations, and

---

[7] As noted in Chapter 2, the *Code of Ethics for Pharmacists* is available online at: www.pharmacist.com/ AM/Template.cfm?Section=Practice_Resources&CONTENTID=2903&TEMPLATE=/CM/ HTMLDisplay.cfm; accessed July 11, 2010.

practice environments that will enable people to avoid having to choose between fulfilling professional obligations and protecting their moral integrity.

The three core professional obligations justify limitations on the exercise of conscience in relation to (1) discrimination, (2) patient harms and burdens, (3) disclosing options, (4) referral and/or facilitating a transfer, and (5) advance notification.

Discrimination and reasons for refusing

There is an important distinction between two types of conscience-based refusals: (1) a refusal to provide a good or service because a health care professional believes that the *good or service* (e.g. EC or abortion) is unethical and (2) a refusal to provide a good or service to specified classes of patients (e.g. African Americans, Muslims, lesbian women, gay men, and unmarried women). Conscience-based refusals of the second kind can be based on invidious discrimination, and when they are, are contrary to the professional obligations of physician, nurses, and pharmacists and are unjustified.

To begin with refusals of the first kind, respect for moral integrity requires granting health care professionals considerable latitude concerning what is and what is not a valid reason for a conscience-based refusal to provide a particular good or service (e.g. EC or abortion).[8] However, this latitude is not unlimited. There are at least two limitations.

First, a provider's conscience-based refusal has little, if any, moral weight if it is undoubtedly incompatible with the goals of her profession.[9] Suppose, for example, after practicing family medicine for several years, a physician converts to Buddhism.[10] Subsequent to his conversion, he believes that pain is the working out of life's karma. In addition, he believes that interfering in the patient's suffering would only contribute to the patient's continued trials on the wheel of rebirth. Based on these beliefs, he refuses to provide pain medication to patients. As a second example, suppose a hospital nurse refuses to provide pain medication because she believes that pain is God's punishment for sin. Arguably, neither practitioner's conscience-based

---

[8] When refusals are conscience-based, a health care professional's moral integrity is at stake, which presents the strongest case for accommodation. However, it might not be feasible in practice to determine whether refusals are based on a practitioner's *core* moral beliefs. Moreover, as I noted in Chapter 1, there may be reasons to accommodate refusals even when they are based on ethical or religious beliefs that are not included within the scope of a practitioner's core moral beliefs.

[9] As the two examples suggest, actual situations in which there is no room for reasonable disagreement about whether a conscience-based refusal is contrary to the goals of a profession are likely to be rare.

[10] This example is based on Thomasine Kushner's description in a personal communication about an actual incident.

objection to providing pain medication merits any moral weight. A person who has a conscience-based objection to relieving pain should not enter fields, such as family medicine or nursing, that are committed to that goal.[11]

Second, conscience-based refusals that are based on demonstrably false clinical beliefs merit little, if any, moral weight. A study of South Dakota pharmacists reported that 36.6 percent of the respondents did not correctly identify the mechanism of action of EC, and 19 percent incorrectly identified it as most similar to that of the abortifacient mifepristone (Van Riper and Hellerstedt 2005). Another study reported that 35.8 percent of New Mexico pharmacists surveyed mistakenly believed that "[o]ral emergency contraception is also known as RU-486" (Borrego *et al.* 2006: 37). Such mistaken beliefs about EC are not limited to pharmacists. For example, similar findings are reported for family medicine physicians and nurses (Wallace *et al.* 2004). Although available evidence supports the conclusion that EC does not have any post-fertilization effects, there may be a low, unknown probability that if neither ovulation nor fertilization is prevented, EC will prevent implantation (Allen and Goldberg 2007; Davidoff and Trussell 2006; Prine 2007). However, the main mechanisms of EC are to prevent or delay ovulation and prevent fertilization. Moreover, unlike the abortifacient, mifepristone, EC does not have a post-implantation effect – i.e. it does not interfere with the development of embryos after implantation (Bastianelli *et al.* 2008; Hansen *et al.* 2007). Suppose a pharmacist's conscience-based objection to dispensing EC is based on a mistaken belief that if implantation takes place, it will terminate the pregnancy. Further, suppose the pharmacist would not object to dispensing EC if he correctly understood that the primary function and most likely effect is to prevent ovulation or fertilization and that it will not interfere with the development of an embryo after implantation.[12] Arguably, the pharmacist's conscience-based objection to EC merits little, if any, moral weight.

To turn to conscience-based refusals to provide a good or service to specified classes of patients, *invidious* discrimination is ethically unacceptable.

---

[11] There is a significant difference between such conscience-based refusals to provide pain medication and those that are based on a consideration of one's training and skills. For example, a physician or nurse with little or no expertise in pain control might refer a patient to a palliative care specialist.

[12] A pharmacist who understands that EC does not have any post-implantation effects might still object to dispensing EC on the grounds that there may be a low, unknown probability that if neither ovulation nor fertilization is prevented, EC will prevent *implantation*. Robert Card argues that it is "simply unreasonable to withhold medication because of the mere possibility that this may contribute to an immoral result" (Card 2007: 8–14 at 11). According to Card, the pharmacist's conscience-based refusal is unreasonable, and in such cases, it is justified to refuse requests for exemptions. For a critical analysis of Card's argument, see (Wicclair 2007: 21–2).

Historically, invidious discrimination on the basis of characteristics such as race, ethnicity, and religion has involved enslavement, genocide, and oppression as well as denial of basic rights and liberties. Such practices were associated with a belief that members of certain racial, ethnic, or religious groups have diminished moral worth and dignity and are not (full-fledged) members of the moral community. Clearly, such extreme forms of invidious discrimination are abhorrent and ethically unacceptable.

There are less extreme, but no less morally unacceptable, forms of invidious discrimination, such as unjustly disadvantaging and denying equal consideration to persons due to their race, ethnicity, or religion. Considering such characteristics, however, does not necessarily involve invidious discrimination. For example, the casting director for a docudrama about Eleanor Roosevelt would not be subject to a charge of invidious discrimination if he were to refuse to consider Oprah Winfrey for the lead role, claiming that as an African American she does not "fit the part." By contrast, if African Americans are excluded from parts that can be played by black or white actresses, and their exclusion is rooted in racial prejudice or bias, it is an instance of invidious discrimination. Similarly, if a health care professional refuses to provide goods and services to African American patients because of racial prejudice or bias, the refusal is an instance of invidious discrimination.

It is a settled view – one based on defensible and widely shared conceptions of justice, equality, dignity, and respect – that racial, ethnic, religious and gender-based prejudice or bias are ethically wrong. Even if it is conscience-based (i.e. rooted in core moral beliefs), no accommodation of such invidious discrimination is warranted. General ethical considerations as well as core values of each of the three professions support a constraint against invidious discrimination on the basis of race, ethnicity, religion, and gender.[13]

As indicated above, the ANA *Code of Ethics for Nurses* includes an unspecified proscription of "prejudice" (Fowler 2008: 147); the APhA includes an unspecified prohibition of "discriminatory practices;" and, in addition to a general proscription of "prejudice," the AMA *Code of Medical*

---

[13] As indicated above, anti-discrimination provisions in the professional codes of the AMA, ANA, and APhA require a commitment by members of each profession to refrain from invidious discrimination. Thus, physicians, nurses, and pharmacists have a *special* obligation as health care professionals not to discriminate. However, in contrast to a health care professional's obligation to give priority to patient health and well-being, the obligation not to discriminate is a *general* ethical obligation (i.e. an obligation that applies to everyone) as well as a professional obligation. That is, a physician, nurse, or pharmacist who practices invidious discrimination violates a general ethical obligation as well as a professional obligation.

Ethics specifically prohibits invidious discrimination on the basis of race, color, religion, national origin, sexual orientation, and gender identity. The AMA added sexual orientation to the specified types of prohibited invidious discrimination in 1993, and gender identity in 2007.[14] This expansion indicates that the scope of prohibited invidious discrimination within a profession can change over time. Such changes correspond to changes in accepted views within and outside the profession about the scope of invidious discrimination.[15] Adding invidious discrimination based on a patient's sexual orientation and gender identity reflects a judgment that a health care professional's moral disapproval is not an acceptable reason for refusing to provide health care goods or services to patients who are gay, lesbian, or transgendered.

It is, of course, possible to question whether a particular specification of the scope of invidious discrimination is justified. For example, although it is a settled view that race-based prejudice is ethically unacceptable, it might be questioned whether moral disapproval of gay, lesbian, or transgendered patients reflects *prejudice or unjustified bias*. Obviously, from the perspective of those who disapprove, their moral disapproval is justified and is not a prejudice or unjustified bias. In response, it might be argued that unless *good reasons* can be presented to defend moral disapproval of gay, lesbian, or transgendered patients, it is warranted to conclude that moral disapproval of them is based on prejudice or unjustified bias.

There may be a less controversial basis for not accommodating refusals to provide health care goods and services to gay, lesbian, and transgendered patients. It is arguable that, putting aside the soundness of the ethical assessment, moral disapproval of gay, lesbian, or transgendered patients is not an appropriate reason for a member of a profession committed to health, well-being, and respect for autonomy and dignity to refuse to provide goods or services to such patients. Indeed, it is arguable that no matter how morally objectionable a patient's character and/or past behavior, it is not justified to deny him access to essential health care goods and services. For example, deliberately withholding medically necessary treatment from convicted terrorists or serial killers cannot be justified ethically

---

[14] The AMA Board of Trustees (BOT) approved adding discrimination on the basis of sexual orientation in 1993 and the HOD approved it five years later. See (Schneider and Levin 1999: 1287–8). The BOT approved the addition of gender identity in 2007 (BOT Report 11, E-9.03, "Recommendations to Modify AMA Policy to Ensure Inclusion for Transgender Physicians, Medical Students, and Patients"). The CEJA approved it in the same year (CEJA Report 2-I-07).

[15] An example outside the health care professions is the explicit prohibition of employment discrimination based on gender identity that was added to the US federal jobs website in January 2010. See (Knowlton 2010: sec. A, p. 15).

by citing their deplorable conduct and extreme lack of moral virtue. As an illustration of a commitment to this principle, executions in the United States are delayed to enable death row prisoners to receive medical treatment for life-threatening illnesses. Clearly, a health care professional's refusal to provide goods or services to convicted terrorists or serial killers cannot be attributed to an unjustified prejudice or bias. Nevertheless, it is arguable that such a refusal would violate a practitioner's professional obligations.

In response, it might be claimed that even though a *virtuous* practitioner would never refuse to provide care due to moral disapproval of a *patient*, as long as another practitioner will provide medically necessary care in a timely fashion, a particular practitioner may refuse to treat a terrorist or serial killer without violating his professional obligations.[16] To be sure, this claim is debatable. Even if accepted, however, it is arguable that the same principle does not apply to refusals based on invidious discrimination. Refusals based on prejudice or unjustified bias, even if conscience-based and even if another practitioner is available to provide medically necessary services in a timely fashion, violate a practitioner's professional obligations and do not warrant accommodation. Accordingly, insofar as a refusal to provide goods and services to gay, lesbian, and transgendered patients is based on prejudice or unjustified bias, it violates the professional obligations of physicians, nurses, and pharmacists and does not warrant accommodation.

This is not the place to defend the claim that moral disapproval of gay, lesbian, and transgendered patients is based on prejudice or unjustified bias. However, even if this claim is accepted, refusals to treat such patients need not be based on moral judgments about them and may not violate a defensible constraint against invidious discrimination. The following actual case involving a lesbian couple who sought fertility treatments illustrates this point.[17]

Guadalupe Benitez and her lesbian partner, Joanne Clark, decided that Ms. Benitez would attempt to become pregnant with the aid of intravaginal self-insemination, a nonmedical process in which a woman inserts sperm into her own vagina. Several efforts failed to produce a pregnancy, and in 1999 Ms. Benitez was diagnosed with polycystic ovarian syndrome, which is associated with irregular ovulation.

---

[16] Those who accept this claim would deny that people who are unwilling to provide health care goods or services to terrorists or serial killers due to moral disapproval should seek a profession outside health care.

[17] This description of the case is based on the accounts provided in a California Supreme Court decision, *North Coast Women's Care Medical Group, Inc.* v *San Diego County Superior Court* (189 P 3d 959 (Cal. 2008)); (Buchanan 2005); and (Moran 2005).

Ms. Benitez then saw Dr. Christine Brody, an obstetrician-gynecologist at the North Coast Women's Care Medical Group (North Coast) in San Diego, California. Dr. Brody agreed to provide some fertility treatments,[18] but she stated at the first appointment that if those treatments were to fail, she could not provide intrauterine insemination (IUI), a medical procedure that involves threading a catheter through the patient's cervix to enable semen to be inserted directly into the uterus. Dr. Brody stated that it would be contrary to her religious beliefs to perform the procedure *on Ms. Benitez*. No public documents about the case explain why Dr. Brody was willing to help Ms. Benitez conceive but drew the line at IUI.

One of the factual issues in dispute is Dr. Brody's reason for refusing to perform IUI on Ms. Benitez. Whereas Dr. Brody alleges that she told Ms. Benitez she would not perform it on an *unmarried* woman, Ms. Benitez claims that Dr. Brody told her that she would not perform IUI on a *lesbian*. From the perspective of California law, this is an important distinction. Ms. Benitez sued Dr. Brody, North Coast, and another physician for violating the Unruh Civil Rights Act (CA Civ. Code § 51 (a)–(f)). At the time, it prohibited discrimination based on sexual orientation, but it did not prohibit discrimination on the basis of marital status.[19]

For the purposes of this analysis, suppose Dr. Brody refused to perform IUI because Ms. Benitez is a lesbian. To be sure, a refusal to provide IUI to a lesbian might be based on moral disapproval of lesbians. However, there are other reasons for denying fertility treatments to lesbian women. For example, a practitioner can refuse to provide or participate in providing fertility treatments on the grounds that it is "unnatural" for lesbian women to have children. It is debatable whether this reason warrants a charge of invidious discrimination. Another reason may be a commitment to provide or participate in providing fertility treatments only when the resulting child will be raised in an environment that is conducive to its proper development, combined with a belief that the proper development of children requires a male and a female parent who are married to each other. This belief may

---

[18] Dr. Brody prescribed Clomid to induce ovulation while Ms. Benitez performed intravaginal self-insemination with sperm from a sperm bank. Dr. Brody also ordered a hysterosalpingiogram, which established that Ms. Benitez's infertility was not a result of blocked fallopian tubes, and she performed a diagnostic laparoscopy, which ruled out endometriosis as the cause.

[19] At the time when Dr. Brody told Ms. Benitez that she would not provide IUI, the Unruh Civil Rights Act did not explicitly prohibit discrimination on the basis of sexual orientation. However, courts had interpreted the statute to include such a prohibition. An amendment enacted in 2005 expressly prohibits discrimination on the basis of sexual orientation and marital status (Ca. Stats. 2005, ch. 420, § 2). Among the legal questions raised by the case is whether the protection of religious liberty in federal and state law exempts individuals from the anti-discrimination provisions of the Unruh Civil Rights Act. The California Supreme Court in 2008 held that there is no such exemption (189 P 3d 959 (Cal. 2008)).

well be unsubstantiated or false, but it need not be based on moral disapproval of lesbians.[20]

Refusing to provide fertility treatments to lesbian women out of a concern for the well-being of children might be compared to refusing to provide *in vitro* fertilization (IVF) or other reproductive technologies to women over a certain age, or who have cancer, out of a concern for the effect of the death of a parent on the well-being of young children. A concern for the well-being of children might not be a good reason for refusing to provide fertility treatments in these circumstances, but it is questionable that such refusals can be said to be based on invidious discrimination. Similarly, a concern for the well-being of children may be a poor reason for denying fertility treatments to lesbian women. However, if the belief that it is in the best interests of children to have a male and female parent who are married to each other is based on the perceived needs of children and not on alleged deficiencies in the moral character, skills, abilities, and the like of lesbian women, refusals to provide fertility treatments to lesbian patients may not be subject to the charge of invidious discrimination. Moreover, even if it can be considered a type of unjustified discrimination, compared to discrimination based on moral disapproval, contempt, disrespect, and the like, it may not rise to the level of seriousness that would warrant inclusion within the scope of a constraint on the exercise of conscience. Whereas it is demeaning, degrading, and a serious insult to one's dignity to be denied health care goods and services due to moral disapproval of one's sexual orientation, the same cannot be said about a denial based on mistaken beliefs about the developmental needs and interests of children.

Reasons for refusing to provide fertility services to lesbian women are not always evident. Accordingly, it can be challenging to determine whether a refusal to provide fertility treatments to lesbian patients is based on moral disapproval. However, a willingness to provide or participate in providing non-reproductive health care goods and services to lesbian patients is evidence that a refusal to provide fertility treatments is not based on moral disapproval and may not fall within the scope of a defensible constraint against invidious discrimination. Consistency is another helpful indicator. For example, if a practitioner's reason for refusing to provide fertility treatments to lesbian patients is based on a belief that children

---

[20] Invidious discrimination based on sexual orientation is involved, however, if the belief about the proper upbringing of children is in turn based on the following two assumptions: (1) children are likely to adopt the sexual orientation of their parents; and (2) it is bad for children to become homosexuals (i.e. an indication of "abnormal" or morally flawed development). The second assumption expresses moral disapproval of gays and lesbians.

require a male and a female parent who are married to each other, then she should also refuse to provide fertility treatments to heterosexual women who are unmarried.

As in the Benitez case, it may be difficult to determine whether conscience-based refusals involve invidious discrimination. First, such determinations require ethical judgments about what constitutes prejudice or unjustified bias, and in some cases controversial ethical assumptions may be needed to justify those judgments. Second, such determinations can require ascertaining intentions and reasons, and such determinations can be elusive. Nevertheless, when conscience-based refusals involve prejudice or unjustified bias, they violate the constraint against invidious discrimination and do not warrant accommodation.

Patient harms and burdens

Depending on the situation, when a physician, nurse, or pharmacist refuses to provide a legal and professionally accepted good or service for reasons of conscience, patients can experience harms and/or burdens that they would not have experienced if the health care professional had provided the good or service. These can range from minor inconvenience if a patient has to receive care from another provider, to substantial harm if a patient is unable to receive timely attention to important and pressing health needs or if the patient's health care choices are thwarted. Core professional obligations prohibit the exercise of conscience from resulting in harms/burdens beyond an acceptable limit. Harms/burdens that exceed this limit are *excessive*, and the corresponding ethical constraint on conscience-based refusals will be referred to as a constraint against excessive harms/burdens.[21]

Unfortunately, there is no bright line separating harms and burdens that are excessive from those that are not. One point is clear, however: It is inconsistent with each of the three professions' commitments to the health, well-being, dignity, and autonomy of patients to maintain that no matter how substantial the harms and burdens that patients might experience, they cannot be excessive when they are the result of the exercise of conscience. The view that the value of maintaining moral integrity always outweighs the

---

[21] This constraint corresponds to a constraint on the legal duty of employers to accommodate conscientious objection by employees. Title VII of the 1964 Civil Rights Act (42 USCS § 2000e *et seq.* (2005)) requires employers to "reasonably accommodate" employees' conscience-based objections by means that do not impose "undue hardship on the conduct of the employer's business." Whereas Title VII places a constraint on employers' legal duty to accommodate conscientious objection by employees that protects *employers*, the constraint against excessive harms/burdens protects *patients*. Employment-related constraints on the exercise of conscience will be discussed in a subsequent section.

interests of patients amounts to conscience absolutism, which is incompatible with core professional obligations in medicine, nursing, and pharmacy. The constraint against excessive harms and burdens is to be understood as proscribing conscience-based refusals that will result in harms and burdens that are incompatible with core professional obligations.

Despite the absence of a bright line separating harms and burdens that are excessive from those that are not, there are clear cases at each end of a harm/burden continuum. Absent the availability of other practitioners who are willing and able to provide the good or service in a timely manner, each of the following conscience-based refusals falls within the excessive range of the continuum: (1) a physician's refusal to perform a life-saving emergency abortion and a nurse's refusal to assist; (2) a physician's refusal to perform an emergency laparotomy for a patient with a ruptured ectopic pregnancy and a nurse's refusal to assist, which can result in serious morbidity or even death; (3) a physician's refusal to offer and a pharmacist's refusal to dispense EC, which can result in an unwanted pregnancy and substantial emotional and physical harm; and (4) a physician's or nurse's refusal to honor a patient's request for palliative sedation, which can thwart a patient's autonomous choices and result in increased pain and suffering. In such cases, where there is a significant risk of substantial harm to patients, the exercise of conscience violates a constraint against excessive harms/burdens.

By contrast, at the other end of the continuum, when a physician, nurse, or pharmacist refuses to provide a good or service for reasons of conscience, others may be readily available to provide it without significantly harming or even inconveniencing patients. For example, suppose a patient with end-stage cancer who is in intractable pain requests palliative sedation from Physician P_1, who refuses for reasons of conscience. The patient is transferred immediately to Physician P_2, who complies with the patient's request. A smooth transfer such as this might result in little or no added burdens to the patient. To be sure, changing physicians in such circumstances can add to an already stressful and emotionally traumatic situation for patients. However, the risk of additional burdens associated with transfer can be prevented if physicians with conscience-based objections inform prospective patients in advance.[22]

Conscience-based refusals by nurses and pharmacists can also involve little, if any, risk of significant harm or inconvenience to patients. For example, if an obstetrics-gynecology nurse has notified supervisors of her conscience-based objection to assisting in abortion and providing

---

[22] I discuss advance notification in a subsequent section.

post-abortion care, and nurses who are willing to assist always are available, she might be able to exercise her conscience without subjecting patients to a significant increase in harms or burdens. Similarly, significant burdens to patients who request EC are unlikely if a pharmacist has notified the pharmacy manager of his conscience-based objection to dispensing it, and arrangements have been made to assure that another pharmacist or pharmacy assistant, who is willing to dispense EC, is always available as a back-up.

Between the two extremes on the harm/burden continuum, there are cases in the middle gray area about which reasonable persons might disagree. A reported actual case involving an Emergency Department (ED) physician and EC may be such a case. An ED physician in a central Pennsylvania town refused to give a rape victim EC because it was against his religious beliefs (Bowman and Fishlock 2006). At the time, EC still required a prescription, and the woman had to travel over 20 miles to another city to get it. This case may well fall in the gray zone.[23] Nevertheless, it is not implausible to claim that the woman's experience – especially considering that she was a rape victim – crossed the line into excessive burdens.[24] At the very least, the constraint against excessive harms/burdens would have required the ED physician to consider the impact on the patient and determine whether it was excessive before refusing to provide EC.

Clearly, the seriousness of a patient's condition and the urgency of the patient's need for the refused good or service are among the factors affecting the magnitude of harms and burdens that will result from a conscience-based refusal to provide a good or service. For example, the potential harm of a refusal to provide an emergency laparotomy generally is greater than the potential harm of a refusal to provide an elective first trimester abortion or fertility services. However, the case of the ED physician's refusal to provide EC illustrates that the magnitude of harms and burdens is context-dependent in another important respect. The availability of alternative means of access to the good or service can be decisive. If another ED physician had been available to give the rape victim EC, she could have

---

[23] Reasonable people might disagree about whether having to drive 20 miles to get EC from another provider is an excessive burden. Arguably, it is an excessive burden to require a hospitalized end-stage Amyotrophic Lateral Sclerosis (ALS) patient to be transported to another facility if she wants to forgo MPNH. This, in effect, was the ruling in *In the Matter of Beverly Requena* 517 A.2d 869 (1986). This case will be discussed in more detail in Chapter 4.

[24] It may not have been foreseeable that the woman would have to drive over 20 miles to get EC. She reportedly called her gynecologist, who wrote a prescription. However, a local pharmacy affiliated with a national chain did not have EC in stock, and she was advised to go to the nearest chain store location that had it in stock.

received it with little or no additional inconvenience, and she would not have experienced the burden of driving 20 miles to get it.

Location can be significant. When a health care professional in a large metropolitan area refuses to provide a legal and professionally accepted good or service for reasons of conscience, there are likely to be other health care professionals who are willing and able to provide the good or service. However, in small rural communities, the number of physicians, nurses, and pharmacists may be very limited and many may have similar ethical or religious beliefs. In such communities, when a practitioner refuses to provide a good or service for reasons of conscience, residents may have to travel substantial distances at considerable inconvenience and expense to receive the good or service and/or experience substantial delays. For example, when the only pharmacist in Broadus, Montana (population 450) decided to stop dispensing oral contraceptives, residents reportedly had to either drive 80 miles to the nearest pharmacy or mail order them (Gease 2007).[25] In an incident involving a young woman in Laconia, New Hampshire, after a pharmacy refused to fill her prescription for EC late at night on a Saturday, she reportedly did not get it filled by another pharmacy before the 72-hour window of maximum effectiveness had long passed (Stein 2005).

Accordingly, the impact on patients and the ethical acceptability of conscience-based refusals can vary depending on the location of practitioners who refuse to provide a good or service. Hence, *applying the same standard of excessive harms/burdens*, although physicians, nurses, or pharmacists in a large metropolitan area may not be obligated to provide or assist in providing a good or service (e.g. EC for rape victims or an emergency laparotomy) against their conscience, practitioners in a small rural community may be obligated to provide or assist in providing the same good or service against their conscience. Choice of practice locations can prevent difficult choices between fulfilling one's professional obligations and maintaining moral integrity.[26]

Access to goods and services from other providers can be substantially limited even in large urban areas. This point is exemplified by the case of

---

[25] This information is from the online edition: www.rapidcityjournal.com/articles/2007/12/17/news/ top/doc4764c55d12c4a942856230.txt; accessed July 10, 2010.

[26] The focus of this book is on ethics and the ethical limits of conscientious objection. It is beyond its scope to consider means to enforce ethical constraints and protect patient access to health care goods and services. Holly Fernandez Lynch takes up this issue in depth. See (Lynch 2008). She argues that it is a responsibility of licensing boards to guarantee that conscientious objection does not inappropriately impede patient access to health care.

Guadalupe Benitez, which was discussed in the previous section. Ms. Benitez went to North Coast to help her become pregnant because it was the only fertility clinic within her health plan's network. Accordingly, although there are several other providers of fertility services in San Diego, California, when Ms. Benitez was unable to receive IUI at North Coast, there were no alternative providers whose services were covered by her health plan. Depending on a patient's financial situation, paying for IUI oneself can be extremely burdensome or even infeasible. Thus, health insurance limitations and a patient's financial situation are additional contextual features that can affect the impact and ethical acceptability of health professionals' conscience-based refusals.[27]

Even though there is no bright line separating harms and/or burdens that are excessive and those that are not, the constraint against excessive harms and/or burdens is not inconsequential. First, it serves to prohibit clear instances of excessive harms and/or burdens. Second, it serves as a reminder that physicians, nurses, and pharmacists who have conscience-based objections to providing a good or service also have obligations to patients that may not be ignored. Third, it expresses the important point that determining whether or not the exercise of conscience is ethically justified is in part context-dependent.

Disclosing options

Despite the Internet and various other resources available to the general public, patients often are dependent on health care professionals for reliable information about goods and services that will meet their health needs and interests. This dependence is a basis for the conventional compromise's disclosure requirement, which obligates a health care professional with a conscience-based objection to providing a good or service to inform patients about the good or service "if it is medically relevant to their medical condition" (D. Brock 2008: 194).[28] Arguably, core professional obligations would justify this requirement if, whenever a health care professional has

---

[27] North Coast reportedly covered "extra expenses" incurred when Ms. Benitez received IVF from another provider, and her insurance company allowed her to receive care from an out-of-network provider. See (Buchanan 2005). These measures significantly reduced the burdens that Ms. Benitez experienced as a result of the refusal of North Coast physicians to provide IUI. Needless to say, patients generally cannot count on providers and health insurance companies to mitigate the financial burden of conscience-based refusals.

[28] The conventional compromise is described toward the beginning of Chapter 2. As specified by Brock, it has three components:
   (1) The physician/pharmacist informs the patient/customer about the service/product if it is medically relevant to their medical condition.

a conscience-based objection to a good or service, her patients would not know that it is a clinically suitable option for them unless the health care professional informs them. However, this generalization does not always hold.

To be sure, there are situations in which disclosure by a health care professional with a conscience-based objection to providing a good or service is essential. For example, suppose a rape victim who presents at an ED does not know that EC can substantially reduce the risk of pregnancy.[29] The ED physician on call has a conscience-based objection to EC and fails to inform her of its availability. As a result, the woman leaves without finding out that taking EC can significantly reduce the risk of pregnancy. Without that knowledge, the woman will not have an opportunity to decide whether or not to take EC. Since she considers it a significant harm to give birth to the rapist's child, she would have taken EC if she knew it was an option. Accordingly, it is inconsistent with the ED physician's core professional obligations to promote patient well-being and autonomy to have done nothing to prevent the woman from leaving without knowing about the option of EC.[30]

To satisfy core professional obligations, a physician with a conscience-based objection to a good or service (g/s) has an obligation to ascertain whether a patient in his care for whom g/s is a clinically suitable option knows that g/s is one of her options. A request for g/s by the patient obviously indicates that she has this knowledge. However, if the physician refuses to provide g/s for reasons of conscience, to prevent the patient from

---

(2) The physician/pharmacist refers the patient/customer to another professional willing and able to provide the service/product.

(3) The referral does not impose an unreasonable burden on the patient/customer.

The compromise approach I propose includes several modifications of the conventional compromise.

The AMA *Code of Medical Ethics* includes the following statement:

The patient has the right to receive information from physicians and to discuss the benefits, risks, and costs of appropriate treatment alternatives. Patients should receive guidance from their physicians as to the optimal course of action. *(Fundamental Elements of the Patient–Physician Relationship, Opinion 10.01)*

This statement is somewhat ambiguous due to the reference to "*appropriate* treatment alternatives." It also does not explicitly require disclosure of all medically accepted options. Accordingly, the AMA statement does not unequivocally and unconditionally require disclosure of a medically accepted option that a physician considers to be "inappropriate" because it is against her conscience.

[29] Studies have reported that many women are either unaware of EC or lack sufficient understanding to use it effectively. See, for example (Abbott 2005: 111–13), (Foster *et al.* 2004: 150–6), (Merchant *et al.* 2007: 367–75). I discuss some of the reported findings of these studies in Chapter 4.

[30] According to an AMA House of Delegates Health Policy statement, "information about emergency contraception is part of the comprehensive information to be provided as part of the emergency treatment of sexual assault victims" (Access to Emergency Contraception, Health Policy 75.985).

mistakenly inferring that g/s is not a clinically suitable option for her, the physician should clearly communicate that the refusal is for conscience-based reasons and not because g/s is medically unsuitable. If the patient does not request g/s, it is not sufficient for the physician to state that there is an option that he cannot disclose because doing so is against his conscience. Such a statement does not give the patient sufficient guidance to determine whether the unidentified option has sufficient potential value to warrant trying to find out what it is. Moreover, when time is of the essence, as in the case of EC, by the time the patient finds out about the option, it may be too late or the probability of its effectiveness may have been significantly reduced. In addition, the patient might continue to worry that she has not identified *the* option that the physician would not disclose. Accordingly, if the physician determines that a patient is not aware of option g/s, the physician is obligated to help the patient acquire information about it. This obligation can be met by informing the patient about g/s. Alternatively, it can suffice to offer to arrange for the patient to see another physician who will provide information about g/s in a timely manner. However, this alternative is pointless if the physician does not believe that there is a significant ethical distinction between providing the information herself and referring the patient to another physician who will.

As observed in Chapter 1, a 2008 AMA CEJA Report, adopted by the AMA House of Delegates (Health Policy 140.863), states that physicians have an obligation to offer palliative sedation when it is an appropriate option:[31]

When symptoms cannot be diminished through all other means of palliation, including symptom-specific treatments, it is the ethical obligation of a physician to offer palliative sedation to unconsciousness as an option for the relief of intractable symptoms. (CEJA Report 5-A-08)

Clearly, an obligation to offer includes an obligation to inform, and an obligation to inform is appropriate insofar as many patients or family members are unlikely to know enough about palliative sedation to warrant waiting for them to initiate a discussion of it. However, it is to be expected that some physicians will have a conscience-based objection to including palliative sedation among the end-of-life options that are presented to

---

[31] Available online at: www.ama-assn.org/ama1/pub/upload/mm/369/ceja_5a08.pdf; accessed July 10, 2010. According to the CEJA Report, palliative sedation to unconsciousness is an option for patients in the "final stages of terminal illness." It is said to be "an intervention of last resort to reduce severe, refractory pain or other distressing clinical symptoms that do not respond to aggressive symptom-specific palliation."

patients who satisfy the AMA criteria, or their surrogates.[32] Nevertheless, no provision is made for such physicians in the AMA policy or the conventional compromise.[33]

The foregoing analysis suggests a weaker disclosure requirement than in the AMA policy – one that provides some accommodation to physicians with conscience-based objections to palliative sedation while giving terminally ill patients who meet the AMA criteria for the procedure, or their surrogates, an opportunity to learn about and choose it. The following is the proposed disclosure requirement:

The attending physician of a patient who meets the AMA criteria for palliative sedation has an obligation to inform the patient or surrogate that palliative sedation is an option or arrange for the patient or surrogate to have an opportunity to learn about it from a qualified health care professional.[34]

This disclosure requirement in relation to palliative sedation is similar to a recommendation in a recent American Academy of Pediatrics (AAP) clinical report on forgoing medically provided nutrition and hydration (MPNH). According to the AAP report, forgoing MPNH is ethically appropriate in some circumstances, and parents should be informed of this option. Informing parents when forgoing MPNH is an acceptable option may be essential, since parents might otherwise not be aware of that option; or they may not consider it because they assume it is not legally, professionally, or ethically acceptable. The AAP clinical report recognizes that some providers

---

[32] A study of 677 Connecticut members of the American College of Physicians reported that 78% believed that it is, and 8% believed that it is not, ethically acceptable to provide terminal (palliative) sedation to terminally ill patients with intractable pain. The remaining respondents were either "neutral" or "unsure" (Kaldjian *et al.* 2004a). A study of 236 residents in three internal medicine residency programs in Connecticut reported that 66% "agreed with terminal sedation." The rest either disagreed with the practice or were unsure. (Kaldjian *et al.* 2004b: 381–7). For a report of the attitudes of nurses based on interviews with 22 nurses see (Rietjens *et al.* 2007: 643–9).

[33] A bill introduced in the California Assembly in February 2008 (AB 2747) would have required attending physicians who determine that a patient is terminally ill to provide the patient with an opportunity to receive information and counseling about all legal end-of-life options, including palliative sedation. That bill included an opt-out by transfer provision for physicians with a conscience-based objection to providing end-of-life care according to patient choices, but no comparable provision for physicians with a conscience-based objection to disclosing one or more end-of-life options. The final bill (California Health and Safety Code § 442.5) excludes an explicit reference to terminal sedation and requires providers to provide information and counseling about end-of-life options only if patients request it. Providers who object to supplying such comprehensive information are instructed to facilitate a referral or transfer. The final bill is available online at: http://info.sen.ca.gov/pub/07–08/bill/asm/ab_2701–2750/ab_2747_bill_20080903_enrolled.html; accessed July 5, 2010.

[34] To satisfy the referral constraint, which will be discussed in the following section, the attending physician also has an obligation to assure that the patient or surrogate has an opportunity to choose and receive palliative sedation.

may object to participation in forgoing MPNH and recommends accommodation: "It is also important to emphasize that care providers must work within their own ethical standards, and pediatricians and other health care providers should not be required to participate in treatment plans to which they have personal ethical objections" (Diekema and Botkin 2009: 818). Nevertheless, the AAP report recognizes an obligation to provide parents with an opportunity to consider the option of forgoing MPNH: "when such an option is legal and ethical by societal standards, parents must be made aware of the option and a referral must be made to caregivers who can assist them to further explore and carry out their wishes" (ibid.). To fulfill this obligation, pediatricians need not themselves inform parents of the option of forgoing MPNH, but they must at least ensure that parents have an opportunity to receive relevant information from another provider.

Does a similar requirement apply to informing patients about the option of physician-assisted suicide in Oregon, Washington, and Montana, states in which physician-assisted suicide is legally permitted? Does the attending physician of a patient who meets the Oregon and Washington statutory criteria for receiving medication to end life have an obligation to inform the patient of that option or arrange for the patient to have an opportunity to learn about it from a qualified health care professional?[35] There is a significant difference between palliative sedation and physician-assisted suicide that warrants a negative answer to both questions.[36] Although physician-assisted suicide is legally permitted in Oregon, Washington, and Montana, it still is not a professionally accepted practice within medicine. Indeed, it is explicitly condemned in the AMA *Code of Medical Ethics* and in House of Delegates Health Policy statements.[37] To be sure, the AMA may be mistaken about physician-assisted suicide, and at some point in the future, the

---

[35] As noted in Chapter 1, statutes approved by voters in Oregon (ORS 127.800–995) and Washington (RCW 70.245.010–904) authorize physicians to dispense or prescribe medication to end life under specified conditions, and a Montana Supreme Court decision held that physicians who provide suicide assistance to competent terminally ill patients who consent are not subject to prosecution for homicide (*Baxter* v *Montana* 2009 MT 449). The Oregon and Washington statutes provide specific guidelines and requirements, but the Montana Supreme Court did not provide comparable detailed guidance.

[36] Montana has a statute that prohibits "aiding or soliciting suicide" (§ 45–5–105, MCA). The minority opinion in *Baxter* v *Montana* cited this statute to support its position that assisted suicide is contrary to public policy. One of the majority's responses was to maintain that physician-assisted suicide does not fall within the anti-solicitation provision of the statute because patients initiate requests for it: "In physician aid in dying, the solicitation comes from the patient himself, *not* a third party physician" (*Baxter* v *Montana* n 35 above at 33). This response suggests that Montana physicians may not be able to count on criminal immunity if they offer suicide assistance or disclose that it is an option.

[37] In the *Code of Medical Ethics*, physician-assisted suicide is said to be "fundamentally incompatible with the physician's role as healer ... " (Physician-Assisted Suicide, Opinion 2.211). One HOD

organization may revise its policies to permit the practice. However, currently, assisted suicide is not a professionally accepted practice; and a physician in Oregon, Washington, or Montana who has a conscience-based objection to it can cite the *Code of Medical Ethics* to rebut the claim that she has a *professional obligation* to inform patients whenever assisted suicide is a legally permitted option for them.

Insofar as physicians often have the primary responsibility for explaining health care options to patients, the disclosure requirement applies most frequently to them. Nevertheless, whenever nurses and pharmacists are gatekeepers of information about clinically suitable options, they have an obligation not to allow considerations of conscience to trump a patient's access to information. For example, suppose it is a nurse's responsibility to counsel patients about their options after prenatal genetic screening, which has revealed Tay-Sachs. A conscience-based objection to abortion does not exempt her from an obligation to either disclose that option to the patient or assure that the patient has an opportunity to receive information about it in a timely fashion from another qualified health care professional. If a nurse is not willing to do either, this may well be a situation in which it is justified to maintain that a person with a particular conscience-based objection should avoid selecting certain practice areas.

Since EC is now available to women 17 years and older without a prescription, pharmacists may be asked for information about post-coital contraception. If a pharmacist with a conscience-based objection is asked whether there is any medication that can be taken to prevent pregnancy after unprotected sex, it would be contrary to her professional obligations if she were to provide false or misleading information with the aim of avoiding complicity for a moral wrong. For example, it would be contrary to her professional obligations to say, "There is no such medication" or "It's too late. There is no safe means to prevent pregnancy after sex." In addition to an obligation not to provide false or misleading information, the pharmacist also has an affirmative obligation to provide accurate information. She can

---

Health Policy states that physician-assisted suicide is "fundamentally inconsistent with the physician's professional role" (Physician-Assisted Suicide, Health Policy 140.952). Another states that it is "fundamentally inconsistent with the physician's role as healer" (Physician-Assisted Suicide, Health Policy 270.965). In addition, the CEJA report on palliative sedation cites the *Code of Medical Ethics* statement that physician-assisted suicide and euthanasia are "fundamentally incompatible with the physician's role as healer" (CEJA Report 5-A-08). Similar to the AMA, the ANA prohibits suicide assistance. The ANA Position Statement on assisted suicide is available online at: www.nursingworld.org/EthicsHumanRights; accessed July 10, 2010. The American Society of Health-System Pharmacists "Statement on Pharmacist Decision-making on Assisted Suicide" permits pharmacists to decide whether or not to participate in suicide assistance (American Society of Health-System Pharmacists, 1999: 1661–4).

discharge this obligation by either providing it herself or assuring that the patient has an opportunity to receive the information from another pharmacy employee without delay.[38]

The proposed interpretation of the disclosure requirement represents a contextual understanding of the obligation to inform patients. As such, it can provide greater protection of conscience than the conventional compromise, but only when its exercise does not fail to satisfy the obligation to assure that patients have a timely opportunity to acquire an understanding of all of their clinically acceptable options.

Referral and/or facilitating a transfer

When health care professionals refuse to provide a legal and professionally accepted good or service for reasons of conscience, there is a continuum of follow-up behavior that can affect patient access significantly. At one end of the continuum, practitioners can actively help a patient obtain access to the good or service by facilitating a transfer to a health care professional who is willing and able to provide it. At the other end of the continuum, providers can actively thwart or impede a patient's access to the good or service. Referral to a practitioner who is willing and able to provide it, a requirement associated with the conventional compromise, falls somewhere between the two extremes.

There are two obvious reasons for a constraint against actively blocking or impeding a patient's access to a legal and clinically suitable good or service. First, such behavior fails to respect patient autonomy. Second, if the patient does not receive the good or service in a timely manner, he is likely to be worse off than he would have been if he had received it in a timely manner. Accordingly, actively blocking or impeding patient access violates the duty to promote patient health and well-being. Moreover, if a patient's health worsens as a result of not receiving the good or service in a timely manner, actively blocking or impeding access to it violates a health care professional's duty not to harm the patient.

Health care professionals who actively block or impede patient access may only intend to avoid *their complicity* in the perceived wrongdoing of others. However, another possible aim is to prevent *the patient* from engaging in behavior that is contrary to the ethical or religious beliefs of

---

[38] Arguably, to require the patient to go to another pharmacy to receive the information about EC would constitute an undue burden and would risk her not receiving it in time to prevent a pregnancy. When time is not a crucial factor, it may suffice to require that pharmacists not allow patients to leave without providing guidance to enable them to get answers to their questions without excessive inconvenience or delay.

the health care professional. If a person believes that an action is seriously immoral, it is understandable if she also is committed to preventing others from performing the action. Nevertheless, it generally is inappropriate for a health care professional to exploit her professional gatekeeping power and authority to impose her ethical or religious beliefs on a patient who does not accept them.[39] Moreover, even if the health care professional's intent is only to avoid *her own complicity* in a perceived moral wrong, the effect can be to impose her ethical or religious beliefs on a patient who does not accept those beliefs, which is contrary to the obligation to respect patient autonomy.

The actions of Neil Noesen, a Wisconsin pharmacist with a conscience-based objection to "participating in the work of contraception," illustrates how a health care professional can cross the line that separates passive non-participation from active blocking or impeding.[40] On a Saturday in 2002, Noesen, who was working as a weekend relief pharmacist in a K-mart in Menomonie, Wisconsin, refused to refill a University of Wisconsin student's prescription for oral contraceptives. The prescription had been filled at that pharmacy in the past and was on file there. The woman (referred to as "AR" in the Wisconsin Pharmacy Examining Board report) had used all of her pills and needed the prescription filled to enable her to begin the new cycle the following day (a Sunday). Noesen did not inform AR that she could go to another pharmacy to request a transfer of her prescription, but she went to a Wal-Mart pharmacy and requested a transfer. When the Wal-Mart pharmacist called Noesen, he refused to facilitate a transfer of

---

[39] Under the Oregon and Washington Death with Dignity Acts, health care providers who are unwilling to provide or assist in providing patients with medication to end their lives are not required to do so and are not required to refer patients to a willing health care provider. This provision is justified insofar as providers do not have a professional obligation to participate in suicide assistance. In both Oregon and Washington, however, unwilling providers are not permitted to *block* or *thwart* a patient transfer by refusing to transfer medical records. Whereas it is the responsibility of patients to find and effect a transfer to willing providers, unwilling providers are legally required to transfer *medical records* (ORS 127.885 §4.01(4); RCW 70.245.190(1)(d)). Writing about Oregon Ballot Measure 16, the 1994 voter initiative authorizing physician-assisted suicide, Mullan, Allen, and Brushwood question whether the opt-out provision applies to pharmacists because the initiative defined "health care provider" as "anyone who is licensed or permitted to '*administer*' health care [emphasis added]" (Mullan, Allen and Brushwood 1996: 1185 at 1188). However, the definition of "health care provider" in the current Oregon and Washington Death with Dignity Acts clearly includes pharmacists: "a person licensed, certified or otherwise authorized or permitted by the law of this state to administer health care or *dispense* medication . . . [emphasis added]."

[40] The description of this incident is based on (Weier 2004), and the Wisconsin Pharmacy Examining Board account: "In the Matter of the Disciplinary Proceedings against Neil T. Noesen, RPH, Respondent." Final Decision and Order (LS0310091PHM). Available at the Protection of Conscience Project website: www.consciencelaws.org/Conscience-Archive/Documents/Noesen%20Pharmacy%20Board%20Order.html; accessed July 10, 2010.

AR's prescription.[41] As a result, AR had to wait until Monday, when the managing pharmacist, who was not available earlier, refilled the prescription. By obstructing AR's access to oral contraceptives, Noesen failed to fulfill his professional obligation to protect AR from harm (e.g. anxiety) and the risk of harm (e.g. the emotional impact of unwanted pregnancy, the health risks of pregnancy and childbirth, and the social and financial consequences of having and caring for an unwanted child).[42]

The Wisconsin Pharmacy Examining Board's "Findings of Fact" included the following statement: "Respondent [Noesen] objected to transferring the prescription for contraceptives to another pharmacist on the basis that it would induce another to do a morally wrong or sinful act pursuant to the doctrines of the Roman Catholic Church."[43] It is not clear whether the perceived "morally wrong or sinful act" in question is the action of AR (e.g. taking contraceptives and/or engaging in perceived "morally wrong or sinful" intercourse), another pharmacist (e.g. dispensing contraceptives and/or complicity in perceived "morally wrong or sinful" intercourse), or both. If Noesen wanted to prevent AR from engaging in behavior that violated his religious beliefs, he inappropriately and intentionally used his professional power and authority to impose his religious beliefs on her. Even if this was not his intent, the effect would have been the same. In either case, refusing to transfer AR's

---

[41] Another reported type of obstruction is a refusal to return a prescription. See, for example, the July 25, 2005 testimony to the House Committee on Small Business by Kim A. Gandy, National Organization for Women president. Available online at: www.now.org/issues/abortion/testimony7-25-05.html; accessed July 10, 2010. According to a news item in the *British Medical Journal*, "The *News & Record*, a North Carolina newspaper, reported that some pharmacists were destroying prescriptions, giving patients speeches on morality, and stalling the patient beyond the point where emergency contraception would be effective" (Tanne 2005: 983).

[42] The Wisconsin Pharmacy Examining Board held that Noesen "engaged in a practice which constitutes a danger to the health, welfare, or safety of a patient and has practiced in a manner which substantially departs from the standard of care ordinarily exercised by a pharmacist and which harmed or could have harmed a patient." Their "Findings of Fact" included the following two statements: (1) "Respondent [Noesen] did not ask AR any questions about her medical condition and did not know whether she had a medical condition that would cause harm to her if she became pregnant." (2) "Respondent [Noesen] did not assess the risk of harm to AR as a result of his refusal to transfer her refill prescription or of his refusal to provide her information about her options to obtain her prescribed medication." The Board imposed the following sanctions: a fine, a reprimand, and practice conditions on Noesen's license. With the exception of the fine, these sanctions were upheld in March 2008 by the Wisconsin Third District Court of Appeals (*Noesen v State Department of Regulation & Licensing, Pharmacy Examining Board* (311 Wis. 2d 237)). The Wisconsin Supreme Court refused to hear an appeal of the lower court decision. See Eric Quade, "State Supreme Court Refuses to Hear Case," *Barron News-Shield*, Barron, WI, June 25, 2008. Available online at: www.zwire.com/site/news.cfm?BRD=1132&dept_id=157671&newsid=19803907&PAG=461&rfi=9; accessed July 10, 2010.

[43] "In the Matter of the Disciplinary Proceedings against Neil T. Noesen, RPH, Respondent." Final Decision and Order (LS0310091PHM).

prescription was an abuse of Noesen's professional power and authority and a violation of his professional obligations.

Typically, accommodations for conscientious objectors enable individuals to refuse to perform actions contrary to their conscience, such as military service, abortions, prescribing and dispensing EC, and providing palliative sedation.[44] The point is to allow individuals to refrain from performing actions against their conscience and preserve their moral integrity. However permitting x to refrain from acting against x's conscience is not to be confused with enabling x to prevent y from performing legal actions that are contrary to x's (but not y's), ethical or religious beliefs.

Noesen also appears to have failed to respect AR's privacy. Her prescription was for Loestrin FE, which can be used for birth control, regulation of the menstrual cycle, or treatment of acne. Noesen's conscience-based objection was limited to its use as a *contraceptive*, and he asked AR whether she intended to use the medication for contraception, arguably failing to respect her privacy. If, as reported in some cases, pharmacists and other health care professionals lecture patients and express moral disapproval and condemnation, they also fail to respect the dignity of patients (Tanne 2005).[45]

As the case of AR and Noesen indicates, when a health care professional refuses to provide a legal and professionally accepted service, patients sometimes do not need referrals in order to obtain access to that good or service. Within a short period of time, AR apparently was able to find a conveniently located pharmacy with a pharmacist who was willing to dispense contraceptives. However, sometimes patients do need assistance to secure timely and convenient access to a safe and effective health care good or service that a practitioner refuses to provide for reasons of conscience. In such situations, refusing to assist a patient is inconsistent with core obligations of each of the three professions (i.e. obligations to promote patient health and well-being and respect patient autonomy and dignity). Depending on the situation, such assistance can involve providing a referral

---

[44] In Chapter 6, I consider accommodations for health care professionals who believe, as a matter of conscience, that they have an obligation to *perform* actions that are prohibited by law, regulations, institutional policies, and so forth.

[45] The AMA *Code of Medical Ethics*, the ANA *Code for Nurses*, and the APhA *Code for Pharmacists* all express the professions' commitment to patient privacy and dignity. The Oregon Board of Pharmacy posted the following statement on its website: "[T]he Board would consider it unprofessional conduct for a pharmacist to lecture a patient about the pharmacist's moral or religious beliefs, to violate the patient's privacy or to destroy, confiscate or otherwise tamper with the patient's prescription." Available online at: www.pharmacy.state.or.us/Pharmacy/Position_Statements.shtml; accessed July 10, 2010.

or facilitating a transfer to a practitioner who is willing and able to provide the good or service.[46] If AR had asked Noesen for the location of the nearest pharmacy that was open and where she could get her prescription filled without delay, he would have had an obligation to provide that information.[47] Arguably, to fulfill his obligation to AR, since it might have been difficult to locate a pharmacy where she could get her prescription refilled in a timely fashion, he should have offered to help her locate a pharmacy. For example, Noesen might have offered to call pharmacies to locate one where AR could go to get her refill without delay. In this situation, Noesen's professional obligation to protect AR would take priority over his interest in avoiding complicity in a perceived wrongdoing.

Chervenak and McCullough identify a situation in which they claim an obligation to protect patients from harm requires referral (Chervenak and McCullough 2008). They maintain that physicians with a conscience-based objection to abortion have an obligation to offer patients who are considering the procedure information about "responsible health care organizations such as Planned Parenthood" (ibid.: 232.e2). They claim that a failure to offer such a referral risks exposing patients to significant harm. An obligation to refer is said to be based on physicians' duty to protect their patients:

Given the sorry history of incompetently performed abortions, which unfortunately is not altogether past, the physician has a fiduciary responsibility to protect the patient from loss of future fertility, health, or even her life. (ibid.)

---

[46] Frader and Bosk maintain that refusing to refer can leave patients worse off: "When HCPs [health care professionals] engage in extensive CO [conscientious objection] and fail to provide their patients an alternative, they risk leaving the patient 'worse off,' a situation that appears to violate the Hippocratic injunction 'to do no harm'" (Frader and Bosk 2009: 62–7 at 66). It remains to ask: Worse off relative to what? Clearly, worse off relative to a patient's condition prior to receiving a good or service is not sufficient. If a patient is ill and/or in pain and does not receive medical care due to a physician's conscience-based refusal to provide it or refer to another physician who will, the patient may experience no increase in pain or decline in health. In this respect, the patient is not worse off. However, if referral to another provider would enable the patient to receive care that improves his condition, and the patient is unlikely to receive that care in a timely fashion without the referral, the physician's failure to refer would leave the patient worse off relative to what his health and well-being would have been if the physician had provided a referral. This is the appropriate comparison to determine whether a refusal to offer to refer leaves a patient worse off.

[47] I consider the obligations of pharmacies (pharmacy licensees) in Chapter 4. I will argue that pharmacies, such as the K-mart pharmacy in which Noesen worked, are obligated to have arrangements in place that enable patients such as AR to get prescriptions filled. The K-mart pharmacy had such an arrangement. The manager had agreed to serve as a back-up to fill prescriptions when Noesen would not. However, the manager was unavailable when AR sought to have her prescription refilled. For additional details, see the previously cited Wisconsin Pharmacy Examining Board account of the occurrence.

Although their assessment of the risk of harm without referral might be questioned, it is hardly debatable that a failure to provide a referral if it is necessary to protect patients from such substantial dangers is contrary to a physician's core professional obligations.

When a transfer of care to another physician or nurse is required to accommodate a conscience-based refusal, hospital and nursing home patients generally cannot be expected to assume responsibility for effectuating it. For example, if, for reasons of conscience, an attending physician refuses to write a Do Not Resuscitate (DNR) order for a competent patient who has requested it, the patient cannot be expected to arrange for a transfer to a physician who is willing to write a DNR order. Even if the patient has family who can assist, it is inappropriate to place on them the responsibility and burden of arranging a transfer. They may lack sufficient practical knowledge, and they already are likely to be under considerable emotional stress and strain. It may be acceptable for the attending physician to delegate to other members of the health care team the specific measures required to effectuate a transfer. However, it is the attending physician's responsibility to set in motion the process and to assure that a smooth and timely transfer takes place. Withdrawing from the case without discharging this responsibility is tantamount to patient abandonment.

When a transfer of care is required to accommodate nurses who practice in hospitals or nursing homes, generally nurse managers or supervisors have the primary responsibility for arranging for substitutes. The responsibilities of nurses with conscience-based objections are twofold: (1) to provide timely notification to nurse managers, which facilitates advance planning;[48] and (2) not to withdraw unless and until patient care has been transferred to another nurse. Withdrawing before a substitute assumes responsibility for patient care is tantamount to patient abandonment.[49]

Sometimes, when practitioners refuse to provide a legal and professionally accepted good or service for reasons of conscience, it may not be feasible to determine reliably whether a patient needs assistance to secure

---

[48] In a subsequent section (Constraints in Relation to Employers), I will defend a requirement to provide advance notification to nurse managers or supervisors. The ANA *Code of Ethics for Nurses* includes the following statement:

The nurse who decides not to take part on the grounds of conscientious objection must communicate this decision in appropriate ways. Whenever possible, such a refusal should be made known in advance and in time for alternate arrangements to be made for patient care. (Fowler 2008: at 160)

[49] The ANA *Code of Ethics for Nurses* includes the following explicit constraint in relation to conscientious objection: "The nurse is obliged to provide for the patient's safety, to avoid patient abandonment, and to withdraw only when assured that alternative sources of nursing care are available to the patient" (ibid. at 160–1).

access to it that is safe, effective, timely, and not excessively burdensome. However, to protect patients adequately and minimize the risk that a provider will fail to fulfill core professional obligations, the default position is an obligation to *offer* to refer or facilitate a transfer. That is, if a practitioner who refuses to provide a legal and professionally accepted good or service has insufficient evidence to warrant concluding that the patient does not need her to provide a referral or facilitate a transfer to secure access to it that is safe, effective, timely, and not excessively burdensome, the practitioner has an obligation to offer to refer and/or facilitate a transfer. This analysis, similar to the foregoing interpretation of the disclosure requirement, represents a contextual understanding of the obligation to refer and/or facilitate a transfer.[50] Both requirements can provide greater protection of conscience than the conventional compromise, but only when its exercise does not fail to satisfy core professional obligations.

Advance notification

The timing of patient notification can significantly affect the impact on patients of conscience-based refusals to provide health care goods or services. Patients are prone to be especially vulnerable and dependent at times when they are in need of a health care good or service. To minimize the negative impact on patients and fulfill core professional obligations to them, whenever feasible and apt, practitioners should provide advance notice to patients of conscience-based objections. Generally, if practitioners have a conscience-based objection to providing a legal good or service within the scope of their professional competence, they should not wait until it becomes a clinically suitable option to inform patients that they cannot provide it for reasons of conscience.[51] Health care professionals may be

---

[50] A study of physician attitudes asked respondents whether physicians who have a conscience-based objection to providing a requested procedure "have an obligation to present all possible options to the patient, including information about obtaining the requested procedure" (Curlin *et al.* 2007: 593–600 at 597). The reported physician responses were: 86% yes; 6% undecided; and 8% no. When responses were correlated with low, moderate, or high degree of "intrinsic religiosity," the percentage of yes responses in each category was: low: 92%; moderate: 84%; high: 81%. The study also asked whether physicians who have a conscience-based objection to providing a requested procedure "have an obligation to refer the patient to someone who does not object to the requested procedure." The reported physician responses were: 71% yes; 11% undecided; and 18% no. When responses were correlated with low, moderate, or high degree of "intrinsic religiosity," the percentage of yes responses in each category was: low: 82%; moderate: 73%; high: 56%. It is at least possible that some physicians who accept a contextual interpretation of an obligation to refer or facilitate a transfer would be inclined to answer "undecided" or even "no" rather than "yes" to a question that did not allow nuanced responses.

[51] The study by Curlin and colleagues in n 50 above did not ask whether physicians should provide advance notification of conscience-based objections. The only additional question was whether it

able to minimize harms and burdens by giving (prospective) patients an opportunity to learn about the provider's conscience-based objections during their initial meeting. It is then that finding another provider is the least upsetting and distressing. Advance notification can also maximize a patient's opportunity to establish a relationship with another practitioner – one who has no conscience-based objection to providing a good or service that the patient someday may want.[52]

To be sure, advance notification has to be exercised with care so as to minimize the risk of unnecessary distress to patients. For example, if a physician informs a patient who presents with a suspicious lump in her breast that he is conscientiously opposed to forgoing medically provided nutrition and hydration (MPNH), the patient is likely to mistakenly infer that she has terminal cancer and is dying. The same observation would apply if a physician were to disclose his conscience-based objection to forgoing MPNH when first informing a patient that she has breast cancer. It would be no less inappropriate to disclose a conscience-based objection to forgoing MPNH in such circumstances than it would be to initiate a discussion of advance directives.

As a practical matter, an obligation to provide advance notification *to patients* applies most often to physicians. There might be some exceptions, such as nurse practitioners, but for the most part the obligation of nurses and pharmacists to provide advance notification of conscience-based objections is owed directly to employers, supervisors, or managers and indirectly to patients. In a subsequent section on employment-related constraints, I will examine the obligation to provide advance notification to employers, supervisors, or managers.

The following hypothetical case illustrates the importance of advance notification:

Mr. M is a 56-year-old man with acute myelomonocytic leukemia (AML). After a careful consideration of the options, he decides to undergo chemotherapy, radiation therapy, and a bone marrow transplant. At first, it seemed that the treatment regimen was successful, but the remission turned out to be only

would be ethical "for the physician to plainly describe to the patient [in response to the patient's request for a procedure] why he or she objects to the requested procedure" (ibid.). The reported physician responses were: 63% yes; 15% undecided; and 22% no. When responses were correlated with low, moderate, or high degree of "intrinsic religiosity," the percentage of yes responses in each category was: low: 56%; moderate: 62%; high: 73%.

[52] This is essentially the approach to conscientious objection that Rebecca Dresser refers to as the "contract model" (Dresser 2005). As she observes, its feasibility is limited to situations in which patients have access to other providers who are willing and able to provide the good or service and patients do not have an immediate need for it.

temporary. After discussing the treatment options and his prognosis with Dr. K, an oncologist, Mr. M decides to forgo any further aggressive treatment. He wants to become a hospice patient so that he can experience as little pain, discomfort, and loss of dignity as possible. Mr. M is competent, he clearly understands the options and the consequences of forgoing additional treatment, and everyone in his family, including his wife, parents, two adult children, and sister, fully supports his decision. Dr. T has been Mr. M's internist for over 20 years, and Mr. M values the relationship that has developed between them. When Mr. M explains his decision to his internist, Dr. T tells Mr. M for the first time that her religious beliefs prevent her from actively or passively hastening the death of patients. She explains to Mr. M that as a result of her religious beliefs she cannot in good conscience continue caring for him if he adheres to his decision to forgo aggressive measures and enter a hospice program. When Mr. M responds that he will not change his mind, Dr. T offers to arrange a transfer to another physician who will care for him according to his wishes.

When a patient has had a long-standing good relationship with a physician, an unwanted transfer to another physician can be a source of distress under any circumstances. However, if, as in the case of Mr. M, the unwanted transfer occurs when a patient has a terminal illness and is dying, such a change can be especially traumatic. Even if Mr. M receives the care he wants from another physician, he may feel abandoned by Dr. T in a time of particular need, and may experience self-doubt and/or anger because his long-time physician disagreed with his decision to the point of refusing to continue caring for him. Mr. M could have been spared these additional burdens at the end of his life if Dr. T had disclosed her views about life-sustaining treatment and end-of-life care earlier – either at an appropriate time after the diagnosis of AML or, preferably, during Mr. M's initial appointment with her (e.g. in the context of a discussion of advance directives). Consistent with an earlier observation, however, Dr. T would need to exercise care so as to avoid unnecessarily increasing Mr. M's distress and anxiety.

Obstetrician-gynecologists and family physicians can spare patients unnecessary additional burdens at a time of increased vulnerability if they do not wait until patients consider or request an abortion to inform them of their conscience-based objections. To prevent unnecessary burdens, physicians can give prospective patients an opportunity to learn about their objection to abortion during the first appointment. To be sure, patients can initiate a discussion, ask questions, and so forth. However, they may be reluctant to inquire about the physician's willingness to perform abortions, or it may not be a concern to them at the time. Hence, physicians with conscience-based objections to abortion bear the responsibility for giving patients an opportunity to learn about their unwillingness to perform the procedure. Pamphlets listing services that a physician does and does not provide can help to inform prospective patients that abortion is not among the services that a physician offers.

To return to a case discussed previously, Dr. Brody provided advance notification to Ms. Benitez by informing her at their initial meeting that she would not perform IUI. In this respect, Dr. Brody appears to have satisfied her advance notification responsibility. However, there is some dispute about the adequacy and accuracy of the information she provided about the availability of other North Coast physicians to perform the procedure for Ms. Benitez. Dr. Brody stated that other North Coast physicians who did not share her religious objections would be available to perform IUI for Ms. Benitez. However, due to a special licensure requirement, when Ms. Benitez opted for donation of "fresh sperm" from a friend rather than frozen sperm from an anonymous donor, no willing North Coast physicians were qualified to perform IUI, and Ms. Benitez received IVF from another provider. This incident vividly demonstrates the importance of providing accurate information about back-up physicians. Even if it was inadvertent, giving Ms. Benitez unreliable information thwarted an aim of advance notification – giving patients early notice about the need to find a willing provider.

Circumstances may not warrant advance notification. However, when it is feasible and apt, it can reduce patients' burdens and harms and enable them to select and establish relationships with health care providers who are willing to provide goods and services that are consistent with patients' health needs and preferences.

ADDITIONAL CONSTRAINTS ON THE EXERCISE OF CONSCIENCE

The foregoing constraints and requirements derive from core professional obligations to *patients*. They strike a reasonable balance between the integrity interests of health care professionals and the health care needs and interests of *patients*. However, there are other interests that need to be considered and that can warrant additional limitations on the exercise of conscience by physicians, nurses, and pharmacists. These include constraints in relation to employers, colleagues who are members of the same profession, and members of other professions.

Constraints in relation to employers

Health care professionals have obligations to patients that justify constraints on their exercise of conscience. Additional constraints are justified when physicians, nurses, and pharmacists are affiliated with institutions, organizations, groups, or businesses as employees, staff members, independent contractors, or consultants. For the sake of conciseness, such physicians, nurses, and pharmacists will be referred to as *employees*, and the institutions, organizations, groups, or businesses with which they are affiliated will be referred to as *employers*.

One additional limitation on the exercise of conscience is a constraint against excessive burdens to employers (e.g. hospitals, nursing homes, medical practices, and pharmacies). Another is a requirement to give advance notification to supervisors when health care professionals foresee that they will not be able to fulfill specified responsibilities due to their ethical or religious beliefs. This will be referred to as an advance employer notification requirement.

Excessive employer burdens

Just as conscience-based refusals can result in burdens to patients, they can have a similar effect on employers. For example, to accommodate a pharmacist with a conscience-based refusal to dispense contraceptives, a pharmacy may be confronted with a choice between hiring an additional pharmacist and losing business; and both choices are likely to involve a significant financial loss. Similarly, to accommodate an obstetrics-gynecology nurse's conscience-based objection to assisting with abortions, a hospital may have to hire an additional nurse who is willing to provide such assistance.

Just as there are ethical limits to patient burdens, so, too, there are limits on the burdens that employers are obligated to accept in order to accommodate conscience-based refusals of physicians, nurses, and pharmacists. Corresponding to the constraint against excessive harms/burdens in relation to patients, there is a constraint against excessive burdens to employers. Title VII of the 1964 Civil Rights Act (42 USCS § 2000e *et seq.* (2005)) recognizes a similar constraint in relation to an employer's *legal* obligation to accommodate an employee's conscience-based objection.[53] It requires employers to "reasonably accommodate" conscience-based objections of

---

[53] Title VII is available online at the US Equal Employment Opportunity Commission (EEOC) website: www.eeoc.gov/laws/statutes/titlevii.cfm; accessed July 10, 2010.

health care professional employees unless it would result in an "undue hardship" on the employer.[54] Although the focus of this book is on ethics and not law, some of the provisions of Title VII can serve as a helpful model for *ethical* guidelines.[55]

Under Title VII, a reasonable accommodation is said to be "any adjustment to the work environment that will allow the employee to comply with his or her religious beliefs."[56] Typical accommodations for health care professional employees include exemptions from specific tasks to which they object (e.g. dispensing EC, assisting with abortions, participating in organ donation after cardiac death (DCD), providing family planning, or genetic counseling) and changes of work assignments or transfers (e.g. transfer from an obstetrics-gynecology unit to a general internal medicine unit or transfer from one location of a pharmacy chain to another).[57] If there are two possible accommodations that do not impose an undue hardship on the employer, and one of them does, and the other does not, involve a loss to the employee of employment-related advantages or benefits, only the latter

---

[54] The explanation of Title VII presented here is based on two EEOC documents: (1) "Guidelines on Discrimination Because of Religion" (29 CFR Ch. XIV § 1605) (hereinafter, EEOC Guidelines); (2) EEOC Compliance Manual, Section 12, "Religious Discrimination" (hereinafter, EEOC Compliance Manual). Both documents are available online at: www.eeoc.gov/laws/types/religion.cfm; accessed July 10, 2010. Based in part on case law, the EEOC, which is responsible for enforcing and implementing Title VII, provides authoritative guidelines for interpreting and applying it.

[55] For an examination of employment law in relation to conscientious objection in health care, see (Davis 1986: 847–78).

[56] EEOC Compliance Manual, p. 46. Title VII prohibits *religious* discrimination in employment:

It shall be an unlawful employment practice for an employer –

(1) to fail or refuse to hire or to discharge any individual, or otherwise to discriminate against any individual with respect to his compensation, terms, conditions, or privileges of employment, because of such individual's race, color, *religion*, sex, or national origin; or

(2) to limit, segregate, or classify his employees or applicants for employment in any way which would deprive or tend to deprive any individual of employment opportunities or otherwise adversely affect his status as an employee, because of such individual's race, color, *religion*, sex, or national origin. (42 USCS §§ 2000e–2(a)) (emphasis added)

However, the EEOC adopted the same broad definition of religion as the US Supreme Court applied in two decisions about conscientious objection to military service:

[T]he Commission will define religious practices to include moral or ethical beliefs as to what is right and wrong which are sincerely held with the strength of traditional religious views. This standard was developed in *United States* v. *Seeger*, 380 U.S. 163 (1965) and *Welsh* v. *United States*, 398 U.S. 333 (1970). The Commission has consistently applied this standard in its decisions. (EEOC Guidelines, p. 204)

[57] The EEOC identifies the following "most common methods" of reasonable accommodation for all types of employment: "(1) flexible scheduling; (2) voluntary substitutes or swaps of shifts and assignments; (3) lateral transfer and/or change of job assignment; and, (4) modifying workplace practices, policies, and/or procedures" (EEOC Compliance Manual, p. 65).

is a reasonable accommodation. For example, a means of accommodating a pharmacist with a conscience-based objection to dispensing EC that reduces her hours from 40 to 30 per week would not be a reasonable accommodation if an accommodation without such a reduction would not impose an undue hardship on the pharmacy business. Similarly, reassigning a hospital obstetrics-gynecology nurse who has a conscience-based objection to assisting with abortions to a position at a lower pay grade is not a reasonable accommodation if a reassignment to a position at the same pay grade would not have resulted in an undue hardship to the hospital. Arguably, corresponding to employers' Title VII *legal* obligation to offer a reasonable accommodation that satisfies the foregoing condition, there is a similar *ethical* obligation.

Title VII also provides useful guidance for determining when accommodations may be denied because they would result in *excessive burdens* to employers. The corresponding Title VII term is *"undue hardship."* Generally, Title VII criteria for determining when employer hardships are *undue* are also suitable for determining when employer burdens are *excessive*.

According to authoritative guidelines issued by the US Equal Employment Opportunity Commission (EEOC), whether or not an employer hardship is *undue* is largely context-dependent.[58] The Commission identifies several factors that are relevant when determining whether or not employer hardships are undue. Each factor requires a threshold, but the EEOC does not provide a general standard for determining in specific cases when the threshold is met. The only general guideline is a necessary condition: An employer hardship is undue only if it is "more than *de minimis*." Taken literally, however, this criterion only requires that a hardship not be insignificant or negligible.[59] In place of general criteria for determining when the threshold is

---

[58] Citing *Tooley* v *Martin Marietta Corp.* (648 F.2d 1239, 1243 (9th Cir. 1981)), the EEOC states: "The determination of whether a particular proposed accommodation imposes an undue hardship 'must be made by considering the particular factual context of each case'" (EEOC Compliance Manual, p. 46). The criteria for determining whether an accommodation is *reasonable* also are context-dependent. Citing *Smith* v *Pyro Mining Co.* (827 F.2d 1081, 1085), which in turn quotes *Redmond* v *GAF Corp.* (574 F.2d at 902–3), the EEOC states:

Ultimately, reasonableness is a fact-specific determination. The reasonableness of an employer's attempt at accommodation cannot be determined in a vacuum. Instead, it must be determined on a case-by-case basis; what may be a reasonable accommodation for one employee may not be reasonable for another ... The term 'reasonable accommodation' is a relative term and cannot be given a hard and fast meaning; each case ... necessarily depends upon its own facts and circumstances, and comes down to a determination of 'reasonableness' under the unique circumstances of the individual employer-employee relationship. (EEOC Compliance Manual, pp. 53–4)

[59] The *Oxford English Dictionary* online offers the following definition of "*de minimis*": "so insignificant as to be unworthy of attention; negligible." Available online (subscription required) at: www.oed. com/; accessed July 10, 2010.

met in relation to a given factor, the Commission provides examples of clear cases in which employer hardships are and are not undue. As in the case of the constraint against excessive harm to patients, here, too, there may be clear cases at each end of the continuum but no bright line separating burdens that are, from those that are not, excessive.

The following are among the relevant factors that the EEOC identifies, which are also appropriate for determining whether employer burdens are excessive: "the type of workplace, the nature of the employee's duties, the identifiable cost of the accommodation in relation to the size and operating costs of the employer, and the number of employees who will in fact need a particular accommodation" (EEOC Manual, p. 57). Accordingly, it would be an undue hardship/excessive burden for a family planning clinic with only two staff nurses to exempt one from offering counseling that included the option of abortion. By contrast, it might not be an undue hardship/ excessive burden for a large pharmacy with more than one pharmacist on duty at all times to accommodate the only pharmacist who refuses to dispense EC for reasons of conscience. However, if 7 of the 9 pharmacists employed by the pharmacy have a conscience-based objection to dispensing EC, accommodating each of them would comprise an undue hardship/ excessive burden. Similarly, it might not be an undue hardship/excessive burden for a large Health Maintenance Organization with salaried physicians to accommodate the only staff obstetrician-gynecologist with a conscience-based objection to elective non-therapeutic abortion if each of the other 6 staff obstetrician-gynecologists is willing to perform elective abortions. However, if the physician who objects to performing non-therapeutic abortions for reasons of conscience is the *only* staff obstetrician-gynecologist, an accommodation that required hiring an additional physician would comprise an undue hardship/excessive burden.[60]

The EEOC distinguishes between accommodations that require temporary increases in payroll expenses and those that require permanent increases:

Generally . . . temporary payment of premium wages (*e.g.*, overtime rates) while a more permanent accommodation is sought, will not constitute more than *de minimis* cost, whereas the regular payment of premium wages or the hiring of additional employees to provide an accommodation will generally cause an undue hardship to the employer. (EEOC Manual, p. 58)

---

[60] In this respect, the situation may be comparable to an obstetrician-gynecologist's refusal to deliver babies.

Accordingly, if a small pharmacy would have to hire an additional employee to accommodate a pharmacist's conscience-based objection to dispensing contraceptives, it would be an undue hardship/excessive burden. By contrast, unless there are extraordinary circumstances, overtime payments by a large pharmacy chain while a transfer is arranged for a pharmacist with a conscience-based objection to dispensing contraceptives does not involve an undue hardship/excessive burden.

According to the Commission, administrative costs associated with accommodations generally do not rise to the level of an undue hardship:

> Generally, the payment of administrative costs necessary for an accommodation, such as costs associated with rearranging schedules and recording substitutions for payroll purposes . . . will not constitute more than *de minimis* cost . . . (ibid.)

This appears to be an acceptable standard in relation to excessive employer burdens, provided it is treated as a presumptive rule that can be rebutted in particular cases.

When an accommodation involves exempting a health care professional from a specific task or a change of assignment, position, or location of employment, whether it will result in an undue hardship/excessive burden for the employer can depend on the availability of substitutes and positions (ibid.: p. 68). Another relevant factor is the effect on the *performance* of other employees (ibid.: p. 59).[61] The relevance of such considerations is illustrated by a second incident involving Neil Noesen, the K-mart pharmacist in Menomonie, Wisconsin who refused to facilitate a transfer of a woman's prescription for oral contraceptives to a Wal-Mart pharmacy.[62] Among the disciplinary measures imposed by the Wisconsin Pharmacy Examining Board for that 2002 incident, Noesen was ordered to give potential employers a written description of any services that he would not provide and the measures that he would take to assure that patients' access to medications was not obstructed. In July 2005, Noesen was hired for a temporary position in a Wal-Mart pharmacy in Onalaska, Wisconsin. The pharmacy agreed to several measures to accommodate his stated conscience-based objection to participating in contraceptive dispensing. These included exempting him from dispensing contraceptives or taking orders for them from customers or physicians. In addition, to enable

---

[61] The EEOC also classifies *burdens* to other employees as *employer* hardships. However, such burdens are considered in a subsequent section (Constraints in Relation to Other Professionals).

[62] The description offered here of this second incident is based on the US Court of Appeals for the Seventh Circuit account (232 Fed. Appx. 581). Two examples in the EEOC Compliance Manual (43 and 44) are based on this second incident (EEOC Compliance Manual, p. 69).

Noesen to avoid any physical contact with prescriptions for contraceptives, other employees pre-sorted prescriptions and placed any for contraceptives in a separate basket.

The accommodations offered by the Wal-Mart pharmacy were not sufficient for Noesen. When he began working there, he refused to interact in person or on the telephone with customers or physicians if they expressed any interest in contraceptives. In such situations, he walked away from customers and put callers on hold, and he refused to notify other pharmacy staff to enable them to take over for him.[63] As an additional accommodation, the pharmacy supervisor offered to require Noesen to assist customers only if they were male or not of childbearing age. However, Noesen refused this offer. The only acceptable accommodation to him was to have another pharmacy employee pre-screen all calls and customers. The pharmacy supervisor offered pre-screening of on-site customers, but not telephone calls. When Noesen rejected this accommodation, he was fired, and he subsequently initiated legal action, claiming violation of Title VII.

Clearly, the accommodations that were offered Noesen were feasible only because other pharmacy employees were available to take on the responsibilities that he was not asked to perform. The hardship/burdens would have been undue/excessive, and it would have been ethically justified to refuse to offer those accommodations if: (1) the pharmacy that hired Noesen was a small pharmacy with only one pharmacist on duty at a time; (2) another full-time pharmacist employed by the Wal-Mart pharmacy in Onalaska already had a conscience-based exemption from dispensing contraceptives; (3) other pharmacists and staff (e.g. interns and technicians) employed by the Wal-Mart pharmacy in Onalaska could not discharge their responsibilities satisfactorily under the arrangements required by the accommodations offered to Noesen.

Indeed, the US Court of Appeals for the Seventh Circuit (232 Fed. Appx. 581) held that refusing to grant Noesen the accommodation he demanded did not violate Title VII, because of the effect it would have had on the performance of other employees: "the diversion of technicians from their assigned duties of data input and insurance verification would impose the undue cost of uncompleted data work on Wal-Mart." The accommodation that Noesen demanded is a clear case of an excessive burden on an employer and a clear case of a justified denial of an accommodation.

---

[63] Noesen clearly failed to satisfy a reasonable requirement proposed by Mullan, Allen and Brushwood: "the employer may require notification by an objector pharmacist to a nonobjector, or other passive involvement by the objector" (1996: 1185–91 at 1189).

Advance employer notification

Advance employer notification enables supervisors to accommodate conscience-based objections with a minimum of inconvenience and disruption. By facilitating continuity of services provided by an institution, organization, group, or business it also serves to minimize the burdens that patients will experience as a result of conscience-based refusals. Finally, since advance notification can enable colleagues who might be asked to substitute to make any necessary professional and personal adjustments, such notification also minimizes inconvenience and disruption to them.

From the perspective of physicians, nurses, and pharmacists with conscience-based objections, providing advance notification to supervisors is unlikely to comprise even a minor burden or inconvenience. On the contrary, insofar as advance notification increases the likelihood that an accommodation will be feasible, it is in the interest of health care professionals who foresee situations in which they will refuse to provide a good or service for reasons of conscience. Accordingly, there are good reasons to accept, and no compelling reasons to reject, an advance employer notification requirement. Although it is an obligation owed directly to supervisors, it is also an indirect obligation to patients and colleagues.

Neil Noesen's brief employment history at the Wal-Mart pharmacy in Onalaska, Wisconsin illustrates the value of advance employer notification. As previously indicated, after the earlier incident at a K-mart pharmacy, the Wisconsin Pharmacy Licensing Board required Noesen to give prospective employers a written description of any services that he would not provide. Before beginning to work, he gave Wal-Mart a written statement explaining that he would "'decline to perform the provision of, or any activity related to the provision of contraceptive articles,' including 'complete or partial cooperation with patient care situations which involve the provision of or counsel on contraceptive articles'" (232 Fed. Appx. 581). This written advance notification enabled the pharmacy manager to reassign responsibilities to other pharmacy employees with the aim of accommodating Noesen. However, as it turned out, Noesen only partially complied with the advance employer notification requirement. He failed to unambiguously communicate that he would refuse to notify other employees if a customer or caller wanted anything related to contraceptives and that the only acceptable accommodation would be for other employees to pre-screen customers and telephone calls.

For several days prior to his dismissal, Noesen walked away when customers indicated an interest in contraceptives, and callers who expressed a similar interest were left on indefinite hold. Accordingly, due to his failure to fully inform the pharmacy supervisor, customers and callers were inconvenienced, and some may have experienced significant delays in receiving their medications. In addition, the supervisor undoubtedly received complaints and may have been subject to criticism for ineffective management. Moreover, it is not clear that Noesen himself benefited from the experience. Even if he earned a few days' income, some of his encounters with customers and colleagues must have been unpleasant; and he risked additional disciplinary action by the Wisconsin Pharmacy Licensing Board.

Although Noesen's case provides only one example of the value of advance employer notification, there is no reason to assume that it is not generalizable. Indeed, it offers a cautionary lesson about the importance of unambiguous prior notification when a physician, nurse, or pharmacist is unwilling to provide a good or service within the scope of his or her profession and/or specialty.

Constraints in relation to other professionals

When physicians, nurses, and pharmacists refuse to provide goods or services for reasons of conscience, other professionals can be affected. These other professionals can be colleagues who are members of the same profession or members of other professions. Limitations on the exercise of conscience are warranted in relation to each.

Members of the same profession

Aside from the possible negative impact on *the performance* of colleagues, granting conscience-based accommodations to physicians, nurses, or pharmacists also can result in *burdens* to their colleagues. To accommodate Noesen, other pharmacy employees had to take on the tasks he refused to perform, which increased their workloads. If an Intensive Care Unit (ICU) nurse is exempted from participating in DCD, other nurses must be available to assist, which might add to their workloads. Similarly, to enable a hospital or nursing home nurse to be exempted from caring for patients who are unable to take nutrition and hydration orally and who themselves or whose family members have decided to forgo MPNH, it might be necessary to switch assignments with another nurse, which may not be a welcome change for the latter. To enable a physician in a group obstetrics-gynecology practice to avoid having to respond to patient requests for information about prenatal genetic testing, a colleague may have to add providing this service for the other physician's patients to her usual responsibilities. Similarly, if an on-call pediatric intensivist refuses to participate in withdrawing life-support for patients who are to undergo DCD, other pediatric intensivists will have to be available to supervise and perform established DCD procedures.

To be sure, a willingness to tolerate some disadvantages to enable colleagues to exercise their conscience and preserve their moral integrity is virtuous and laudable. However, there are limits to the increased burdens that colleagues can be expected to accept. Just as an employer may justifiably refuse to accommodate an employee's conscience-based objection if the resulting burdens to the employer would be excessive, so, too, a physician, nurse, or pharmacist may justifiably refuse to accept changes in his or her conditions of practice intended to accommodate the conscience-based objections of a colleague if such changes would be excessively burdensome. When accommodating a conscience-based objection of a practitioner would be excessively burdensome to his or her colleagues, supervisors may justifiably deny the accommodation. Once again, there may be no bright line separating burdens that are and are not excessive, but wherever the line is drawn, accommodations may be refused if they would result in excessive burdens to colleagues.

Although the EEOC classifies burdens to other employees as *employer* hardships, the Commission does recognize the principle that accommodations may be refused if they would result in undue hardships to other employees.[64] Some of the Commission's criteria for distinguishing between hardships that are and are not undue apply as well to the ethical distinction between excessive and non-excessive burdens.[65] The Commission rightly observes that not all complaints rise to the level of undue hardships/ excessive burdens. Those based on "general disgruntlement, resentment, or jealousy," for example, do not rise to that level (EEOC Manual, p. 63). By contrast, a hardship/burden is undue/excessive if it "causes co-workers to carry the accommodated employee's share of potentially hazardous or burdensome work" (ibid.: pp. 59–60).

On the basis of these general criteria it is at least possible to identify clear cases in which burdens are, and are not, excessive. Suppose, for example, that Burke, a pharmacist who has a conscience-based objection to

---

[64] According to the Commission, "courts have found undue hardship [to employers] where the accommodation . . . infringes on other employees' job rights or benefits . . . or causes co-workers to carry the accommodated employee's share of potentially hazardous or burdensome work" (EEOC Compliance Manual, pp. 59–60).

[65] Some of the Commission's criteria are specific to contract law (e.g. rights based on collective bargaining agreements and seniority systems).

dispensing contraceptives, is employed by a pharmacy in which there are always two pharmacists on duty. Unlike Noesen, Burke is willing to talk to customers, answer the telephone, and refer any customers or calls related to contraceptives to the second pharmacist. So that the workload of the other pharmacist does not increase, as a *quid pro quo* Burke offers to allow the second pharmacist to refer customers and calls to him provided they do not involve contraceptives. Except for Cassidy, all of the other pharmacists are willing to accept the arrangement. When the pharmacy owner-manager tries to persuade Cassidy to accept the arrangement by pointing out that his working conditions will not change significantly, Cassidy responds, "I don't care. I don't see why I should accommodate Burke. Who does she think she is anyway? Just because she went to Harvard doesn't mean she deserves special treatment. Moreover, since she got a raise and I didn't, I'll be darned if I'm going to help her out." To arrange the pharmacy work schedule so that Burke and Cassidy would never be on the same shift would impose excessive burdens on the pharmacy owner-manager as well as the other pharmacists. Under these conditions, the pharmacy owner-manager cannot justify refusing to accommodate Burke by claiming that it would impose excessive burdens on Cassidy. In this case, it is at least arguable that insofar as accommodating Burke will impose no significant burden on Cassidy: (1) Cassidy *should* cooperate; and (2) if Cassidy is unwilling to cooperate, and there is no good reason for the owner-manager not to replace Cassidy with someone who will cooperate, the owner-manager *should* replace Cassidy. A possible good reason for not replacing Cassidy with someone who will cooperate is that doing so would impose excessive burdens on the owner-manager.

By contrast, suppose accommodating a pediatric intensivist's refusal to participate in withdrawing life-support for patients who are to undergo DCD would require another pediatric intensivist, who is a single parent, to double his on-call time and double the amount he pays for child care. In this situation, the head of the ICU can justifiably refuse to accommodate the intensivist by claiming that it would impose excessive burdens on her colleague. Similarly, a nursing supervisor can justifiably refuse to accommodate a nurse in the following situation. Due to an adolescent clinic nurse's religious beliefs, when asked about birth control and/or means to prevent sexually transmitted diseases (STDs), she will provide nothing more than "abstinence only" counseling. To accommodate the nurse, and provide clinic patients counseling about contraceptives and means to prevent STDs, it would be necessary for another nurse to significantly increase her workload and double her weekend on-call schedule. Arguably such an accommodation would impose excessive burdens on the second nurse.

Members of other professions

When practitioners from more than one health care profession are members of the same team, a conscience-based refusal by a member of one profession (e.g. a nurse) can result in burdens to members of another profession (e.g. a physician) that are comparable to those experienced by members of the same profession (e.g. other nurses). For example, as a result of a nurse's refusal to assist in providing palliative sedation or participate in the care of a patient awaiting DCD, the attending physician might have to temporarily assume increased responsibilities for patient care. Accordingly, the excessive burden constraint also applies to how a conscience-based refusal by a member of one profession affects members of other professions, and accommodations may be denied if the burdens to members of other professions are excessive. Advance notification of supervisors and other members of the health care team can provide an opportunity to plan ahead and thereby avert disruptions and burdens that are a result of last-minute refusals and requests for accommodations.

Even when practitioners are not on the same health care team or affiliated with the same institution or organization, members of one profession (e.g. physicians) can claim that conscience-based refusals by members of another profession (e.g. nurses or pharmacists) inappropriately interfere with their professional practice. Physicians have been the most consistent and outspoken source of such complaints, which have tended to focus on pharmacists' conscience-based objections to filling prescriptions and their alleged inappropriate intrusion into the physician–patient relationship. As an indication of the scope and intensity of physician concern, the AMA House of Delegates took up the issue of conscience-based refusals by pharmacists at their June 2005 meeting. According to an account in *American Medical News*, an internist who attended the meeting "voiced concerns that pharmacist refusals upset the physician–patient relationship" and stated that the phenomenon "is a very important issue for the AMA to get engaged in."[66] The House of Delegates (HOD) approved a resolution that addressed the issue. Some provisions of the resolution are incorporated into an HOD Directive (Preserving Patients' Ability to Have Legally Valid Prescriptions Filled, Directive of the HOD 120.975), and the remaining provisions are incorporated into an HOD Health Policy (Preserving Patients' Ability to Have

[66] From amednews.com (subscription required for the complete article): www.ama-assn.org/amed-news/2005/07/11/prsd0711.htm; accessed July 10, 2010.

Legally Valid Prescriptions Filled, Health Policy of the HOD, 120.947).
One provision states:

> [The AMA] supports legislation that requires individual pharmacists or pharmacy
> chains to fill legally valid prescriptions or to provide immediate referral to an
> appropriate alternative dispensing pharmacy without interference. In the event
> that an individual pharmacist or pharmacy chain refers a patient to an alternative
> dispensing source, the individual pharmacist or the pharmacy chain should return
> the prescription to the patient and notify the prescribing physician of the referral.
> (Health Policy of the HOD, 120.947)

Another provision expresses the AMA's commitment to secure legal author-
ization for physicians to dispense medications when pharmacist refusals
interfere with patient access:

> [The AMA will] in the absence of all other remedies, work with state medical
> societies to adopt state legislation that will allow physicians to dispense medication
> to their own patients when there is no pharmacist within a thirty mile radius who is
> able and willing to dispense that medication. (Directive of the HOD, 120.975)

Physicians can object to refusals by pharmacists to fill valid prescriptions
for one or both of the following reasons: (1) Such refusals are an inappropriate interference with the authority of physicians to decide which medications should be accessible to patients. Physicians, not pharmacists, are the
appropriate gatekeepers for prescription drugs;[67] (2) Such refusals inappropriately limit patient access to prescription medications. There is merit
to each of these reasons, and objections based on both are satisfactorily
addressed by several of the previously examined constraints and requirements based on obligations to patients. These include a constraint against
excessive patient harms/burdens, a constraint against obstruction (e.g.
efforts to prevent patients from getting prescriptions filled by other pharmacies and/or pharmacists), and a qualified transfer/referral requirement. If
the exercise of conscience is consistent with these constraints and requirements, pharmacists will not inappropriately intrude on the physician–
patient relationship, and they will not inappropriately limit the access of
patients to prescription medications.

Physicians can object to conscience-based refusals by nurses to carry out
their orders for similar reasons: (1) Such refusals are an inappropriate
interference with the authority of physicians and an improper intrusion

---

[67] This objection to a "moral veto" based on pharmacists' personal ethical or religious beliefs does _not_
imply that it is improper for them to detect clinical mistakes (e.g. improper dosages), identify
potentially harmful drug interactions, or identify and report suspected violations of _professional_
ethical standards.

into the physician–patient relationship;[68] (2) Such refusals inappropriately limit patient access to medical goods and services. As in the case of conscience-based refusals by pharmacists, there is merit to both of these reasons, and objections based on both are satisfactorily addressed by several of the previously examined constraints and requirements based on obligations to patients. These include a constraint against excessive patient harms/burdens, a constraint against obstruction (e.g. efforts to prevent patients from receiving a good or service that is against a nurse's conscience), and a transfer/referral requirement (specifically, a requirement to withdraw only if a substitute has assumed responsibility for patient care). If the exercise of conscience is consistent with these constraints and requirements, nurses will not inappropriately intrude on the physician–patient relationship, and they will not inappropriately limit the access of patients to medical services.

Organizational policies and procedures

Conscientious objection policies are appropriate for larger health care organizations, such as hospitals, nursing homes, and pharmacy chains. They also may be appropriate for group practices and independent pharmacies, depending on the size and structure of the organization. Organizational conscientious objection policies can promote consistency and minimize discontent and contention due to ambiguity, confusion, and unrealistic expectations. Conscientious objection policies can include: (1) substantive criteria that will be used to determine whether or not an accommodation will be granted; (2) procedures that will be used to determine whether the criteria are satisfied in particular instances; and (3) a process for appealing decisions.

The constraints and requirements identified in this chapter provide the basis for a set of ethically justified substantive criteria for determining whether to grant or deny accommodations. Although some organizations may opt to forego substantive criteria and limit policies to procedural rules, this approach increases the risk of actual and perceived arbitrariness. Moreover, it fails to provide guidance to practitioners concerning when they can and cannot expect to be granted accommodations. The availability of substantive guidelines when practitioners are deciding whether or not

---

[68] This objection to a "moral veto" based on nurses' personal ethical or religious beliefs does *not* imply that it is improper for them to detect, prevent, and/or report physician clinical mistakes or behavior that violates *professional* ethical standards. For a discussion of the nurse's responsibility to detect, prevent, and/or report physician errors, see (Kroeger-Mappes 2001: 161–8).

to join an organization can forestall unpleasant adversarial encounters at a later date.

A policy with general substantive criteria is far superior to one that only identifies the services or goods that qualify for accommodations. Whether or not accommodations are appropriate is not merely a function of the good or service. Other relevant factors include impact on patients, colleagues, and organizational efficiency and effectiveness. Accordingly, if a policy merely identifies goods and services that qualify for accommodations, it will fail to provide sufficient guidance. Moreover, due to advances in medical science and technology and, in many western societies, a population that is increasingly multicultural, it may not be possible to anticipate the kinds of goods and services that will occasion requests for conscience-based exemptions in the future. Hence, it may be short-sighted to adopt a policy that provides an inclusive list of goods and services that qualify for conscience-based exemptions. Nevertheless, a partial list may be appropriate if there are certain measures such as performing or assisting with abortions or withdrawing or assisting with withdrawing life-sustaining treatment, for which, with some qualifications, exemptions will be more or less routinely granted. In such cases, however, it is insufficient merely to identify the qualifying measures. In addition, conditions that must be met to receive accommodations to those measures should be specified. For example, a hospital policy might explicitly state that: (1) physicians who have a conscience-based objection to withdrawing life-sustaining treatment will not be obligated to do so if a transfer to another physician can be arranged; and (2) nurses who have a conscience-based objection to withdrawing life-sustaining treatment will not be obligated to do so if another nurse is available to assist.

In some situations there may be no need for a formal review process to determine whether a health care professional will receive an accommodation. For example, in lieu of a formal review process, a policy may require only that there is a willing and able substitute. This, for example, is the typical approach in relation to physicians with conscience-based objections to withdrawing life-sustaining treatment. However, when accommodations require more pervasive standing reallocations of responsibilities within an organization, a policy might require formal requests and specific advance approval. Requests can be oral or written, and in either case, health care professionals might be asked to provide an explanation of their conscience-based objections. The review process might be the responsibility of one person (a supervisor or manager) or a committee (e.g. a hospital ethics committee).

A formal review process that requires health care professionals who request accommodations to explain their reasons provides an opportunity to distinguish between genuine conscience-based objections (or objections based on firmly held ethical and/or religious beliefs) and requests for exemptions that are based on other concerns, such as health, safety, or a desire to avoid onerous tasks. In addition, a review process can serve to identify demonstrably false clinical beliefs and provide an opportunity to correct them. A review process also can provide opportunities to probe a practitioner's sincerity and determine whether invidious discrimination underlies requests for exemptions. It is justified to deny requests for conscience-based exemptions on grounds of insincerity or invidious discrimination. However, to deny requests merely because they are deemed to be based on "unsound values" would thwart the goals of conscience-based exemptions.[69]

A formal appeals process may not be suitable for smaller organizations, such as an independent pharmacy. However, for larger organizations, such as hospitals or nursing homes, an appeal process can help to reduce the perception of arbitrariness as well as actual arbitrariness. It can also add another measure to promote the important aim of properly determining when it is and is not justified to deny requests to accommodate conscience-based objections.

CONCLUSION

Despite the importance and value of moral integrity and other reasons for accommodating conscience-based refusals, physicians, nurses, and pharmacists have core professional obligations that restrict the exercise of conscience. The exercise of conscience may not involve invidious discrimination or result in excessive harms/burdens to patients. In addition, health care professionals may not cross the line that separates refusal from obstruction. Finally, health care professionals have qualified obligations to disclose options, provide referrals and/or facilitate transfers, and provide timely notification to patients or prospective patients. Depending on the circumstances, fulfilling these obligations can require acting against a provider's conscience.

---

[69] Two examples discussed earlier, the Buddhist family medicine doctor and the nurse who object to providing pain medication for reasons of conscience, are exceptions to this general rule. However, both are extreme cases and are likely to occur only rarely, if ever.

Additional constraints and requirements apply to relations with employers and other health care professionals. The exercise of conscience by health care professional employees may not result in excessive burdens to employers or other practitioners. In addition, the exercise of conscience by a member of one profession should not inappropriately cross professional boundaries. The primary aim of this constraint is to protect patients – a common goal of each of the professions – and not to protect the "turf" of a particular profession. Finally, to minimize disruption and preventable harms and burdens, health care professionals should provide advance notification of foreseeable conscience-based refusals to employers and colleagues.

Although formal conscientious objection policies may not be suitable for smaller health care organizations, such as independent pharmacies and group practices, they can facilitate important goals if they are adopted by larger organizations, such as hospitals, nursing homes, and pharmacy chains. Organizational conscientious objection policies can promote consistency and minimize discontent and contention due to ambiguity, confusion, and unrealistic expectations. They also can help to ensure that health care professionals will be denied accommodations for their conscience-based objections when and only when it is justified to do so.

An important component of a conscientious objection policy is a set of substantive criteria that will determine whether an accommodation will be granted or denied. Depending on the size and structure of the organization, a policy may also include procedures that will be used to determine whether the criteria are satisfied in particular instances and a process for appealing decisions.

CHAPTER 4

Pharmacies, health care institutions, and conscientious objection

The focus of previous chapters has been on conscience-based refusals by individual physicians, nurses, and pharmacists. This chapter will consider conscientious objection in relation to pharmacies and health care institutions. Even if it is acknowledged that it is appropriate to accommodate individual pharmacists with conscience-based objections to dispensing a medication when the constraints and requirements proposed in Chapter 3 are satisfied, it remains to consider whether *pharmacies* may justifiably refuse to stock and dispense a medication for reasons of conscience. Similarly, even if it is acknowledged that it is appropriate to accommodate conscience-based objections of individual physicians, nurses, and pharmacists who practice in health care institutions (e.g. hospitals and nursing homes) when those constraints and requirements are satisfied, it remains to consider whether *institutions* may justifiably refuse to provide a service for reasons of conscience.

PHARMACIES

Dispensing obligations of pharmacy licensees

Pharmacies are licensed by states, are granted a monopoly to dispense medications that require prescriptions, and are subject to regulation. State boards of pharmacy confer licenses to operate pharmacies with the justified expectation that they will promote specified ends – typically, the public health, safety, and welfare. These are the ends identified in a Model State Pharmacy Act.[1] The Model Act's "Legislative Declaration" (Section 102) includes the following statement: "The Practice of Pharmacy in the State of _____ is declared a professional practice affecting the public health,

---

[1] National Association of Boards of Pharmacy, "Model State Pharmacy Act and Model Rules of National Association of Boards of Pharmacy" (August 2009). Available online at: www.nabp.net/publications/model-act/; accessed July 10, 2010.

safety, and welfare and is subject to regulation and control in the public interest." The subsequent section, the "Statement of Purpose," includes the following provision:

It is the purpose of this Act to promote, preserve, and protect the public health, safety, and welfare by ... the licensure, control, and regulation of all sites or Persons, in or out of this State, that Distribute, Manufacture, or sell Drugs (or Devices used in the Dispensing and Administration of Drugs), within this State ...[2]

Since state pharmacy boards are authorized to grant and revoke licenses and to assign penalties, it is in the interest of pharmacy licensees to conform to a state board's requirements. However, licensees also have an *obligation* to promote the public health, safety, and welfare. At least three accounts can be given of this obligation (Wicclair 2006). First, the obligation can be said to derive from a *commitment* by licensees to promote the public health, safety, and welfare and to comply with the relevant requirements when they accept a license to operate a pharmacy. Licenses are granted with the legitimate expectation that pharmacies will promote those ends and satisfy the relevant requirements, and when licensees accept a license to operate a pharmacy, they agree to do so. This agreement or commitment generates corresponding obligations, and a failure to fulfill these obligations is a failure to honor a commitment. Second, an obligation to promote the public health, safety, and welfare can be said to derive from considerations of *reciprocal justice*. A license to operate a pharmacy confers certain rights and privileges on the licensee, and when licensees accept and enjoy these rights and privileges, they incur reciprocal obligations, including an obligation to promote the public health, safety, and welfare. When licensees fail to fulfill these reciprocal obligations, they do not merit the rights and privileges associated with a license to operate a pharmacy. Third, an obligation to promote the public health, safety, and welfare might be derived from general ethical principles, such as beneficence, non-maleficence, and justice, together with certain assumptions about the connection between pharmaceuticals and well-being, the potential for harm if they are not properly dispensed, the vulnerability of people who are ill and require medications, and so forth.

Pharmacies can fail to promote the public health, safety, and welfare by exposing patients to harm due to unsanitary facilities and/or equipment, poor

---

[2] A comment to Section 102 underscores the commitment to the public health, safety, and welfare by stating that pharmacy is a profession and not a commercial business:

Pharmacy is a learned profession affecting public health and welfare and should be declared as such by the State Legislature. The Practice of Pharmacy ..., from time to time, has been erroneously viewed, even by government agencies, as a commercial business rather than a profession.

record keeping, inadequate supervision of employees, and the like. Most of the rules and regulations promulgated by state boards of pharmacy are directed at preventing such harms. However, pharmacies also can fail to promote the health and welfare of the public by not dispensing pharmaceuticals that satisfy the health needs of the populations they serve. From the perspective of public health and welfare, it seems no less important to ensure that pharmacies dispense drugs that promote the health needs of the populations they serve than it is to prevent harm to patients from medications they receive. Whereas improperly prepared, stored, and/or dispensed pharmaceuticals can cause pain, suffering, poor health, and even death, a failure to dispense them can have similar consequences. Accordingly, if pharmacy licensees can fail to discharge an obligation to promote the public health, safety, and welfare when pharmacies dispense drugs that expose patients to a risk of harm, it seems reasonable to hold that they can also fail to discharge that obligation when pharmacies do not dispense medications that promote the health needs of the populations they serve.

Licensing boards in a few states explicitly require non-specialized pharmacies to stock and dispense medications that meet the health care needs of the communities they serve. The Pennsylvania State Board of Pharmacy mandates that a pharmacy "maintain a supply of drugs and devices adequate to meet the needs of the health professions and the patients it is intended to serve" (49 Pa. Code § 27.14).[3] The Massachusetts Board of Registration in Pharmacy imposes the following requirement:

Except as provided by exemptions ... with respect to restricted pharmacies and ... nuclear pharmacies ... [t]he pharmacy or pharmacy department shall maintain on the premises at all times a sufficient variety and supply of medicinal chemicals and preparations which are necessary to compound and dispense commonly prescribed medications in accordance with the usual needs of the community.[4] (247 CMR § 6.02)

Citing this requirement, the Massachusetts Board in February 2006 ordered Wal-Mart to stock the emergency contraceptive (EC) Plan B (Mohl 2006). In what it cited as a "business decision," Wal-Mart had decided in 1999 not to stock Preven (another type of EC), a year after its approval by the FDA (Canedy 1999).[5]

As the exemptions cited by the Massachusetts Board suggest, stocking and dispensing requirements should be sensitive to differences in pharmacies.

---

[3] Available online at: www.pacode.com/secure/data/049/chapter27/s27.14.html; accessed July 10, 2010.
[4] Available online at: www.mass.gov/Eeohhs2/docs/dph/regs/247cmr006.pdf; accessed July 10, 2010.
[5] Preven (also known as the Yuzpe regimen) combines progestin (levonorgestrel) and estrogen (ethinyl estradiol) and Plan B is a progestin (levonorgestrel) only EC. In clinical trials, Plan B was found to be more effective and to have fewer side effects than Preven. See (Ho and Kwan 1993: 389–92), (Task Force on Postovulatory Methods of Fertility Regulation 1998: 428–33).

Whereas some are in outpatient retail settings, others are located in clinics, hospitals, or other institutional settings. In addition, some specialize in certain types of products (e.g. diabetic supplies or nuclear medicines) and/or serve restricted populations (e.g. clients of family planning clinics or members of groups or organizations). Even in relation to general, full-service community pharmacies, one might cite the fact that, depending on the nature of the specific population, health needs can vary significantly. Thus, for example, post-menopausal women do not need birth control, and a pharmacy located in a retirement community is not likely to receive requests to fill prescriptions for contraceptives. Absent need and demand, there is no obligation to dispense; and if the limited range of medications dispensed by a specialized pharmacy does not include a certain type of drug (e.g. contraceptives) it cannot be expected to dispense them.

How can the pharmaceutical needs of a community be ascertained? A former Massachusetts Board president-elect answered that they can be determined "by the prescriptions that are presented" (Mohl 2006). This answer is both simple and plausible. Moreover, putting aside considerations of conscience (which will be considered in the following section), the action of the Massachusetts Board appears to be justified. Insofar as a medication such as EC is among the health needs of a community served by a pharmacy, it is arguable that the pharmacy's obligation to promote the public health, safety, and welfare includes an obligation to stock and dispense it.

It might be objected, however, that the Massachusetts Board's action in relation to Wal-Mart is a special case due to the number of customers affected by its decision not to sell EC. In 1999, the year Wal-Mart announced its decision not to dispense EC, it was the fifth-largest pharmaceutical distributor in the United States (Canedy 1999). Hence, the number of customers affected by an independent community pharmacy's decision not to dispense EC pales in comparison to the number of customers affected by Wal-Mart's decision. In response, it can be claimed that this objection misses the point of the Massachusetts Board's action. It cited "the usual needs of the community." Accordingly, the requirement applies to *each pharmacy*, small as well as large, and independent as well as chain enterprises. To fulfill its obligation to promote the public health and welfare, every non-specialized pharmacy must dispense prescription and restricted distribution medications that satisfy the health needs of the community it serves.[6]

---

[6] As explained in Chapter 1, although levonorgestrel-based EC (e.g. Plan B and Plan B One-Step) is available without prescription for women 17 years and older, women still must request it at the pharmacy counter and provide proof of their age if asked. In addition, it can be sold only by pharmacies and health clinics. Accordingly, it remains a restricted distribution medication. Ulipristal acetate-based EC (ella) requires a prescription regardless of age.

In response, it can be claimed that individual pharmacies may have a policy not to dispense a prescription or restricted distribution medication without failing to fulfill the licensees' obligation to promote the health and welfare of the populations they serve as long as individuals who need the medication can get it at some other pharmacy without experiencing excessive burdens (e.g. undue delay and inconvenience). This answer suggests that pharmacy boards adopt a *general public availability* standard rather than a *pharmacy-by-pharmacy* standard to determine whether pharmacy licensees are discharging their obligation to promote the health and welfare of the populations they serve. According to a general public availability standard, a particular pharmacy may adopt a policy not to dispense a prescription or restricted distribution medication for which there is a need and demand among the population it serves without failing to discharge the licensee's obligation to promote the public health and welfare as long as that policy does not deny members of the population timely and convenient access to the pharmaceutical. There are two reasons in favor of pharmacy boards using a pharmacy-by-pharmacy standard rather than a general public availability standard.

One reason is fairness. It is likely to be economically advantageous for pharmacies to avoid dispensing low demand, low profit margin, and/or controversial medications. For example, dispensing EC might prompt protests, boycotts, and patient flight that would significantly decrease sales and profits. As noted, when Wal-Mart announced that its pharmacies would not dispense EC, it was characterized as a "business decision" (Canedy 1999). To be sure, this statement may not have expressed accurately the exclusive or primary reason for Wal-Mart's decision, but it is not far-fetched to imagine that continuing to dispense EC could have had a negative impact on Wal-Mart's "bottom line." In any event, pharmacies that dispense low demand, low profit, and/or controversial drugs may incur significant burdens that are avoided by pharmacies that do not dispense them. In such cases, licensees of non-dispensing pharmacies would be released from an obligation to dispense only if other licensees endure burdens that they could avoid by not dispensing. Accordingly, one might claim that licensees of non-dispensing pharmacies are "free riders" who do not assume a fair share of the burdens of fulfilling the obligation to promote the public health and welfare.

It might be objected, however, that as long as some pharmacy licensees are *willing* to accept the burdens associated with dispensing, the charge of unfairness is groundless. To evaluate this objection, it may be helpful to consider a claim that is sometimes made about unfairness in relation to military service. It has been said that a disproportionate number of American soldiers fighting in Iraq and Afghanistan are economically disadvantaged and are bearing an unfair share of the burdens of fighting those wars. Assuming for the sake of argument that a disproportionate number of American soldiers fighting in Iraq and Afghanistan are economically disadvantaged, the charge of unfairness cannot be refuted by simply pointing out that all American soldiers fighting in Iraq and Afghanistan *volunteered* for military service. Indeed, some have proposed reinstituting the military draft as a means to eliminate the perceived unfair distribution of the burdens of military service. To be sure, in the case of military service, the worry about fairness is based in part on a concern that the choices and opportunities of economically disadvantaged American young men and women, especially during a recession, are relatively limited. However, even if the choices and opportunities of licensees of pharmacies that dispense controversial drugs such as EC are not similarly limited, and even if licensees freely decide to discharge their obligations to the populations they serve, it still is possible to question the fairness of the resulting distribution of the burdens of promoting the public health and welfare.

The second reason for preferring a pharmacy-by-pharmacy standard to a general public availability standard has to do with the elusive and controversial nature of the determinations that the latter would require pharmacy boards to make. A general public availability standard would require pharmacy boards to monitor the operations of pharmacies and public access to prescription and restricted distribution medications to determine whether the standard is satisfied. This monitoring, in turn, would require the collection of data to determine whether, as a result of pharmacy dispensing policies, either (1) some people cannot get a prescription or restricted distribution medication, or (2) for some people, obtaining a prescription or restricted distribution medication is excessively burdensome. The latter determination would require identifying and applying criteria to ascertain whether burdens, such as travel times and distances, delays, and inconvenience, are "excessive." Moreover, if more than one non-dispensing pharmacy could provide effective, timely, and convenient access to a particular individual or group of persons (e.g. residents of a particular geographic area) criteria would need to be identified to determine whether all, or only some – and if so, which – licensees of the non-dispensing pharmacies have an obligation to dispense. It is unclear whether it is feasible for pharmacy boards to make the requisite determinations; and even if it would be possible, doing so would require the use of controversial criteria. Accepting the view that licensees of all general, full-service pharmacies have an obligation to dispense prescription and restricted distribution medications that satisfy the health needs of the populations they serve avoids the charge of unfairness, as well as a need to make determinations that require controversial criteria and for which there may be inadequate data. Accordingly, again putting aside considerations of conscience, pharmacy boards can justifiably claim that the following is a reasonable specification of pharmacy licensees' obligation to promote the public health, safety, and welfare:

If a prescription or restricted distribution medication promotes the health needs of the population served by a general, full-service pharmacy, licensees of all such pharmacies serving that population have an obligation to dispense it.

Conscience-based objections and the obligations of pharmacy licensees

If a pharmacy licensee has a conscience-based objection to dispensing a prescription or restricted distribution medication that satisfies a health need of the population the pharmacy serves, may the pharmacy nevertheless be required to dispense it? To answer this question, it is first necessary to distinguish between independent pharmacies and large retail chains such as Wal-Mart, Rite Aide, CVS, and Walgreens. If claims of conscience are made on behalf of retail chain pharmacies, there are many people, such as the chief executive officer, other corporate executives, corporate office staff, other employees, and share holders, whose moral integrity might be at stake, and they might advance conflicting claims of conscience. Whereas some might believe that their moral integrity would be compromised if the company's pharmacies were to dispense a certain type of medication (e.g. EC), others might believe that their moral integrity would be compromised if the company's pharmacies did not dispense it. Then, too, from the perspective of the moral integrity of some executives, corporate office staff, other employees, and share holders, it might not matter at all whether the company's pharmacies dispense the drug. Moreover, whereas people in certain corporate positions (e.g. the CEO, other high-ranking executives, and members of the board of directors) may have greater authority to set corporate policy, there is no good reason to think that their moral integrity carries any more moral weight than the moral integrity of others connected with the organization. To be sure, corporations may have mission statements that promote specified goals and values, and they can be held accountable for their actions and inactions by means of fines and other penalties. Moreover, in some contexts, it may be appropriate to treat corporations as "persons" from the perspective of law.[7] Nevertheless, it is doubtful that one can refer plausibly to the "conscience" of a corporation independently of the appeals to conscience of its individual members. Accordingly, it is doubtful that reasons for granting exemptions to enable the exercise of conscience apply to large retail pharmacy chains that do not dispense controversial pharmaceuticals such as EC.[8]

However, it remains to consider independent pharmacies and the type of case in which a claim of conscience is arguably both clearest and strongest – when it is advanced by individual pharmacy licensees. An actual case of this type involves a family-owned pharmacy in Olympia, Washington.[9] The pharmacy is located in Ralph's Thriftway, a full-service supermarket owned by Ken Stormans and his three children. According to the Ralph's Thriftway website, it is a "one-stop supermarket" with a variety of departments as well as a post office, a Starbucks, and a Subway; and it is "one of Thurston County's most popular supermarkets."[10] Accordingly, there is no reason to doubt that the community served by the Stormans' pharmacy includes women who may have occasion to need and want EC. Nevertheless, the Stormans refused to stock and dispense Plan B for reasons of conscience.[11]

Consistent with the compromise approach presented in Chapter 3, it might be suggested that Stormans' pharmacy should be permitted to refuse to dispense Plan B if: (1) there is at least one other pharmacy where patients can get convenient and timely access to Plan B; and (2) if requested, Stormans' pharmacy will refer patients to a pharmacy where they can get convenient and timely access to Plan B. If Stormans' pharmacy were to

---

[7] In *Citizens United* v *Federal Election Commission* (558 U.S. _____ (2010)), the US Supreme Court affirmed its previous determination that First Amendment free speech protections apply to corporations. See Adam Liptak, 'Justices, 5–4, Reject Corporate Spending Limit', *New York Times*, January 22, 2010, sec. A, p. 1. In a controversial 5–4 ruling, the court overturned two of its prior decisions and held that legal restrictions on corporate expenditures for advocating the election or defeat of political candidates ("electioneering communications") violate First Amendment political speech protections. The decision is available online at: www.supremecourt.gov/opinions/09pdf/08–205.pdf; accessed July 10, 2010.

[8] By contrast to for-profit business enterprises, health care institutions with a religious mission (e.g. Catholic hospitals) can attempt to justify refusals to offer goods and services by appealing to their identity and integrity, and such claims can bear a family resemblance to appeals to conscience by individuals. I will examine such institutional "appeals to conscience" in the following section.

[9] The description of the case presented here is based on information in the US Court of Appeals for the Ninth Circuit decision in *Stormans, Inc.* v *Selecky*, 526 F.3d 406 (9th Cir. 2008). Available online at: www.ca9.uscourts.gov/datastore/opinions/2009/07/08/07–36039.pdf; accessed July 10, 2010.

[10] www.ralphsthriftway.com/index.html; accessed July 10, 2010.

[11] A growing number of pharmacies reportedly are refusing to stock and dispense contraceptives and/or EC. See (Stein 2008b: sec. A, p. 1).

satisfy these two conditions, its refusal to dispense Plan B would not impose excessive harms or burdens on women who seek access to EC.

However, even if Stormans' pharmacy were to satisfy these two conditions, a Washington State Board of Pharmacy regulation that came into effect on July 26, 2007 would not permit the pharmacy to refuse to dispense Plan B. The regulation states in part:[12]

Pharmacies have a duty to deliver lawfully prescribed drugs or devices to patients and to distribute drugs and devices approved by the U.S. Food and Drug Administration for restricted distribution by pharmacies, or provide a therapeutically equivalent drug or device in a timely manner consistent with reasonable expectations for filling the prescription. . . (WAC 246–869–010)

Washington State Board of Pharmacy regulations do not provide an exemption for pharmacy licensees such as the Stormans who have conscience-based objections to dispensing Plan B.[13] As the Board of Pharmacy explained its regulations in a "Concise Explanatory Statement:"

[P]harmacies are required to maintain at all times a representative assortment of drugs in order to meet the pharmaceutical needs of its patients. Pharmacies would not be considered to be in compliance if their policy/procedure and/or practice is to refer patients to another pharmacy when dealing with prescriptions for which the pharmacy/pharmacist has a personal objection.[14]

Accordingly, although it may be infeasible for pharmacies to stock all prescription and restricted distribution medications, the Board of Pharmacy held that stocking decisions should be tailored to meet the needs of

---

[12] Available online at: http://apps.leg.wa.gov/wac/default.aspx?cite=246–869–010; accessed July 10, 2010.

[13] The Stormans and two pharmacists who worked in other pharmacies filed a lawsuit in the US District Court for the Western District of Washington, claiming that the Washington regulations violated their constitutional rights and Title VII of the 1964 Civil Rights Act (*Stormans, Inc.* v *Selecky*, 524 F. Supp. 2d 1245 (W. D. Wash. 2007)). The District Court granted a temporary injunction against the regulations. The Ninth Circuit Court of Appeals reversed the injunction, and remanded to the District Court (*Stormans, Inc.* v *Selecky*, 526 F.3d 406 (9th Cir. 2008)). Washington Pharmacy Board regulations do not require *pharmacists* to dispense EC. However, the two pharmacists who joined the Stormans' lawsuit claimed that requiring all pharmacies to dispense EC would likely result in their loss of employment because their employers would have to hire additional staff in order to accommodate them, and the employers were unlikely to do so. As of July 2010, there has been no court ruling on whether the Washington Board of Pharmacy regulations violate the claimants' legal rights, which is the main substantive legal question in the case. A discussion of this legal question is beyond the scope of this book.

[14] Available online at: http://74.125.93.132/search?q=cache:QynuJ-eFM38J:listserv.wa.gov/cgi-bin/wa%3FA3%3Dind07%26L%3DWSBOP-NEWSLETTER%26E%3Dbase64%26P%3D996798%26B%3D------_%253D_NextPart_001_01C7B787.E08C1DA8%26T%3Dapplication%252Fmsword%3B%2520name%3D%2522Concise%2520Explanatory%2520Statement.doc%2522%26N%3DConcise%2520Explanatory%2520Statement.doc%26attachment%3Dq+Concise+Explanatory+Statement+washington+board+of+pharmacy&cd=2&hl=en&ct=clnk&gl=us; accessed July 10, 2010.

the population a pharmacy serves, and a decision not to stock a particular item may not be based on reasons of conscience. In its "Concise Explanatory Statement," the Board of Pharmacy stated that it had enacted the new regulations "to promote patient safety and access to health care . . ."[15]

Is the Board of Pharmacy's decision not to approve exemptions for pharmacy licensees such as the Stormans, who have conscience-based objections to dispensing a prescription or restricted distribution medication, a reasonable specification of a pharmacy licensee's obligation to promote the public health, safety, and welfare? To answer this question, it is first necessary to distinguish between medications such as Plan B that are standard of care and those that are not. As noted in Chapter 1, in 2008 Washington became the second US state to authorize physician-assisted suicide. It is arguable that even in Washington, Oregon, and Montana (the three states in which physician-assisted suicide is legally permitted), there is no medical condition for which "medication to end life" is standard of care. As indicated in Chapter 3, physician-assisted suicide is contrary to the *Code of Medical Ethics* and AMA policy. In addition, a study of Washington state family physicians based on data collected in 1997, several years before physician-assisted suicide was legalized, reported that 58 percent of the respondents stated that they would not provide suicide assistance to patients even if it were legal (Hart *et al.* 2003). Under such circumstances, even though physician-assisted suicide is legally permitted, it is implausible to claim that medication to end life is standard of care in Washington. Insofar as medication to end life is not standard of care for any medical condition in Washington, it is implausible to justify denying an exemption to a pharmacy licensee with a conscience-based objection to dispensing medication to end life by claiming that dispensing it is included within the scope of the licensee's obligation to promote the public health, safety, and welfare. Accordingly, it is arguable that the Washington regulations should be understood to apply only to prescription and restricted distribution medications such as Plan B that are standard of care.

It might be objected that the Washington Board of Pharmacy regulations are more stringent than is needed to adequately protect the public health, safety, and welfare. If some pharmacies such as Stormans refuse to dispense

---

[15] This goal is consistent with The Washington State Board of Pharmacy's charge to promulgate "rules for the dispensing, distribution, wholesaling, and manufacture of drugs and devices and the practice of pharmacy for the protection and promotion of the public health, safety and welfare" (RCW 18.64.005). Available online at: http://apps.leg.wa.gov/RCW/default.aspx?cite=18.64.005; accessed July 10, 2010.

Plan B for reasons of conscience, there are likely to be other pharmacies which stock and dispense it.[16] Accordingly, it might be claimed, regulations should provide an exemption for pharmacy licensees who object to dispensing Plan B for reasons of conscience if the population served by a pharmacy will still have timely and convenient access to Plan B at other pharmacies.

Previously, I argued that a policy of exempting licensees of general, full-service pharmacies from an obligation to dispense a drug that promotes a community's health needs may place an unfair burden on other licensees in the same community. However, what if this exemption is limited to *conscience-based* decisions not to dispense certain pharmaceuticals? If, contrary to fact, the Stormans had decided not to dispense Plan B for "business reasons," and other pharmacies dispensed it despite the risk of associated burdens (e.g. exposure to protests and boycotts, loss of business, and decreased profits), it would not be implausible to claim that the other pharmacy licensees carried an unfair share of the burdens of meeting the community's health needs and the Stormans were free riders. But the Stormans' refusal was based on reasons of *conscience*. Is it plausible to advance a similar claim in relation to such conscience-based refusals to dispense Plan B?[17]

Even if dispensing Plan B imposes significant burdens on pharmacy licensees who have no conscience-based objections and dispense it, one also has to consider the "moral burden" of dispensing Plan B to pharmacy licensees such as the Stormans who do have conscience-based objections. The question, then, is whether, from an ethical perspective, preserving the Stormans' moral integrity is more important than equitably distributing the burdens of satisfying a community's health needs. As long as the burdens incurred by the licensees of dispensing pharmacies are not excessive, it is at

---

[16] In its opinion lifting the temporary injunction against the Washington State Board of Pharmacy regulations, the US Court of Appeals for the Ninth Circuit presented the results of a survey conducted by the Board and cited in the District Court opinion:

Seventy-seven percent of Washington pharmacies, responding to a sample survey of 121 pharmacies conducted before the adoption of the challenged new rules, typically stock Plan B. Those who did not cited low demand (15 percent) or an easy alternative source (2 percent). Only two pharmacies (2 percent) surveyed did not stock the drug because of personal, religious, or moral objections. If the survey is accurate and representative, that translates into approximately 27 of the 1,370 licensed pharmacies in Washington. (*Stormans, Inc.* v *Selecky* (526 F.3d 406 at 411–12))

[17] If refusals were to be permitted for reasons of conscience, but not for business reasons, pharmacy licensees might claim the former even when the refusal is based on the latter. The hurdles to accurately determining whether appeals to conscience are genuine and sincere might provide another reason for pharmacy boards to adopt a pharmacy-by-pharmacy standard and a reason for not permitting exemptions – even for alleged conscience-based refusals.

least arguable that moral integrity can trump equitably distributing the burdens of dispensing Plan B.

Although considerations of fairness alone may fail to justify the Washington Board of Pharmacy's decision not to grant an exemption to pharmacy licensees such as the Stormans who have conscience-based objections to dispensing Plan B, there is another rationale that may provide a justification. Recall that the stated objection to not providing exemptions to pharmacy licensees with a conscience-based objection to dispensing Plan B is based on the assumption that patients will have timely and convenient access to the medication at other pharmacies. Determining whether this condition is satisfied involves applying what was referred to above as a *general public availability* standard. But it was argued that the determinations required to ascertain whether this standard is satisfied are likely to be controversial and infeasible. Accordingly, a pharmacy board may not be able to determine reliably whether exempting pharmacy licensees with conscience-based objections from an obligation to dispense Plan B will thwart some patients' timely and convenient access to it.[18] Absent reliable means to assure that permitting such conscience-based objections will not deny women timely and convenient access to Plan B, a pharmacy board might decide not to allow them in order to protect the public health, safety, and welfare.

An earlier draft of the Washington State Pharmacy Board regulations granted unconditional exemptions for conscience-based refusals to dispense medications.[19] Absent conditions to ensure that conscience-based exemptions do not deny patients timely and convenient access to Plan B and other prescription or restricted distribution medications, regulations that grant such exemptions do not provide sufficient protection to patients. To be sure, compared to the two extremes of granting unconditional conscience-based exemptions and not granting any conscience-based exemptions, it would be preferable to grant exemptions with conditions to protect patient access. However, if it is not feasible for pharmacy boards to formulate and effectively monitor and enforce compliance with rules that are designed to offer such protections, it is at least arguable that they may justifiably adopt

---

[18] In effect, Holly Fernandez Lynch proposes that medical licensing boards apply a general public availability standard to prevent the exercise of conscience by physicians from resulting in excessive restrictions on patient access to medical services. See (Lynch 2008). My objections to that standard apply to her recommended approach as well.

[19] An account of the rule-making process is included in the District Court decision: *Stormans, Inc.* v *Selecky*, 524 F. Supp. 2d 1245 (W. D. Wash. 2007). Pressure from the governor reportedly played a significant role in eliminating the exemption for conscience-based refusals.

regulations that do not grant exemptions for conscience-based objections. Reasonable people may disagree, but this conclusion is supported by the following considerations. First, boards of pharmacy grant licenses with the legitimate expectation that pharmacy licensees will promote and protect the public health, safety, and welfare. Second, timely and convenient access to prescription and restricted distribution medications, including EC, promotes and protects the public health, safety, and welfare. Third, although a policy of not granting conscience-based exemptions to pharmacy licensees may restrict professional practice options for individuals with conscience-based objections to dispensing a medication such as EC, it does not require anyone to compromise his or her moral integrity. For example, individuals with conscience-based objections to EC can protect their moral integrity by not owning and operating a pharmacy in a state that does not grant conscience-based exemptions to pharmacy licensees – or at least by not owning and operating a pharmacy that serves a population with an interest in timely and convenient access to EC. In any event, since a pharmacy licensee has an obligation to promote the public health, safety, and welfare, a pharmacy may justifiably refuse to stock and dispense a medication for reasons of conscience only if members of the population in its service area have timely and convenient access to the medication at other pharmacies.

Finally, it is worth noting that the Washington State Board of Pharmacy appropriately distinguishes between the obligations of pharmacy licensees and pharmacists. To protect the public health, safety, and welfare, the Board requires pharmacy licensees to dispense EC and other prescription or restricted distribution medications despite conscience-based objections. However, the Board does not impose a similar requirement on individual pharmacists – provided the pharmacy in which a pharmacist practices can accommodate the pharmacist's conscience-based objections without failing to satisfy its dispensing obligations.[20]

HEALTH CARE INSTITUTIONS

Health care facilities such as hospitals and nursing homes sometimes refuse to provide goods and services or honor patients' decisions to forgo life-sustaining treatment for reasons that appear to resemble appeals to

---

[20] One of the two pharmacist-plaintiffs in *Stormans, Inc.* v *Selecky* was accommodated for the 5 months that the Washington State Board of Pharmacy regulations were in effect before the District Court temporary injunction. The other pharmacist-plaintiff secured employment at a pharmacy that was able to accommodate her by arranging for another pharmacist to be on duty with her at all times.

conscience. For example, based on the *Ethical and Religious Directives for Catholic Health Care Services* (ERD), Catholic hospitals and nursing homes have refused to forgo MPNH, and Catholic hospitals have refused to provide EC and perform abortions or sterilization procedures.[21] I will consider three categories of institutional refusals: (1) refusals to offer EC to victims of sexual assault who present at the emergency department (ED); (2) refusals to honor decisions to forgo MPNH; and (3) refusals to provide medical interventions in emergency situations that will terminate or risk terminating a pregnancy. A preliminary question, however, is whether such institutional refusals can be conceptualized as *conscience-based*.

Can refusals by health care institutions be conscience-based?

If taken literally, it would be implausible to claim that institutions can have and exercise a conscience. Institutions do not appear to have the characteristics that would warrant ascribing to them those capacities. According to George Annas, "Hospitals are corporations that have no natural personhood, and hence are incapable of having either 'moral' or 'ethical' objections to actions" (Annas 1987: 21). To be sure, institutions are not living, conscious organisms. They lack awareness and do not have the capacity to think, form intentions, or feel good or bad. Moreover, in contrast to health care professionals, institutions cannot *experience* the effects of a loss of moral integrity, and they cannot *experience* guilt or *suffer* from injury to their identity. Nevertheless, claims can be advanced on behalf of health care institutions that bear a family resemblance to appeals to conscience by individuals and warrant substantial deference.

In some cases, a health care institution's mission can be considered an analogue to the conscience of a physician, nurse, or pharmacist. As Kevin Wildes puts it:

[A]n institution can have a moral identity and conscience. A necessary condition for talking about institutional conscience is the moral identity of an institution. One way to explore this moral identity is to look at the mission of an institution. (Wildes 1997: 416)

Although most, if not all, hospitals and nursing homes have mission *statements*, only some can purport to have genuine *missions* (i.e. a commitment to goals, values, and principles) that comprise a distinct *identity* and provide

---

[21] See (United States Conference of Catholic Bishops 2009). Available online at: www.usccb.org/ meetings/2009Fall/docs/ERDs_5th_ed_091118_FINAL.pdf; accessed July 9, 2010. The previous (4th) edition of the ERD came into effect in June 2001.

the basis for what might be considered analogues to appeals to conscience.[22] Health care institutions with a commitment to religious principles often have genuine missions, and a paradigm example is provided by Catholic hospitals and nursing homes whose mission involves a commitment to the ERD.[23] For such health care institutions, adherence to the ERD is essential to their identity and integrity.[24] Accordingly, a failure to adhere to the ERD would comprise a failure to maintain the institution's identity and integrity that is analogous to the loss of moral integrity when health care professionals fail to adhere to their core moral values.[25]

Even if it is plausible to contend that a health care institution can have an identity and that certain actions can result in a loss of its identity and (moral) integrity, it remains to ask why it should matter whether an institution is able to preserve its identity and moral integrity. Unlike

[22] Mission statements, according to William Stempsey, "are the primary means by which institutions express their identity and serve as standards to measure the integrity with which an institution lives out its identity" (Stempsey 2001: 3–14 at 14). Although it would be implausible to attribute this function to all mission statements, it might be credible to limit the claim to the mission statements of health care institutions, such as those that adhere to the ERD, that involve a commitment to goals, values, and principles which comprise the institution's identity.

[23] For an account of mission statements associated with a hospital's "Catholic identity," see (O'Rourke 2001: 15–28). Although other religions can provide the basis for conceptions of institutional identity and integrity, this analysis will be limited to Catholic health care institutions. Due to their strong commitment to maintaining their Catholic identity, they have been a major source of institutional appeals to conscience. Moreover, a significant percentage of community hospitals in the United States are Catholic (12.4%); Catholic hospitals account for more than 20 percent of admissions in 22 states; and there are Catholic hospitals in all but 6 states. Information from the Catholic Health Association online: www.chausa.org/Pages/Newsroom/Fast_Facts/; accessed July 9, 2010.

[24] Ana Smith Iltis provides an analysis of institutional integrity according to which it "can be understood as the coherence between what an institution claims to value (its stated moral character), what an institution does (its manifest moral character), and an institution's fundamental moral commitments (its deep moral character)" (Smith Iltis 2001: 95–103 at 98). According to Smith Iltis, "when there is a lack of coherence between an institution's manifest moral character and its identity, then the institution has failed to maintain its integrity" (ibid.: 101).

[25] For the purpose of this discussion, I am only considering aspects of a Catholic hospital's identity that affect the kinds of interventions that it does and does not offer. Accordingly, I am not considering theological commitments or "transcendent goals." Some commentators claim that the commitment to spiritual goals is fundamental. William Stempsey expresses a view along these lines:

Any hospital might refuse to allow abortion and physician-assisted suicide, but Catholic hospitals refuse these things because they are fundamentally inconsistent with Christian values. Directive 1 of the ERD (1995) states: "A Catholic institutional health care service is a community that provides health care to those in need of it. This service must be animated by the Gospel of Jesus Christ and guided by the moral tradition of the Church." This is unambiguous. Catholic health care is not the same as secular health care. To hold that Catholic hospitals have lost their identity because their surgical procedures do not look different from those in secular hospitals is a conclusion based upon a false dichotomy. The question is. Is the care animated by Gospel values? (Stempsey 2001: 3–14 at 11)

H. Tristram Engelhardt, Jr. laments the increasing secularization of Catholic hospitals, which is characterized by a failure to give priority to their spiritual mission. See (Engelhardt, Jr. 2001: 151–61).

individuals, institutions cannot have or lose self-respect or a sense of dignity, and they cannot experience a loss of identity or moral integrity as a harm or injury. Hence, it might seem that in contrast to individuals, there is no sound basis for valuing the preservation of institutional identity and integrity. Accordingly, although it might be conceded that there are grounds to accommodate individual physicians, nurses, and pharmacists who accept the ERD, it might be maintained that there is no ethical basis for a similar accommodation for health care institutions. For example, it might be conceded that protecting the identity and moral integrity of individual ED physicians and nurses with conscience-based objections to EC provides a good reason for reasonable accommodation. However, it might be argued that preserving the identity and (moral) integrity of a Catholic hospital that is committed to the ERD fails to provide a good reason to support exempting its ED from an obligation to offer EC to rape victims.

In response, there are several reasons for enabling health care institutions to maintain their identity and integrity and exempting them from general institutional obligations that would compromise their identity and integrity. First, it can be important to physicians, nurses, pharmacists and other personnel to be able to practice and work in a *community* that shares a commitment to a core set of goals, values, and principles. Practicing or working in an institution that permits actions that violate a health care professional's core values might compromise her moral integrity. At the very least, it can contribute to considerable moral distress. Second, it can be important to patients to receive care in a facility that is committed to their fundamental values. Even if a patient's moral integrity is not at stake, it can be a considerable source of distress to be cared for in a facility that engages in practices that are inconsistent with one's fundamental ethical or religious values. Third, even when they are not hospital or nursing home patients, members of a faith community may have an interest in the existence of health care institutions that exemplify its fundamental principles. Fourth, it might be claimed that the existence of health care institutions dedicated to upholding perceived moral ideals is intrinsically valuable. To be sure, there are exceptions. For example, there is nothing intrinsically valuable about health care institutions such as Nazi hospitals that were committed to "racial purity" and other clearly unacceptable goals. However, excluding such outliers, it nevertheless might be claimed that, generally, a society with health care institutions whose identity is based in part on perceived moral ideals is a better society than one without such health care institutions. Fifth, it might be claimed such institutions are instrumentally valuable insofar as they sustain and nourish diversity. Finally, it might be claimed that insofar as such institutions have a *social* mission, which is perhaps especially true of religiously affiliated facilities, they promote social justice and contribute to social welfare. For example, in a section of the ERD entitled "The Social Responsibility of Catholic Health Care Services," the Third Directive states:

> In accord with its mission, Catholic health care should distinguish itself by service to and advocacy for those people whose social condition puts them at the margins of our society and makes them particularly vulnerable to discrimination: the poor; the uninsured and the underinsured; children and the unborn; single parents; the elderly; those with incurable diseases and chemical dependencies; racial minorities; immigrants and refugees ...[26]

In view of this social mission, it might be claimed that enabling Catholic health care institutions to maintain a coherent identity and integrity benefits the community. If Catholic hospitals are not able to maintain their distinctive identity, they might decide to close their doors rather than compromise their integrity, which would leave more vulnerable members of the community worse off. Moreover, in some communities, the closing of one health care facility can substantially reduce convenient access to health services for all residents.

Arguably, these reasons provide grounds for exempting Catholic health care institutions from an obligation to provide a good or service such as EC, abortion, or sterilization if doing so would compromise the institution's identity and integrity. However, there are limits to such accommodations. Similar to pharmacies, and for similar reasons, hospitals and nursing homes have obligations and responsibilities to patients, including obligations to promote their health, protect them from harm, and respect their autonomy. First, hospitals and nursing homes are licensed by states with a legitimate expectation that they will protect patients from harm, promote their health, and respect their autonomy; and corresponding obligations can be said to derive from a commitment by licensees when they accept a license to operate a facility.[27]

---

[26] A review of 25 Catholic hospital mission statements reportedly revealed a consistent commitment to social justice. See (Shannon 2001: 49–65).

[27] In August 2009, the Joint Commission, which provides accreditation for hospitals in the United States, adopted a revised mission statement. According to that statement, its mission is "[t]o continuously improve health care for the public, in collaboration with other stakeholders, by evaluating health care organizations and inspiring them to excel in providing safe and effective care of the highest quality and value." Available online at: www.jointcommission.org/NR/rdonlyres/2F04C126–906D-4155-B16F-1F1A6570C387/0/jconlineAug1209.pdf; accessed July 9, 2010. This mission statement identifies general patient-centered goals for hospitals and nursing homes that seek Joint Commission accreditation. Accordingly, Joint Commission accreditation requirements provide a *prudential* reason for hospitals and nursing homes to protect patients from harm, promote their health, and respect their autonomy.

Second, those obligations can be said to derive from considerations of reciprocal justice. A hospital or nursing home license confers certain exclusive rights and privileges on the licensee, and when licensees accept and enjoy these rights and privileges, they incur reciprocal obligations, including obligations to protect patients from harm, promote their health and respect their autonomy. Third, those obligations might be derived from general ethical principles, such as respect for autonomy, beneficence, non-maleficence, and justice, together with certain assumptions about the connection between safe and effective health care and health, the potential for harm if patients do not receive timely and competent health care, the vulnerability of people who are ill and require health care, and so forth.

Accordingly, obligations to patients set limits to identity and integrity preserving refusals by health care institutions. In successive sections, I will consider whether health care institutions have potentially identity and integrity compromising obligations to: (1) offer access to EC to rape victims who present in the ED; (2) honor patient or surrogate decisions to forgo MPNH; and (3) provide standard of care emergency medical treatment to pregnant patients.

Emergency contraception

Levonorgestrel-based EC (e.g. Plan B and Plan B One-Step), which must be taken within 72 hours of unprotected intercourse (Anonymous 2002), is available without prescription for women 17 years and older. In August 2010, the US FDA approved ella (ulipristal acetate), which is effective up to 120 hours after unprotected intercourse. It requires a prescription.[28] Despite the availability without a prescription of levonorgestrel-based EC to women 17 years and older, hospital EDs are likely to remain a frequent access point to EC for victims of sexual assault. Yet many studies report that most Catholic hospitals in the United States do not provide EC even to rape victims (Harrison 2005; Nunn *et al.* 2003; Polis *et al.* 2005).[29] Some

---

[28] Information about ella is available at Drugs@FDA: www.accessdata.fda.gov/scripts/cder/drugsatfda/: accessed October 20, 2010.

[29] One exception is a study of Massachusetts Catholic hospitals which reported that respondents in only 3 of 9 hospitals stated that EC was not available for sexual assault victims (Temin *et al.* 2005). The California study reported that in 66% of the 44 Catholic hospitals, EC is not provided under any circumstances (Polis, Schaffer and Harrison 2005: 174–8). However, data for the study predates a California law requiring provision of EC to rape victims. Accordingly, the situation may have changed in California and other states that have subsequently adopted similar legislation. On the other hand, some Catholic EDs reportedly violated existing state EC requirements, so there appears to be a gap between legal requirements and actual practice. See (Nunn *et al.* 2003: 38–41). It is noteworthy that all of the studies reported that a significant percentage of non-Catholic hospitals do not provide EC for rape victims.

Catholic hospitals that offer EC to rape victims reportedly do so only with conditions, such as requiring a negative pregnancy test or police notification. Some of the studies reported that most Catholic hospitals that do not provide EC also do not refer to practitioners who do; and even when referrals are provided, they often turn out to be unhelpful to patients. These studies used telephone calls to determine whether an ED will provide EC to a patient who requests it, and they were not designed to determine whether the option of EC is disclosed to assault victims who present at an ED. However, a small pilot study of 28 Catholic and 30 non-Catholic hospitals did ask whether hospital policy prohibits a discussion of EC with rape victims (Smugar *et al.* 2000). The study reported that none of the non-Catholic hospitals had such a policy. By contrast, 12 Catholic hospitals had such a policy (one did not respond to the question). However, the study found a significant difference between policy and practice in several of the Catholic hospitals that, according to respondents, had a policy prohibiting discussing EC with rape victims. In 4 of the hospitals, ED staff reportedly discussed EC in violation of hospital policy; in 2 hospitals, patients received information about EC from a provider outside the ED; and rape counselors provided information about EC in the ED in 2 hospitals.[30]

Since some women will no longer require a prescription for EC, when considering the obligations of Catholic hospitals in relation to rape victims who present at an ED, it is necessary to distinguish between rape victims who do and those who do not need a prescription.[31] There are two categories

---

[30] The study also found significant differences in the practices of Catholic hospitals in relation to providing prescriptions for and dispensing EC. Such variation is not surprising if, as some commentators have claimed, the ERD (specifically Directive 36) does not provide unambiguous guidance in relation to EC for victims of sexual assault. See (ibid.). Directive 36 states:

Compassionate and understanding care should be given to a person who is the victim of sexual assault. Health care providers should cooperate with law enforcement officials and offer the person psychological and spiritual support as well as accurate medical information. A female who has been raped should be able to defend herself against a potential conception from the sexual assault. If, after appropriate testing, there is no evidence that conception has occurred already, she may be treated with medications that would prevent ovulation, sperm capacitation, or fertilization. It is not permissible, however, to initiate or to recommend treatments that have as their purpose or direct effect the removal, destruction, or interference with the implantation of a fertilized ovum.

Directive 36 includes the following footnote:

It is recommended that a sexually assaulted woman be advised of the ethical restrictions that prevent Catholic hospitals from using abortifacient procedures. Cf. Pennsylvania Catholic Conference, "Guidelines for Catholic Hospitals Treating Victims of Sexual Assault," *Origins*, 22 (1993): 810.

[31] Levonorgestrel-based EC, which must be taken within 72 hours of unprotected intercourse (Anonymous 2002), is available without prescription for women 17 years and older. As noted in

of women who will require a prescription: (1) women under the age of 17 and (2) women who need EC that is effective past 72 hours. Reasonable people might disagree about whether Catholic hospitals have an obligation to provide EC to rape victims who need a prescription. However, at the very least, it is the responsibility of all hospitals, including Catholic hospitals, to ensure that rape victims who present at the ED have an opportunity to receive information about EC without delay and have timely and convenient access to it if they decide to take it.

Optimally, to minimize delay and additional emotional distress, information about EC should be offered and, if requested, provided on site. If information is provided on site, it need not be by hospital staff. For example, a hospital might have a standing arrangement with a rape crisis or counseling center to make personnel available to explain EC to patients in the hospital. Off-site alternative arrangements can suffice, but only if they assure that rape victims have an opportunity to make informed decisions about and receive EC in a convenient and timely manner. For example, hospitals might offer to arrange for patients to be transported at no charge to a rape crisis or counseling center. However, hospitals that pursue this option have an obligation to disclose the following information to rape victims: (1) there is a medication to prevent pregnancy; (2) the medication should be taken as soon as possible, but no later than 72 hours (levonorgestrel-based EC) or 120 hours (ulipristal acetate-based EC) after the sexual assault; and (3) it is contrary to the hospital's mission to provide additional information or the medication, but the hospital will provide free transportation to an organization that can give a full explanation about the medication and facilitate timely and convenient access to it. In view of the trauma of rape, and the urgency of the situation, however, it is at least arguable that if a rape victim objects to having to go elsewhere for information about EC, hospitals should provide it.

If hospitals provide information about EC but do not provide the medication, if requested, they should at least provide information about conveniently located pharmacies that dispense it. If there are no nearby pharmacies that stock EC and are open 24/7, hospitals arguably have an obligation to stock a supply so that the medication can be given to rape victims if needed to prevent excessive inconvenience or delay.

Chapter 1, after this book was in production, the FDA approved ella (ulipristal acetate), which is effective up to 120 hours after unprotected intercourse. It requires a prescription. Accordingly, for women who can benefit from ella's additional protection, the approach should be the same as that recommended for women under the age of 17. Information about ella is available at Drugs@FDA: www.accessdata.fda.gov/scripts/cder/drugsatfda/: accessed October 20, 2010.

For rape victims who need a prescription, hospitals that do not routinely provide prescriptions for EC have an obligation to assure that such patients have a timely and convenient opportunity to get a prescription for it. Again, this obligation might be discharged by offering to provide free transportation to a rape crisis or counseling center. However, if there are no alternative means to ensure that rape victims have an opportunity to receive prescriptions for EC without excessive delay or inconvenience, hospitals have an obligation to provide them.

Fulfilling these obligations might require some Catholic hospitals to compromise their identity and integrity. Nevertheless, there are several reasons for ascribing these obligations to all hospitals, including those whose identity and integrity might be compromised.

First, some rape victims may depend on the ED for timely information about EC. Studies have reported that many women are either unaware of EC or lack sufficient understanding to use it effectively. A study of Californian women between the ages of 18 and 44 reported that 36.5 percent of the respondents stated that there was nothing women could do in the three days after intercourse to prevent pregnancy, and an additional 11.6 percent stated that they did not know (D. G. Foster *et al.* 2004). A second study reported that only 67 percent of women respondents answered that there is something that women can do after sexual intercourse to prevent pregnancy (Abbott 2005). Moreover, among the women who knew that EC could prevent post-coital pregnancy, only 74 percent knew that it should be taken within 72 hours after intercourse, and almost half of them mistakenly believed that it must be taken immediately or within 24 hours.[32] A third study reported that 85.3 percent of respondents were unable to answer correctly two questions that were designed to test comprehension of the concept of EC (Merchant *et al.* 2007).[33] Since there currently is a 72–120-hour

---

[32] These studies suggest that it cannot be assumed that rape victims will know that a prescription EC can provide protection up to 120 hours after intercourse.

[33] One question asked: "If a woman has had vaginal sexual intercourse with a man (without using birth control), can she take birth control pills AFTERWARDS to prevent pregnancy?" The second question asked respondents whether they agree or disagree with the following statement: "A woman can take birth control pills shortly AFTER having vaginal intercourse with a man to prevent pregnancy." Since the questions referred to "birth control pills" rather than "emergency contraception," "the morning after pill," or simply "medication," they may have failed to accurately test respondents' understanding of the "concept of EC." The study also asked respondents whether they agree or disagree with the following statement: "Taking birth control pills AFTER having sexual intercourse with a man causes an abortion." Only 9.8% expressed their agreement. However, before concluding that over 90% of the respondents had an accurate understanding of the mechanism of EC, one has to consider the possibility that their responses might have been significantly different if the statement had referred to "emergency contraception" or "the morning after pill" rather than "birth control pills."

window of maximum effectiveness of EC, if women do not leave the ED with an adequate understanding of emergency contraception, even if they acquire that knowledge later, it may be too late to enable them to substantially reduce the risk of pregnancy. Moreover, since patients generally can reasonably expect that physicians will tell them about all clinically relevant options, it might not even occur to rape victims to look for other options on their own (e.g. from their obstetrician-gynecologist or on the Internet). Accordingly, if an ED does not make available an opportunity for a rape victim to receive information about EC, she may not be able to make an informed choice about whether or not to take a medication that significantly reduces the risk of becoming pregnant. Since sexual assault victims who present at an ED are likely to be traumatized, distraught, and especially vulnerable, even if a rape victim is aware of EC, an offer to review and explain her options may enhance her ability to make an informed decision.

Second, deciding whether or not to become pregnant is undoubtedly among the most intimate, personal, and important life choices that a woman can make. EC obviously cannot undo or reverse the violation of a rape victim's bodily integrity and personhood. However, it can at least restore her ability to control whether or not she will become pregnant and in this respect restore her control over her own body and procreative future. Moreover, if a rape victim does not have an opportunity to choose EC and prevent a pregnancy, she may be confronted later with a difficult choice between giving birth to a child genetically related to her rapist and having an abortion. Whereas providing information about and access to EC can be a substantial benefit to rape victims, a failure to offer an opportunity to receive information about and access to it can result in additional substantial harm. Hence, timely knowledge about EC and access to it can be of utmost importance to the health and well-being of rape victims.

Third, any delay in offering means to prevent pregnancy can be unbearable to rape victims. It is unreasonable to expect anxious rape victims who insist on knowing *now* to patiently wait until they can be transported to another location to find out how they can lower the risk of becoming pregnant. Moreover, it would be insensitive at best and cruel at worst in effect to tell a rape victim who is fearful of becoming pregnant and insists on taking immediate preventive measures: "Since no conveniently located pharmacies that dispense EC are open now, you will have to wait until tomorrow to do anything about it."

Fourth, offering EC to rape victims who present at an ED is standard of care (Amey and Bishai 2002; Smugar *et al.* 2000). It is explicitly endorsed in policies of the American College of Emergency Physicians (ACEP) and the

AMA. An ACEP policy statement entitled, "Management of the Patient with the Complaint of Sexual Assault," states: "A victim of sexual assault should be offered prophylaxis for pregnancy and for sexually transmitted diseases, subject to informed consent and consistent with current treatment guidelines."[34] The policy statement provides an accommodation for conscience-based objections, but it clearly limits accommodations to those that will not interfere with the obligation to assure that rape victims receive a timely offer of EC:

Physicians and allied health practitioners who find this practice morally objectionable or who practice at hospitals that prohibit prophylaxis or contraception should offer to refer victims of sexual assault to another provider who can provide these services in a timely fashion.

An AMA policy statement affirms that "information about emergency contraception is part of the comprehensive information to be provided as part of the emergency treatment of sexual assault victims."[35]

Finally, withholding information about EC is contrary to the reasonable expectations of rape victims who present at an ED. It is a reasonable expectation that hospital EDs will offer standard of care treatment (Nunn *et al.* 2003). Thus, insofar as offering EC is standard of care for rape victims, not assuring that this option is presented to them in a timely fashion is contrary to a reasonable expectation. Surely, patients can reasonably expect that a hospital will neither condone nor permit staff to intentionally withhold information about clinically appropriate options.

For all of these reasons, it is arguable that: (1) a hospital's general obligations to promote patients' health, protect them from harm, and respect their autonomy are appropriately specified to include an obligation to implement measures to ensure that rape victims who present at the ED have an opportunity to receive information about EC without delay and have timely access to it if they decide to take it; and (2) this obligation applies to all hospitals, including those whose identity and integrity might be compromised by fulfilling it.

Medically provided nutrition and hydration (MPNH)

Many hospitals and nursing homes that have refused to honor patients' or surrogates' decisions to forgo MPNH have claimed that doing so would

---

[34] Available online at: www.acep.org/practres.aspx?id=29562; accessed July 9, 2010.
[35] Access to Emergency Contraception, House of Delegates Health Policy 75.985.

compromise their identity and integrity as a *Catholic* institution. A 2004 papal allocution that addressed MPNH fueled a debate about its meaning as well as the permissibility of forgoing MPNH.[36] In 2007, in response to two questions from the US Conference of Catholic Bishops (USCCB) seeking clarification of the papal allocution, the Congregation for the Doctrine of the Faith (CDF) provided the Vatican's official answers.[37] Although some took these answers to comprise an almost absolute prohibition of forgoing MPNH, the debate continued.[38] In November 2009, responding to the CDF's answers, the USCCB revised the ERD.[39] Although it remains to be seen how these revised directives will influence actual practice in Catholic health care institutions in the United States, their impact is not likely to be an increase in the willingness of Catholic health care institutions to forgo MPNH. It therefore is important to consider whether institutions have an obligation to honor patients' decisions to forgo MPNH even when doing so would compromise their perceived identity and integrity.

The refusal of a Catholic hospital in New Jersey to honor Beverly Requena's decision to forgo MPNH is a representative and frequently cited case that provides an excellent vehicle to address this question.[40] Ms. Requena was a 55-year-old woman with amyotrophic lateral sclerosis

---

[36] See, e.g. (Shannon and Walter 2004: 18–20); (Repenshek and Slosar 2004: 13–16); and (Shannon and Walter 2005: 4). The papal allocution is available online at: www.vatican.va/holy_father/john_paul_ii/ speeches/2004/march/documents/hf_jp-ii_spe_20040320_congress-fiamc_en.html; accessed July 9, 2010.

[37] Congregation for the Doctrine of the Faith, "Responses to Certain Questions Concerning Artificial Nutrition and Hydration (August 1, 2007)." Available online at: www.vatican.va/roman_curia/ congregations/cfaith/documents/rc_con_cfaith_doc_20070801_risposte-usa_en.html; accessed July 9, 2010.

[38] A headline in a September 14, 2007 *International Herald Tribune* article on the CDF statement proclaimed: "Vatican reiterates that it considers removal of feeding tubes immoral." For another interpretation, see (Sulmasy 2007: 16–18).

[39] Nancy Frazier O'Brien, "Bishops Approve Revised Directives on Withdrawal of Food, Water" (Catholic News Service, November 19, 2009). Available online at: www.catholicnews.com/data/ stories/cns/0905131.htm; accessed July 9, 2010. Directive 58, the revised section of the ERD on MPNH states:

In principle, there is an obligation to provide patients with food and water, including medically assisted nutrition and hydration for those who cannot take food orally. This obligation extends to patients in chronic and presumably irreversible conditions (e.g., the 'persistent vegetative state') who can reasonably be expected to live indefinitely if given such care. Medically assisted nutrition and hydration become morally optional when they cannot reasonably be expected to prolong life or when they would be "excessively burdensome for the patient or [would] cause significant physical discomfort, for example resulting from complications in the use of the means employed." For instance, as a patient draws close to inevitable death from an underlying progressive and fatal condition, certain measures to provide nutrition and hydration may become excessively burdensome and therefore not obligatory in light of their very limited ability to prolong life or provide comfort (footnotes deleted).

[40] The description of the case provided here is based on the trial court opinion by Judge Reginald Stanton in *In re Requena*, 517 A.2d 886 (N. J. Super. Ct. Ch. Div. 1986).

(ALS) or Lou Gehrig's disease, which is "a rapidly progressive, invariably fatal neurological disease that attacks the nerve cells (*neurons*) responsible for controlling voluntary muscles."[41] She entered the hospital in April 1985 and her condition progressively deteriorated. Over time, she required ventilator support, lost the ability to communicate by speaking, and was paralyzed from the neck down. As her physical condition worsened, how- ever, she retained her decision-making capacity, and she decided that when she was no longer able to swallow, she did not want to receive nutrition and hydration medically. Ms. Requena was first hospitalized in Riverside Hospital, but several months later it merged with St. Clare's Hospital, a Catholic hospital. The combined health system (St. Clare's/Riverside Medical Center) adopted a Catholic identity, and when notified of Ms. Requena's decision, the administration stated that withholding MPNH was contrary to the hospital's "pro-life values." The hospital board affirmed this position when it unanimously approved the following resolution:

BE IT RESOLVED by the Board of Trustees that it does hereby reaffirm the policy of the former St. Clare's Hospital that food and water are basic human needs and that such fundamental care cannot be withheld from patients in the Medical Center and that neither the Medical Center nor personnel will participate in the withholding or withdrawal of artificial feeding and/or fluids.[42]

It might appear that there is an obvious resolution of this conflict between the hospital's interest in maintaining its identity and integrity and Ms. Requena's interest in not receiving MPNH against her wishes: a transfer to another facility that will honor her decision to forgo MPNH and care for her in accordance with her wishes. In cases such as this, however, transfer often is not feasible. Other facilities may be unwilling to accept patients in Ms. Requena's condition; or if there are facilities that are willing to accept such patients and provide care for them in accordance with their wishes, considerations of safety may rule out transporting a patient to another facility, or the patient's insurance network might not include any of the other facilities. It is arguable that if a transfer is infeasible, a hospital has an obligation to honor a patient's decision to forgo MPNH even if doing so compromises its identity and integrity. The alternative, initiating MPNH

---

[41] National Institutes of Health, National Institute of Neurological Disorders and Stroke. Available online at: www.ninds.nih.gov/disorders/amyotrophiclateralsclerosis/detail_amyotrophiclateralsclerosis.htm; accessed July 9, 2010.

[42] *In re Requena*, n 40 above, 889. Judge Stanton criticized the hospital for not soliciting more input from staff and implies in his decision that some members of Ms. Requena's health care team were willing to honor her decision. Thus, this is a clear case of an *institutional* refusal based on an appeal to its identity and integrity.

against a patient's explicit wishes, would be an unacceptable violation of a vulnerable patient's autonomy, dignity, and bodily integrity. Further, insofar as a patient has made an informed decision to forgo MPNH, it is arguable that in addition to infringing her autonomy, providing MPNH contrary to her wishes is a harm.

In Ms. Requena's case, however, St. Clare's/Riverside Medical Center was able to find another facility, St. Barnabas Hospital, which would care for her in accordance with her wishes. It was said to be possible to transport her to the other facility safely, and insurance coverage did not appear to be an issue. If the care that Ms. Requena would have received at St. Barnabas would have been substantially inferior to that provided at St. Clare's/Riverside Medical Center, it might be argued that the latter facility had an obligation not to transfer her or initiate MPNH against her wishes, even if its identity and integrity would have been compromised. In support of this conclusion it can be claimed that: (1) transferring Ms. Requena to St. Barnabas Hospital would violate St. Clare's/Riverside Medical Center's obligation to protect patients from harm; (2) providing MPNH against her wishes would violate her dignity and bodily integrity and would harm her; and (3) both actions would comprise unacceptable violations of a vulnerable patient's autonomy.

In Ms. Requena's case, however, it was alleged that the quality of her care would not decline at St. Barnabas Hospital. Indeed, a physician who treated her at St. Clare's/Riverside Medical Center also had privileges at St. Barnabas Hospital and could continue to participate in her care there. Nevertheless, Ms. Requena refused to consent to a transfer. In response, St. Clare's/Riverside Medical Center sought a court order compelling her to leave the facility. The trial court judge, Reginald Stanton, ruled against the hospital. He provided the following account of Ms. Requena's reasons for wanting to stay in St. Clare's/Riverside Medical Center:

During her 17-month stay at the Hospital, she has received care which is both professionally good and personally compassionate. She has developed trust in and affection for the nurses, the respiratory technicians and the other staff members at the Hospital. She is familiar with the physical surroundings.[43]

Under these circumstances, did the hospital have an obligation to continue to care for Ms. Requena according to her wishes even if it would compromise its identity and integrity?

---

[43] Ibid.

The change in MPNH policy during Ms. Requena's hospitalization might be cited to support an affirmative answer. When she was admitted to Riverside Medical Center prior to its merger with St. Clare's Hospital, the former facility did not have a policy against forgoing MPNH. As a result, it might be claimed that Ms. Requena had a reasonable expectation that Riverside Medical Center would respect her treatment wishes. At the very least, she did not have any reason to believe that her wishes would not be respected should she decide against MPNH, and she did not have an opportunity to avoid having to transfer to another facility should she decide against MPNH. In addition, although the merger took place in late 1985, it was not until July 1986, and only after her decision to forgo MPNH was communicated to hospital administration, that Ms. Requena was informed of the new policy. In view of these special circumstances, then, it might reasonably be claimed that St. Clare's/Riverside Medical Center had a special obligation to honor Ms. Requena's wishes.[44]

It is at least arguable, however, that a hospital's obligation to honor a patient's decision to forgo MPNH is not contingent on such special circumstances. Judge Stanton plausibly claimed that an involuntary transfer would be burdensome to Ms. Requena: "It would be emotionally and psychologically upsetting to be forced to leave the Hospital. The removal would also have significant elements of rejection and casting out which would be burdensome for Mrs. Requena."[45] Moreover, as Thomas Shannon and James Walter rightly observe: "[t]he decisionmaking process at the end of life is difficult enough as it is. It is a time fraught with tension, pain, suffering, sorrow, guilt, and grieving" (Shannon and Walter 2004: 20). Accordingly, it is not implausible to claim that if a dying patient objects to a transfer, refusing to honor a patient's decision to forgo MPNH is contrary to a hospital's obligation to respect patient autonomy and prevent harm (e.g. excessive burdens). Although reasonable people might disagree, it is at least not implausible to claim that this obligation obtains even if fulfilling it requires a hospital to compromise its identity and dignity.[46]

---

[44] Steven Wear claims that Judge Stanton would not have required St. Clare's/Riverside Medical Center to honor Ms. Requena's decision if she had received advance notice of the hospital policy: "he [Judge Stanton] allows that if only the hospital had given Ms. Requena prior notice of its abhorrence to such an enterprise, he would have sustained its insistence that she be transferred elsewhere" (Wear 1991: 225–30 at 226). Although Judge Stanton cited the lack of advance notice in support of his decision, it was only one of several reasons, and he did not cite it as a necessary condition.

[45] *In re Requena*, n 40 above, 889.

[46] Wear appears to disagree. Although he concedes that St. Clare's/Riverside Medical Center had a "fiduciary responsibility to meet the needs of its patients," he questions whether this responsibility applies to honoring Ms. Requena's decision to forgo MPNH and places the burden of proof on those

To reduce the incidence of such conflicts between patient treatment decisions and policies designed to protect an institution's identity and integrity, institutions can provide an opportunity for patients to learn about policies that might conflict with their end-of-life care preferences prior to admission. However, there are a number of limitations to this strategy. First, patients' choices of hospitals may be substantially limited and/or influenced by a wide range of factors, such as insurance restrictions, location, and quality and range of services. Second, despite a facility's sincere efforts, there are substantial obstacles to effectively communicating MPNH and general end-of-life decision-making policies to prospective patients. Third, one cannot reasonably expect most patients to know when selecting a hospital whether or not they will decide to forgo MPNH if and when they lose the ability to eat and drink. People in an advanced stage of a terminal progressive illness such as ALS that is known to lead eventually to loss of the ability to swallow may have made a decision about MPNH prior to admission, but even such patients can change their minds over time. If people selecting a nursing home have not lost their decision-making capacity, compared to prospective hospital patients, they may be more prepared to consider a facility's MPNH policy. Accordingly, nursing homes may be able to significantly reduce conflicts involving end-of-life decision-making if their policies are clearly explained to prospective residents and patients. Nevertheless, one cannot reasonably expect that a nursing home's MPNH policy will be the decisive factor in selecting a nursing home.

Pregnant patients and emergency medical conditions

It is a settled matter that hospitals generally may refuse to permit physicians to perform abortions in their facilities if doing so is contrary to an institution's ethical or religious mission. There are several reasons that can be given to support the special status of institutional abortion refusals. First, for some health care institutions (e.g. Catholic hospitals) abortion is ethically equivalent to killing innocent persons and therefore is among the most serious ethical wrongs. For such institutions, performing abortions would completely negate their identity and integrity. Second, abortion is one of the most, if not the most, contentious and divisive ethical issues in the United States.

---

who answer in the affirmative: "But how does this institution's commitment to care for the sick, however hopefully leavened by empathy and compassion, necessarily entail that it is thereby obliged to starve a patient to death on demand? This requires argument, which has not been provided" (Wear 1991: at 230). Wear's description of Ms. Requena's decision assumes that honoring it requires an *unethical* action (*starving* a patient to death), which begs the question.

Accordingly, unless access to abortion services is unduly restricted, it might be thought reasonable to adopt a policy of toleration and permit institutions to refuse to make their facilities available for abortions. Third, ethical judgments about abortion are associated with fundamental beliefs about the value and meaning of human life, personhood, autonomy, and sex. Accordingly, it might be claimed, institutional refusals to permit abortions have a special moral status.

Nevertheless, there are emergency medical conditions (e.g. incomplete miscarriage, ectopic pregnancy, pre-eclampsia, placenta previa, placental abruption, sepsis, thromboembolism, and underlying cardiac disease made life-threatening by pregnancy) for which standard of care can involve procedures that either require or risk terminating a pregnancy. In such circumstances, if medically indicated procedures are withheld to maintain a hospital's identity and integrity, patients may be exposed to serious risks of substantial harm, including death. Can a hospital's obligations to its patients limit the risks to which pregnant patients may be exposed to maintain the hospital's identity and integrity?

Lori Freedman, Uta Landy, and Jody Steinauer present case studies of miscarriage management in Catholic hospitals that provide a concrete context for addressing this question (Freedman *et al.* 2008). They focus on cases in which, although still alive, fetuses were pre-viable and could not be saved. In such circumstances, according to the authors, hospital policy did not permit interventions that would terminate a pregnancy without ethics committee approval. In some of the case studies, despite physicians' concerns about the risks to pregnant patients, the ethics committee denied permission. For example, an obstetrician-gynecologist gave the following account of one case:

She [the patient] was very early, 14 weeks. She came in . . . and there was a hand sticking out of the cervix. Clearly the membranes had ruptured and she was trying to deliver . . . There was a heart rate, and [we called] the ethics committee, and they [said], "Nope, can't do anything." (ibid.: 1776)

In this case, the ethics committee denied approval because the fetus's heart was still beating, and the patient was transported 90 miles to another hospital where the fetus was extracted.

In another case, despite the obstetrician-gynecologist's concern that delay would result in an unacceptable increased risk of morbidity and mortality, an ethics committee did not approve a uterine evacuation for a patient in her ninth week of pregnancy. As the obstetrician-gynecologist described the situation:

The pregnancy was in the vagina … [S]he's septic to the point that I'm pushing pressors on labor and delivery trying to keep her blood pressure up, and I have her on a cooling blanket because she's 106 degrees. And I needed to get everything out. And so I put the ultrasound machine on and there was still a heartbeat, and [the ethics committee] wouldn't let me because there was still a heartbeat. This woman is dying before our eyes. (ibid.: 1777)

In the judgment of the obstetrician-gynecologist, the risk of delay to the patient was so great that he violated hospital protocol and snapped the umbilical cord to stop the fetus's heart. After the heart stopped, the ethics committee criterion was satisfied, and he was able to perform the uterine evacuation without any additional violation of hospital protocol. Nevertheless, he reported that the patient almost died:

She was so sick she was in the [intensive care unit] for about 10 days and very nearly died … She was in DIC [disseminated intravascular coagulopathy] … Her bleeding was so bad that the sclera, the white of her eyes, were red, filled with blood. (ibid.: 1777)

The obstetrician-gynecologist was so upset by the experience that he resigned and accepted a position at a non-sectarian academic medical center.

The study reports that there is considerable variation in ethics committees' interpretation of the ERD and the criteria they use to decide whether to approve procedures, such as uterine evacuation, that result in the termination of pregnancies. For the purposes of this discussion of institutional refusals, it is not necessary to explain and evaluate alternative interpretations of the ERD. The question is not whether a particular ethics committee's interpretation of the ERD is justified. Rather, the question to be considered is whether withholding or delaying emergency medical treatment to protect a hospital's identity and integrity – as an ethics committee conceives them – can violate a hospital's obligations to patients.

Any answer to this question is likely to be controversial. However, at the very least it seems reasonable to maintain that when pregnant patients experience emergency medical conditions, time permitting, a hospital's obligations to protect patients from harm, promote their health, and respect their autonomy include an obligation to explain all clinically relevant options, including those that are not offered because providing them would compromise the hospital's identity and integrity and, if feasible, to offer a transfer. More specifically, hospitals that refuse to provide a clinically relevant option have an obligation, time permitting, to offer patients or surrogates:

(1) an explanation of the patient's condition;

(2) an explanation of all clinically relevant options and the associated risks and benefits of each;

(3) the reasons why the hospital will not offer one of the options;

(4) if applicable, disclosure that, clinically, the option not offered by the hospital is standard of care;

(5) when feasible and risks are not excessive, transfer to a hospital that will provide the option and an explanation of the risks and benefits of transfer; and

(6) answers to questions about any of the clinically relevant options.

None of these obligations prevents a hospital from refusing to offer a medical procedure such as abortion that is incompatible with its mission. Moreover, some patients or surrogates might decide, for religious or other reasons, to remain in the hospital and accept an option it does offer. Accordingly, fulfilling these obligations when a hospital refuses to offer a clinically relevant option that is contrary to its core mission might not compromise its identity and integrity. However, even if a hospital's identity and integrity are compromised, these obligations are a reasonable specification of a hospital's general obligations to protect patients from harm, promote their health, and respect their autonomy.

A more difficult question concerns a hospital's obligations when a transfer is not feasible because a pregnant patient is too unstable and any delay in providing treatment that is contrary to a hospital's core mission would expose her to an excessive risk of harm (e.g. morbidity, mortality, and increased pain and discomfort). For example, suppose, as may have been the situation in the second of the two case studies, the alternatives are limited to: (1) providing a procedure that is standard of care in obstetrics-gynecology and will compromise a hospital's identity and integrity, and (2) withholding the procedure to maintain the hospital's identity and integrity and exposing a patient to an excessive risk of mortality or morbidity. It is at least arguable that a hospital that refuses to offer the first option fails to fulfill its obligations to the patient.[47] In other words, when withholding medically indicated emergency treatment will expose a pregnant patient to an excessive increased risk of mortality or morbidity, notwithstanding a hospital's

---

[47] According to an American College of Obstetricians and Gynecologists Ethics Committee Opinion, individual practitioners have a similar corresponding obligation: "In an emergency in which referral is not possible or might negatively affect a patient's physical or mental health, providers have an obligation to provide medically indicated and requested care regardless of the provider's personal moral objections" (American College of Obstetricians and Gynecologists Committee on Ethics 2007: 1203–8 at 1207).

interest in maintaining its identity and integrity, it has an obligation to offer the medically indicated emergency treatment. Arguably, this obligation is a reasonable specification of the general obligations to protect patients from harm, promote their health, and respect their autonomy.[48]

There are several possible criteria for determining whether an increased risk of mortality or morbidity due to not receiving standard of care is "excessive," including: (1) *any* additional risk; (2) any additional risk above an objective standard that is independent of the hospital's interest in maintaining its identity and integrity; (3) any additional risk above an objective standard that factors in the hospital's interest in maintaining its identity and integrity; (4) any additional risk above that which a patient or surrogate is willing to accept. Reasons can be given to support each of these standards. However, it is likely that these reasons will include controversial ethical assumptions. Accordingly, reasonable people may well disagree about the appropriate standard of excessiveness. Nevertheless, reasonable people should agree that there is some threshold of additional risk to which hospitals may expose patients to maintain their identity and integrity without violating their obligations to patients.

CONCLUSION

Although large retail pharmacy chains cannot plausibly advance appeals to conscience, owners of independent community pharmacies can and do have genuine conscience-based objections to stocking and dispensing controversial pharmaceuticals such as EC. However, since a pharmacy licensee has an obligation to promote the public health, safety, and welfare, a pharmacy may justifiably refuse to stock and dispense a medication for reasons of conscience only if members of the population in its service area have timely and convenient access to the medication at other pharmacies. Accordingly, it is at least arguable that absent reliable means to assure that permitting conscience-based refusals to stock and dispense will not deny patients timely and convenient access to EC and other prescription or limited distribution medications, to protect the public health, safety, and welfare pharmacy boards may decide not to grant exemptions.

Health care institutions such as hospitals and nursing homes do not have characteristics that would appear to warrant ascribing to them the capacity to have and exercise a conscience. Nevertheless, they can attempt to justify

---

[48] To enable a hospital to discharge this obligation without requiring staff physicians and nurses to act against their consciences, it might have back-up arrangements with outside practitioners.

refusals to offer goods and services by appealing to their identity and integrity, and such claims can bear a family resemblance to appeals to conscience by individuals and can warrant substantial deference. Health care institutions, however, have obligations to prevent harm to patients, promote patient health, and respect patient autonomy. These obligations set limits to identity- and integrity-maintaining refusals to offer EC, forgo MPNH, and offer medically indicated treatments in emergency situations.

First, hospitals have an obligation to ensure that rape victims, no matter their age, who present at the ED have an opportunity to receive information about EC without delay and have timely and convenient access to it if they decide to take it. Second, if a hospital's mission does not permit forgoing MPNH, and a transfer to another facility is feasible, the hospital may satisfy its obligation to a patient who decides to forgo MPNH by offering a transfer. However, if a transfer is infeasible, or it is not accepted by the patient, it is at least arguable that refusing to honor a patient's decision to forgo MPNH is contrary to the obligation to respect patient autonomy and prevent harm (e.g. excessive burdens). Finally, when pregnant patients experience emergency medical conditions, time permitting, hospitals have an obligation to explain all clinically relevant options, including those that are not offered because providing them would compromise the hospital's identity and integrity and, if feasible, offer a transfer. When withholding medically indicated emergency treatment will expose a pregnant patient to an excessive increased risk of morbidity or mortality, notwithstanding a hospital's interest in maintaining its identity and integrity, it has an obligation to offer the medically indicated emergency treatment.

CHAPTER 5

Students, residents, and conscience-based exemptions

Just as practitioners can object to providing services that are against their conscience, students and residents can have conscience-based objections to participating in educational activities. Among medical, nursing, and pharmacy students, the former have been in the forefront of efforts to secure exemptions from activities that violate their ethical or religious beliefs.[1] Accordingly, their experience can serve as a model for students of nursing and pharmacy.

In 1996, the Medical Student Section of the American Medical Association (AMA) introduced a resolution calling on the AMA to adopt a policy in support of exemptions for students with ethical or religious objections.[2] In that resolution, students identified abortion, sterilization, and procedures performed on animals as examples of activities that might prompt requests for conscience-based exemptions. In response to the student initiative, the Council on Medical Education (CME) recommended the adoption of seven "principles to guide exemption of medical students from activities based on conscience."[3] The House of Delegates

---

[1] Consistent with the understanding of conscience-based refusals adopted in previous chapters, students and residents can be said to request *conscience*-based exemptions from educational activities only if their objection is based on their *core* moral beliefs. My focus in this chapter is on conscience-based exemptions. Nevertheless, some of the reasons that are presented for granting conscience-based exemptions also apply to ethical or religious objections that do not involve core moral beliefs. Similarly, reasons that justify refusing requests for exemptions that are conscience-based also apply to requests for exemptions that are not based on core moral beliefs. If it is justified to refuse to grant a *conscience*-based request for an exemption, it would be justified to refuse a request for a similar exemption for ethical or religious reasons that is *not* based on core moral beliefs.

[2] AMA Student Section Resolution 7-I-96, "Respect for Individual Student's Beliefs."

[3] CME Report 9 (I-98), "Conscience Clause: Final Report." With two exceptions, the recommended principles are procedural. The exceptions are a requirement that patient care not be compromised and a requirement that students "learn the basic content or principles underlying procedures or activities that they exempt." However, even the latter requirement has a procedural escape clause: "Any exceptions to this principle should be explicitly described by the school." Citing differences among medical schools in "core mission, religious affiliation, state legal and regulatory requirements,

adopted these principles in their entirety (AMA Policy H-295.896, "Conscience Clause: Final Report").[4]

Among residency programs, it is likely that obstetrics and gynecology programs generally have the most experience related to conscience-based exemptions. Although some family medicine residency programs provide abortion training, historically obstetrics and gynecology residency programs have been the primary providers of graduate medical training pertaining to performing abortions. Since abortion has been a primary target of conscience-based refusals in health care, it is to be expected that some obstetrics and gynecology residents have ethical or religious objections to abortion training. Beyond abortion training, obstetrics and gynecology residency programs provide training in reproductive medicine generally, and, as noted in Chapter 1, according to the American College of Obstetricians and Gynecologists (ACOG) Committee on Ethics, this is an area in which "[c]onscientious refusals have been particularly widespread" (American College of Obstetricians and Gynecologists Committee on Ethics 2007). Accordingly, the discussion of conscience-based exemptions for residents will focus on obstetrics and gynecology residents and residency programs.

REASONS FOR GRANTING CONSCIENCE-BASED EXEMPTIONS

Why should medical, nursing, and pharmacy schools and obstetrics and gynecology residency programs grant, or at least seriously consider, students' or residents' requests for conscience-based exemptions? Why, it might be asked, isn't it justified to respond by dismissing such requests, reminding students and residents that they are, after all, *students/residents*, and pointing out that all students/residents must complete the applicable

organizational structures, and student body characteristics," the Council on Medical Education Report explicitly declines "to define, *a priori*, a set of activities for which medical students may be granted an exemption because of conscience."

[4] The National Student Nurses Association (NSNA) "Bill of Rights and Responsibilities for Students of Nursing" includes two sections that might be understood to *indirectly* address conscience-based exemptions. Section 5 states: "Students should be free to take reasoned exception to the data or views offered in any course of study and to reserve judgment about matters of opinion, but they are responsible for learning the content of any course of study for which they are enrolled." Section 8 states: "The student should have the right to have a responsible voice in the determination of his/her curriculum." Available online at: www.nsna.org/publications/billofrights.aspx; accessed July 10, 2010. By contrast, the 1996 Medical Student Section resolution explicitly endorsed a policy that recognizes conscience-based exemptions.

curricular requirements? There are several reasons for rejecting this response.

First, a policy of categorically denying students' and residents' requests for conscience-based exemptions may have the unintended consequence of diminishing their ethical sensitivity. To be sure, ethics education requires familiarizing students and residents with the accepted standards of the profession. However, if faculty and administrators discount students' and residents' ethical and religious beliefs, they may inadvertently communicate the message that ethics does not matter. That is, students and residents might come to believe that success requires unquestioning accommodation to the established culture and suspension of ethical judgment. Accordingly summarily dismissing students' and residents' conscience-based objections might discourage ethical analysis and desensitize them to ethical concerns. To prevent such desensitization, it may not be necessary to grant requests for conscience-based exemptions. In some cases, it may suffice to provide students and residents with an opportunity to present and explain their objections and, if an exemption is denied, to explain the reasons for that decision.

Training on recently deceased patients can serve to illustrate how disregarding students' and residents' ethical concerns might promote decreased ethical sensitivity. Medical students and residents commonly practice procedures, such as intubation and placement of central lines, after patients die. Frequently, these training procedures were performed without the pre-mortem consent of patients or the consent of family members (Denny and Kollek 1999; Fourre 2002). The absence of consent generated considerable discomfort on the part of some medical students and residents.[5] Suppose students and residents who object to practicing on newly deceased patients without consent are admonished to "get over" their "discomfort." The unintended message to them might be to put aside their ethical concerns, and the unintended result might well be an overall decrease in their ethical sensitivity. Presumably, an aim of professional education and training is to reinforce and nurture, rather than extinguish or decrease, ethical sensitivity.

Studies of medical students suggest that a concern about desensitization is not unfounded. A survey of clinical medical students at the University of

---

[5] A study of parents' willingness to consent to practicing intubation on newly deceased infants included the following comment by a resident: "As long as parents agree to allow intubation, I feel comfortable about doing it. Once, as a medical student we practiced on a deceased patient without family permission and I felt very uncomfortable doing it" (Benfield *et al.* 1991: 2360–3 at 2362). Apparently, this was not an uncommon response among medical students and residents.

Toronto reported that 47 percent of respondents (48 of 103) replied that they felt pressured to act unethically very frequently, frequently, or occasionally (Hicks *et al.* 2001). According to the authors, students reported that clinical preceptors infrequently initiated a discussion of ethical issues, and students were not encouraged to express their ethical concerns. The authors suggest that this inattention to students' ethical perceptions and concerns is one of the "deleterious aspects of the 'hidden curriculum' which currently hinder the ethical growth of medical students" (ibid.: 710). Another study reported that medical students experience "ethical degradation" during their clinical clerkships (Feudtner *et al.* 1994). Sixty seven percent felt bad or guilty about something they did during a clinical clerkship; 62% believed they had experienced an erosion or loss of some of their ethical principles; and 38% were displeased with their ethical development. One possible explanation for the students' reported ethical deterioration may be their perception that an exploration of their ethical concerns would not have been welcomed by other members of the health care team. Sixty-five percent of the student respondents reported feeling either very or somewhat uncomfortable challenging other members of the health care team. It is noteworthy that in a concluding section entitled "Can Ethical Erosion Be Prevented?" the authors offer the following assessment:

Physicians who ask students about their ethical dilemmas, listen carefully to what they say, and then respond with sensitivity are agents of reform. So, too, are physicians who promote an environment during their private and group interactions where it is both safe and acceptable for students to challenge team members about the ethical implications of various courses of action. (ibid.: 678)

Admittedly, these claims – and corresponding claims pertaining to teachers and mentors of students of nursing and pharmacy as well as obstetrics and gynecology residents – may apply most unequivocally when students and residents accept and advocate "mainstream" bioethics. However, insofar as it is undesirable to communicate the message that ethics is not important in clinical practice, the foregoing claims also may serve as a caution against routinely dismissing the conscience-based objections of ethical "outliers." Students or residents who are outliers in relation to a limited set of ethical beliefs also can hold a wide range of mainstream ethical beliefs, and by dismissing objections based on the former, teachers and mentors may unintentionally promote desensitization in relation to the latter.

　　Second, since students and residents may have valuable ethical insights, sometimes granting conscience-based exemptions can serve as a catalyst for improving the ethical environment within a school or residency program and possibly even within the profession. Initially, only a few ethical outliers might seek exemptions for reasons of conscience. However, taking their conscience-based objections seriously and granting them exemptions may initiate a process of re-examination that eventually results in an ethically improved environment for all students or residents.

This point is illustrated by medical student opposition to the use of animals, one of the issues identified in the 1996 AMA Medical Student Section resolution. Prior to that year, a growing number of medical students objected to the use of animals for instruction, and some medical schools granted exemptions to individual students (Dodge 1989). Prompted in part by student protests, medical schools found alternative instructional aids, such as videos and computer simulations, some of which were also more cost-effective. A 1987 survey by the American Medical Student Association and the Physicians Committee for Responsible Medicine found that 53% of medical schools used animals in physiology classes, 25% used animals in pharmacology labs, and 19% used animals in surgery courses (ibid.). According to the Physicians Committee for Responsible Medicine, as of July 2010 only seven US medical schools used animal laboratories for student training.[6] It would be difficult to justify continuing to require students to dissect and perform procedures on live animals who are eventually killed if there are alternatives that are more cost-effective and no less sound educationally. In this case, then, student objections appear to have acted as a catalyst of ethical improvement – a process that began by granting conscience-based exemptions to individual students.[7]

Training on newly deceased patients is another area in which medical students' ethical objections have served as an impetus for constructive change. A medical student initiative prompted a review by the AMA Council on Ethical and Judicial Affairs (CEJA) of the practice of training on newly deceased patients without consent.[8] The resulting CEJA report, which recommended requiring consent, was the basis for Opinion 8.181,

---

[6] Information posted online at: www.pcrm.org/resch/meded/ethics_medlab_list.html; accessed July 7, 2010.
[7] In 1993 the American Medical Student Association (AMSA) urged that "all medical school classes and laboratories involving the use of live animals be optional for students, who for moral or pedagogical reasons, feel such use is either unjustified or unnecessary." In 2007, AMSA issued a statement in which it "[s]trongly encourages the replacement of animal laboratories with non-animal alternatives in undergraduate medical education." Both statements are available online at: www.pcrm.org/resch/meded/ethics_med_AMSA.html; accessed July 10, 2010.
[8] A resolution introduced by the Medical Student Section during the AMA's House of Delegates Interim Meeting in 2000 requested that: "[The] American Medical Association study the issue of using deceased patients for training or other educational purposes and develop ethical guidelines

"Performing Procedures on the Newly Deceased" (Council on Ethical and Judicial Affairs of the American Medical Association 2002). In this case, students initiated a process that resulted in a policy that reflects respect for deceased patients and sensitivity to the interests and emotional well-being of grieving family members. More recently, Harvard medical students protested alleged faculty conflicts of interest (Wilson 2009). Among other things, they objected to lectures about drugs by faculty members who are paid consultants for the pharmaceutical companies that manufacture those drugs. Following their protests, Harvard convened a committee, which includes three students, to re-examine its conflict of interest policies. The students' protests attracted considerable media attention and may stimulate a re-examination of conflict of interest policies at other medical schools and, more generally, training programs in the health professions. Neither the Harvard medical students' protest against alleged conflicts of interest nor the medical students' initiative in relation to training on the recently deceased is an instance of conscientious objection. However, both illustrate how trainees' sensitivity to ethical problems can initiate a constructive ethical re-examination of accepted practices.

Third, a policy of categorically refusing all requests for conscience-based exemptions can undermine the goal of maintaining a diverse student or resident population and, thereby, present a barrier to achieving diversity in the corresponding professions. For example, a policy of categorically dismissing Muslim students' or residents' requests for exemptions from a curricular requirement that is contrary to their religious beliefs will tend to discourage observant Muslims from attending a school or residency program. As a result, observant Muslims are unlikely to be included in the populations of schools or residency programs with such a policy, which will present an obstacle to observant Muslims who aspire to become health care professionals.

Finally, denying students' or residents' requests for conscience-based exemptions fails to respect, and threatens to undermine, their moral autonomy and moral integrity. There are several reasons for respecting and not undermining a student's or resident's moral integrity.[9] First, moral integrity is a generally recognized value. People tend to value moral integrity, and students and residents are no exception. For students and residents with conscience-based objections, maintaining their moral integrity can be of utmost importance to them. Second, insofar as maintaining

---

regarding this practice" (Resolution 1, I-00, "Requesting Consent for Invasive Procedures in the Newly Deceased Patient," Proceedings of the American Medical Association's 2000 Interim Meeting of the House of Delegates).

[9] I provide a more detailed discussion of reasons for respecting moral integrity in Chapter 1.

moral integrity requires adherence to a person's core moral beliefs – beliefs that in part define one's identify or self-conception – its loss can be experienced as "self-betrayal" and diminished self-respect. Third, even when students' and residents' ethical or religious concerns are given a sympathetic hearing, insofar as denying their requests undermines their moral integrity, it can also promote moral desensitization.

REASONS FOR DENYING CONSCIENCE-BASED EXEMPTIONS

Even if it would be mistaken to categorically deny students' and residents' requests for conscience-based exemptions, it would be no less mistaken to automatically grant them. There are competing values and interests that need to be considered when determining whether or not to grant such exemptions. The following are the primary considerations that can justify denying conscience-based exemptions: established core educational requirements, "local" core curricula, non-discrimination, impact on patients, and impact on substitutes and supervisors.

Established core educational requirements

Core educational requirements are one basis for denying conscience-based exemptions. Since core educational requirements for a particular profession purport to identify the essential components of a curriculum for that profession, it generally is justified to deny conscience-based exemptions from those requirements. For example, when medical students requested exemptions from dissecting and practicing procedures on animals, had there been no alternatives that satisfied the corresponding core educational objectives, it would have been justified to deny their requests.

Accreditation standards for schools of medicine, nursing, and pharmacy and obstetrics and gynecology residency programs express each profession's conception of core educational requirements. Since professions have considerable discretion in setting entry requirements and standards of competence, accreditation standards generally provide an authoritative basis for identifying core educational requirements for each discipline.[10] Accreditation organizations have the ultimate authority to decide whether a particular institution satisfies the relevant set of standards. Nevertheless,

---

[10] There are external checks and balances that place limits on the discretion of accreditation organizations.

institutions retain significant discretion in relation to interpreting established standards and designing curricula that satisfy them.

If granting a conscience-based exemption will result in a student's or resident's failure to satisfy a component of the discipline's established core requirements, a school or residency program *may* justifiably deny the exemption. However, when core curriculum requirements are not *fully* satisfied, a school or residency program might nevertheless determine that *partial* satisfaction in special cases can be *sufficient*. For example, schools or residency programs might grant exemptions to accommodate students and residents with disabilities. Similar accommodations might be made for students and residents with conscience-based objections to participating in an activity without which a core requirement will not be fully satisfied.[11] It seems appropriate for schools and residency programs at least to retain limited discretion in relation to such judgments in individual cases. Ultimately, however, the appropriate accreditation organization has the authority to determine whether a program's criterion of sufficiency is within an acceptable range.

Utilizing the respective accreditation standards, core educational requirements will be examined for medical, nursing, and pharmacy students as well as obstetrics and gynecology residents.

Medical students
The Liaison Committee on Medical Education (LCME) is the accrediting authority for medical education programs leading to the M.D. degree in the United States and Canada. Its "Functions and Structure of a Medical School: Standards for Accreditation of Medical Education Programs Leading to the M.D. Degree" (June 2008) stipulates that each medical school's curriculum "must include the contemporary content of those disciplines that have been traditionally titled anatomy, biochemistry, genetics, physiology, microbiology and immunology, pathology, pharmacology and therapeutics, and preventive medicine" (ED-11, p. 8).[12] Since learning

---

[11] It is not necessarily inconsistent for schools or residency programs to grant exemptions from a core requirement (e.g. a requirement to perform certain kinds of physical examinations) to students or residents with physical disabilities and not to grant similar exemptions to students or residents with ethical or religious objections. In the former case, students and residents may be willing to satisfy the requirement, but they are physically unable to do so. In the latter case, students and residents may be physically able to satisfy the requirement but are unwilling to do so. Accordingly, it might be claimed, it is only when students and residents request a conscience-based exemption that they fail to acknowledge its status as an essential component of professional training and practice.

[12] The LCME accreditation standards are available online at: www.lcme.org/functions2008jun.pdf; accessed July 10, 2010.

basic human anatomy is a core requirement, it would be justified to deny a student's request for a conscience-based exemption from all activities that involve observing and touching bodies and body parts or even viewing images of them. LCME standards also state that if medical schools do not require students to complete clerkships offering clinical experience in family medicine, internal medicine, obstetrics and gynecology, pediatrics, psychiatry, and surgery; they "must ensure that their students possess the knowledge and clinical abilities to enter any field of graduate medical education" (ED-15, p. 8). It would be justified, then, to deny conscience-based exemptions from activities needed to satisfy this requirement.

The American Association of Medical Colleges (AAMC) offers another set of curricular guidelines for medical students in a 1998 report entitled "Learning Objectives for Medical Student Education-Guidelines for Medical Schools" (Medical School Objectives Project 1998).[13] The report, which was produced by the AAMC Medical School Objectives Project (MSOP), includes a list of knowledge, skills, and abilities that each student must acquire and demonstrate prior to graduation, including the following:

Knowledge of/about:

- the normal structure and function of the body and of each of its major organ systems;
- the molecular, biochemical, and cellular mechanisms that are important in maintaining the body's homeostasis;
- the various causes of maladies and the ways in which they operate on the body;
- the altered structure and function (pathology and pathophysiology) of the body and its major organ systems that are seen in various diseases and conditions;
- the most frequent clinical, laboratory, roentgenologic, and pathologic manifestations of common maladies; and
- relieving pain and ameliorating the suffering of patients.

The ability to:

- obtain an accurate medical history that covers all essential aspects of the history, including issues related to age, gender, and socio-economic status;
- perform both a complete and an organ system-specific examination, including a mental status examination;

---

[13] The AAMC report is available online at: https://services.aamc.org/publications/index.cfm?fuseaction=Product.displayForm&prd_id=198&cfid=1&cftoken=32975D3D-9FEB-7545-A14A9722B4D2FFFD; accessed July 10, 2010.

- perform routine technical procedures including at a minimum venipuncture, inserting an intravenous catheter, arterial puncture, thoracentesis, lumbar puncture, inserting a nasogastric tube, inserting a foley catheter, and suturing lacerations;
- interpret the results of commonly used diagnostic procedures;
- reason deductively in solving clinical problems;
- construct appropriate management strategies (both diagnostic and therapeutic) for patients with common conditions, both acute and chronic, including medical, psychiatric, and surgical conditions, and those requiring short- and long-term rehabilitation;
- recognize patients with immediately life-threatening cardiac, pulmonary, or neurological conditions regardless of etiology, and to institute appropriate initial therapy;
- recognize and outline an initial course of management for patients with serious conditions requiring critical care; and
- communicate effectively, both orally and in writing, with patients, patients' families, colleagues, and others with whom physicians must exchange information in carrying out their responsibilities.

The stated aim of the MSOP was "to develop a consensus within the medical education community on the attributes that medical students should possess at the time of graduation, and to set forth learning objectives that can guide each medical school as it establishes objectives for its own program" (Medical School Objectives Project 1998: 13). Skeptics might question whether the listed objectives reflect a genuine consensus within the medical community, and even when there is a genuine consensus, one can still request reasons and/or challenge conclusions. Nevertheless, all accredited medical schools in the United States and Canada are members of the AAMC, which has the recognized authority to establish curricular guidelines. Moreover, none of the items included in the knowledge and skill set proposed by the MSOP appears to be arbitrary or controversial. It is therefore warranted to treat that knowledge and skill set as an authoritative basis for identifying essential components of medical education.[14] Accordingly, it would be justified to deny conscience-based exemptions

---

[14] In the UK, the General Medical Council (GMC) in a publication entitled "Tomorrow's Doctors" identifies a core set of cognitive knowledge and skills that all medical school students must acquire. The current 2003 edition remains in effect until 2011/12, when a revised 2009 edition is to be implemented. Both editions are available at: www.gmc-uk.org/education/undergraduate/tomorrows_doctors.asp; accessed July 10, 2010. A GMC Education Committee Position Statement entitled "Core Education Outcomes" explains that this core set of cognitive knowledge and skills is to be understood as an exceptionless constraint on conscience-based exemptions that may be granted to medical students: "*Tomorrow's Doctors* lists the knowledge, skills, attitudes and behaviour that must

from activities required to satisfy MSOP knowledge and skill set objectives. For example, it would be justified to deny a conscience-based exemption to a student who refuses to perform the specified "routine technical procedures" and acquire the corresponding skills.

Both the LCME standards and the AAMC curricular guidelines provide a basis for denying a conscience-based exemption to a student who refuses to participate in any activities that involve observing and touching bodies and body parts or even viewing images of them. But, what about more realistic cases in which a student refuses only to touch cadavers or perform examinations on members of the opposite sex?[15] The answer in both cases requires a determination of the extent to which the refusal at issue will result in a student's failure to satisfy established curricular standards. For example, if required knowledge and skills are usually acquired from dissecting human cadavers and there are no effective alternative means for students to satisfy those requirements, established curricular standards would support denying an exemption to students with conscience-based objections to dissecting human cadavers. Similarly, if required knowledge and skills are usually acquired from examining members of the opposite sex, and if there are no effective alternative means for students to satisfy those requirements, established curricular standards would support denying an exemption.[16]

Neither the LCME nor the AAMC standards provide a basis for denying conscience-based exemptions from participating in abortions. However, when determining whether granting a conscience-based exemption is compatible with established curricular standards, it can be important to distinguish between two kinds of exemptions: (a) exemptions from observing or assisting in the provision of a health service, and (b) exemptions from learning about indications, contraindications, benefits, risks, complications, and so forth. Even if it is compatible with established curricular standards to grant students exemptions from *observing* or *participating* in the provision of a service that violates their ethical or religious beliefs, to satisfy those standards it may still be necessary for students to *understand* relevant basic

be demonstrated in order to graduate with a medical degree. There is no provision to avoid any of these requirements." The Position Statement is available online at: www.gmc-uk.org/Core_Education_Outcomes_1.0.pdf_25396917.pdf; accessed July 10, 2010.

[15] Some Muslim students in the UK reportedly have refused to treat patients of the opposite sex. See Daniel Foggo and Abul Taher, "Muslim Medical Students Get Picky," *Times Online*, October 7, 2007. Available at: www.timesonline.co.uk/tol/news/uk/health/article2603966.ece; accessed July 10, 2010.

[16] Non-discrimination might provide another basis for denying requests for conscience-based exemptions from performing physical examinations on members or the opposite sex. I consider this reason below.

science and clinical information.[17] Such cognitive knowledge is essential for identifying the appropriate standard of care and is needed to inform, counsel, and refer patients. Moreover, it is required for proper follow-up care, treatment of complications, and so forth. In relation to abortion, a medical school curriculum committee might interpret established standards to require an understanding of the relevant basic science, clinical indications, methods, complications, and post-abortion care. This appears to be a reasonable interpretation of established curricular standards and therefore does not exceed a school's legitimate interpretive discretion. Accordingly, a medical school might justifiably deny conscience-based exemptions from activities designed to achieve the specified cognitive goals related to abortion.

Generally, it is warranted to deny conscience-based exemptions from course or clerkship requirements that aim to increase cognitive knowledge and understanding and do not require students to perform actions (excluding reading and attending lectures and seminars) that violate their ethical or religious beliefs. Without such cognitive knowledge conditions cannot be properly diagnosed and the appropriate standard of care cannot be identified. For example, some Muslim students in the United Kingdom reportedly have refused to learn about alcohol-related or sexually transmitted diseases because it offends their religious beliefs.[18] Without such knowledge, however, they will not be able to perform satisfactory differential diagnoses because they will not recognize the specific symptoms of alcohol-related or sexually transmitted diseases. In addition, without comprehensive cognitive knowledge and understanding, students and practitioners may not be able to accurately determine which, if any, services and medications are incompatible with their ethical or religious beliefs. For example, without an understanding of the mechanisms of Plan B, no informed decision can

---

[17] As noted above, this position is endorsed by the AMA (H-295.896, "Conscience Clause: Final Report"). It is reiterated in an AMA policy entitled "Medical Student Education on Termination of Pregnancy Issues:"

The AMA encourages education on termination of pregnancy issues so that medical students receive a satisfactory knowledge of the medical, ethical, legal and psychological principles associated with termination of pregnancy, although observation of, attendance at, or any direct or indirect participation in an abortion should not be required. (H-295.911)

The University of Manitoba Faculty of Medicine Conscientious Objection Policy includes a similar provision: "An objection to participate in any service or delivery of care does not exempt the student from the responsibility to learn about its indications, contraindications, benefits, and risks. A student will not be exempted to demonstrate this knowledge on any examination." The policy is available online at: www.medicine.usask.ca/education/undergrad/curriculum_committee/cc_phaseAD/minutes/U%20of%20M%20Conscientious%20Obj.pdf; accessed July 10, 2010.

[18] Foggo and Taher n 15 above.

be made about whether a conscience-based objection to abortifacients applies to it.

Nursing students

Most baccalaureate nursing programs are accredited by the Commission on Collegiate Nursing Education (CCNE), based on "The Essentials of Baccalaureate Education for Professional Nursing Practice" (2008) developed by the American Association of Colleges of Nursing (AACN).[19] As described on the AACN website, it offers "a comprehensive set of core standards for baccalaureate-degree nursing education programs."[20] It provides an authoritative basis for determining whether conscience-based exemptions are incompatible with general core educational requirements for baccalaureate programs. The last of the nine Essentials, "Baccalaureate Generalist Nursing Practice," provides a comprehensive list of "practice focused outcomes that integrate the knowledge, skills, and attitudes delineated in Essentials I-VIII into the nursing care of individuals, families, groups, communities, and populations in a variety of settings" (p. 29). Accordingly, Essential IX provides the primary basis for determining whether conscience-based exemptions are incompatible with CCNE standards.

Two common areas in which practicing nurses have sought conscience-based exemptions are abortion and contraception. None of the 22 practice-focused outcomes listed in Essential IX specifically addresses either. The emphasis is on general skills and competencies rather than specific content areas or services, and individual schools have considerable discretion in designing curricula that satisfy CCNE standards. Essential IX does include a 34-item "Sample Content," but neither abortion nor family planning is included. The section on "Expectations for Clinical Experiences within the Baccalaureate Program" calls for a broad range of clinical experience in a variety of settings, but it does not identify specific procedures or services. Accordingly, a school could not plausibly cite Essential IX to justify denying students' requests for conscience-based exemptions from activities related to abortion or family planning.

One of the practice-focused outcomes identified in Essential IX is an ability to "[r]ecognize the relationship of genetics and genomics to health, prevention, screening, diagnostics, prognostics, selection of treatment, and monitoring of treatment effectiveness … " (p. 31). Courses designed to

[19] Available online at: www.aacn.nche.edu/Education/bacessn.htm; accessed July 11, 2010.
[20] www.aacn.nche.edu/Education/bacessn.htm; accessed July 11, 2010.

satisfy this outcome might occasion requests for conscience-based exemptions. For example, a nursing school might include within its required curriculum a course that includes units on pre-implantation and prenatal genetic screening. If students request a conscience-based exemption, may the school justifiably cite as a reason for denying their requests that granting them is incompatible with the CCNE's conception of core education requirements? To determine the answer to this question, it will be helpful first to recall an observation offered in relation to medical students that applies as well to nursing students: Generally, it is warranted to deny conscience-based exemptions from course or clerkship requirements that aim to increase cognitive knowledge and understanding and do not require students to perform actions (excluding reading and attending lectures and seminars) that violate their ethical or religious beliefs. Hence, as long as cognitive requirements are reasonably related to a practice-focused outcome endorsed by the CCNE, its core curriculum standards provide a basis for denying requests for conscience-based exemptions from those cognitive requirements. However, since the relevant CCNE outcome is *cognitive* (an ability to *recognize*), it cannot justify denying requests for exemptions from participating in activities related to pre-implantation or prenatal genetic screening, such as assisting in the procedures or counseling.

Another Essential IX practice-focused outcome that might occasion requests for conscience-based exemptions is an ability to "[i]mplement patient and family care around resolution of end of life and palliative care issues, such as symptom management, support of rituals, and respect for patient and family preferences" (p. 31). This practice-focused outcome appears to provide an unambiguous basis for denying requests for exemptions by students who have ethical or religious objections to learning the fundamentals of palliative care and the management of dying patients. It is noteworthy that unlike the outcome standard related to genetics and genomics, this outcome standard does not appear to be limited to cognitive abilities. Accordingly, this CCNE practice-focused outcome may also provide a reason for denying requests for exemptions from participating in end of life care.[21]

Pharmacy students

The Accreditation Council for Pharmacy Education (ACPE) is the accreditation agency for US professional degree programs in pharmacy.

---

[21] There is considerable institutional variability in the end-of-life activities in which nursing students participate. Accordingly, whether or not participation in end-of-life care is required may depend in part on a school's "local core curriculum," the subject of a subsequent section.

Its "Accreditation Standards and Guidelines for the Professional Program in Pharmacy Leading to the Doctor of Pharmacy Degree" (2006) provides authoritative core curriculum standards for schools of pharmacy.[22] Accordingly, it is generally justified to deny conscience-based exemptions from activities that are essential to satisfying those requirements.

The primary focus of conscientious objection by practicing pharmacists has been contraceptives.[23] Some have refused to dispense all contraceptives and others have refused to dispense certain types of contraceptives, especially EC. A key question in relation to pharmacy students, then, is whether core educational requirements provide a basis for refusing requests for conscience-based exemptions from educational activities associated with contraceptives.

The ACPE provides separate standards for course work and practice experiences. Standard 13 lists a set of core competencies that are to be acquired by course work. It identifies biomedical sciences, pharmaceutical sciences, social/behavioral/administrative sciences, and clinical sciences as the "scientific foundation necessary for achievement of the professional competencies" (p. 20). Although there is no specific requirement that students learn scientific and clinical facts about contraceptives (e.g. benefits and risks, contraindications, side-effects, and interactions with other medications), there are several general standards that appear to support such a requirement. One is Standard 9, which addresses curriculum goals: "The college or school's professional degree program curriculum must prepare graduates with the professional competencies to enter pharmacy practice in any setting to ensure optimal medication therapy outcomes and patient safety . . . " (p. 15). Another is found in Standard 12, which requires students to develop an ability to "[p]rovide patient care . . . based upon sound therapeutic principles and evidence-based data, taking into account . . . emerging technologies, and evolving biomedical, pharmaceutical, . . . and clinical sciences that may impact therapeutic outcomes" (p. 18). The same standard (Guideline 12.1) requires pharmacy schools to ensure that graduates "are competent to . . . *provide patient-centered care,* through the ability

---

[22] The ACPE accreditation standards are available online at: www.acpe-accredit.org/pdf/ ACPE_Revised_PharmD_Standards_Adopted_Jan152006.pdf; accessed July 11, 2010.

[23] Pharmacists in Oregon and Washington, states in which statutes authorize pharmacists to fill prescriptions for "medication to end life" (typically barbiturates) have refused to dispense it. Since barbiturates have other potential uses (e.g. for anesthesia and treatment of anxiety, insomnia, and convulsions), it is essential for all pharmacists to learn the relevant scientific and clinical facts. Without such knowledge, a pharmacist would not be able to distinguish between lethal and non-lethal dosages, understand possible side-effects, and so forth.

to ... design, implement, monitor, evaluate, and adjust pharmacy care plans that are patient-specific ... and are evidence-based" (pp. 18–19).

These standards suggest two reasons for requiring *all* students, including those with conscience-based objections, at least to learn basic scientific and clinical facts about contraceptives: First, contraceptives appear to fall within the scope of general requirements to acquire pharmacy-related knowledge and competencies. Second, even if a student will only work in pharmacies that grant a conscience-based exemption from dispensing contraceptives, patients seeking to have prescriptions filled for other medications may be taking contraceptives. In such cases, a pharmacist may need knowledge about contraceptives to fulfill the responsibilities identified in the cited ACPE standards. For example, knowledge about contraindications and drug interactions may be necessary to "ensure optimal medication therapy outcomes and patient safety" (Standard 9, p. 15). An additional reason for requiring all students to learn basic scientific and clinical facts about contraceptives is not directly related to ACPE standards: Without an accurate understanding of the mechanisms of various contraceptive medications and devices, students will not be able to make an informed determination about which, if any, are contrary to their ethical and religious beliefs.

A study of College of Pharmacy students at the University of Arkansas for Medical Sciences suggests that there is actual cause for concern in relation to students' knowledge about contraceptives (Ragland and West 2009). The following are among the study's reported findings: Thirty-four percent of all students who responded believed falsely that EC works by disrupting a newly implanted ovum, and 32% indicated they did not know its pharmacological mechanism. Thirty-five percent mistakenly identified Plan B as the abortifacient RU-486 (mifepristone), and only 26.7% affirmed that they were competent to instruct patients concerning the proper use of EC. As one might expect, generally fourth-year students were more knowledgeable than third-year students, third-year students were more knowledgeable than second-year students, and second-year students were more knowledgeable than first-year students. For example, the percentage of first-, second-, third-, and fourth-year students, who knew that EC does not work by disrupting a newly implanted ovum was 31.2%, 46.3%, 45.1%, and 62.5% respectively. Nevertheless, it is hardly reassuring that only 62.5% of fourth-year student respondents rejected this false belief about EC and a substantial number of them did not feel competent to provide patients with information about EC. Indeed, the study's authors report that in response to the study, the curriculum was revised to include more educational material about EC.[24] It is noteworthy that 29.9% of the students expressed being uncomfortable dispensing EC for moral or religious reasons. The study does not provide data to determine the percentage of these students who did not understand the pharmacological mechanism of EC.[25]

Practice experience requirements are the subject of Standard 14, which begins with the following general statement:

The college or school must provide a continuum of required and elective pharmacy practice experiences throughout the curriculum, from introductory to advanced, of adequate scope, intensity, and duration to support the achievement of the professional competencies presented in Standard 12. The pharmacy practice experiences must integrate, apply, reinforce, and advance the knowledge, skills, attitudes, and values developed through the other components of the curriculum. (p. 21)

Standard 14 also requires that students receive practice experiences in each of the following settings: community pharmacy, hospital or health-system pharmacy, ambulatory care, inpatient/acute care general medicine. Accordingly, students might be assigned to a setting in which abortifacients, EC, and/or other contraceptives are dispensed. It is doubtful that ACPE standards provide a justification for refusing to grant conscience-based exemptions from assisting in dispensing such medications. Indeed, Guideline 14.2 appears to recommend accommodation, albeit not specifically to conscience-based refusals: "When assigning students to preceptors and practice sites, the college or school should strive to avoid circumstances or relationships that could adversely affect the student/teacher relationship and the desired outcomes" (ibid.). Although ACPE standards alone may not provide a basis for denying exemptions to students with conscience-based objections to assisting in dispensing abortifacients, EC, and/or other contraceptives, granting them is contingent on being able to find suitable locations for students that will enable them to satisfy practice experience requirements.

---

[24] As noted in Chapter 3, studies suggest that many practicing pharmacists also are misinformed about EC.

[25] These results are consistent with the reported findings of an earlier study of pharmacy students. See (Evans, Patel and Stranton 2007: 711–16). One section of the survey included several statements that students were asked to identify as either true or false. Of the 752 students from 18 schools of pharmacy who completed the survey, 32% and 25%, respectively, did not correctly identify the following statements as false: (1) "Oral emergency contraception is also known as RU-486." (2) "Oral emergency contraceptives interrupt an established pregnancy."

Obstetrics and gynecology residents

The Accreditation Council for Graduate Medical Education (ACGME) is responsible for the accreditation of all US residency programs. Its "Program Requirements for Graduate Medical Education in Obstetrics and Gynecology" (2008) provides authoritative core curriculum standards for obstetrics and gynecology residents. Accordingly, it is generally justified to deny conscience-based exemptions from activities that are essential to satisfying those requirements.

Abortion training is undoubtedly the primary focal point of conscientious objection in relation to obstetrics and gynecology residents. As the following two sentences indicate, the status of abortion training in ACGME Program Requirements is mixed: "No program or resident with a religious or moral objection shall be required to provide training in or to perform induced abortions. Otherwise, access to experience with induced abortion must be part of residency education" (IV-A-2-d, p. 15).[26] The second sentence suggests that abortion training is a component of a core obstetrics

---

[26] Despite the ACGME requirement that unless a residency program or a resident has an ethical or religious objection, "access to experience with induced abortion must be part of residency education," a significant percentage of obstetrics and gynecology residency programs did not provide routine abortion training to residents several years after the requirement first took effect in 1996. A study of obstetrics and gynecology residency programs in 2004 reported the following results: 51% provided routine abortion training (i.e. required with an opportunity to opt out); 39% offered optional abortion training; and 10% offered no abortion training. See (Eastwood *et al.* 2006: 303–8). The same study offered comparisons with prior years. For 1998, it reported the following results: 31% of obstetrics and gynecology residency programs provided routine abortion training; 23% offered optional abortion training; and 44% offered no abortion training. However, this comparison is misleading. For the 2004 study, questionnaires were sent to residency program directors and the response rate – after three requests – was 73%. The authors of the 1998 study also contacted many programs several times to increase the response rate. See (Almeling, Tews and Dudley 2000: 268–71, 320). The authors noted that programs that responded to the first request reported higher rates of routine abortion training than programs that had to be contacted two or more times. Accordingly, the authors of the 1998 study calculated results twice, using alternative assumptions about non-responding programs: (a) they were similar to responding programs; and (b) none offered abortion training. When the authors of the 2004 study compared their results with the results of the 1998 study, they used the data based on the assumption that non-responding programs did not offer abortion training. The 1998 study reported the following results with the assumption that non-responding programs were similar to responding programs: 46% of obstetrics and gynecology residency programs provided routine abortion training; 34% offered optional abortion training; and 19% offered no abortion training. The authors of the 2004 study calculated that if non-responding programs did not offer abortion training, 34% (not 10%) of programs would not offer any abortion training. They do not provide a similar calculation for the other two categories (routine and optional abortion training). Accordingly, the appropriate comparisons between the percentage of obstetrics and gynecology residency programs that did not offer abortion training in 1998 and 2004 are either: (a) 19% in 1998 and 10% in 2004; or (b) 44% in 1998 and 34% in 2004. Hence, the decrease in the percentage of residency programs that do not offer abortion training is significantly less than the authors of the 2004 study suggest.

and gynecology residency curriculum.[27] However, the first sentence unequivocally states that residents with conscience-based objections cannot be required to perform induced abortion. Hence ACGME accreditation standards incorporate into core curriculum requirements an exemption for any resident who has a conscience-based objection to performing induced abortions. Clearly, then, those standards cannot justify denying a resident's request for a conscience-based exemption from performing induced abortions.

Although ACGME program requirements exempt residents with ethical or religious objections from *performing* induced abortions, *all residents* are required to receive training in managing abortion-related *complications*: "Experience with management of complications of abortion must be provided to all residents" (IV-A-2-d, p. 15).[28] Hence, according to current ACGME standards, conscience-based exemptions justifiably may be denied if residents refuse to receive such training.

The ACGME program requirements list "genetics, including experience with genetic amniocentesis and patient counseling" as one of the core competencies related to patient care (IV-A-5-a-2-a-ii, p.16). Some patients, when informed of amniocentesis results, will decide to have an abortion. Accordingly, although ACGME program requirements do not provide a basis for denying residents' conscience-based objections to performing induced abortions, they do provide a basis for denying conscience-based exemptions from training related to a genetic test that can occasion abortion decisions. Current ACGME program requirements also provide grounds for denying exemptions to training for amniocentesis counseling.

Another potential focal point of conscientious objection within obstetrics and gynecology residency programs is family planning. The ACGME program requirements list "clinical skills in family planning" as one of the core competencies related to patient care (IV-A-5-a-2-b-vii, p.18). Family planning is also among the core competencies related to medical knowledge:

[Residents] will have a structured didactic and clinical educational experience in all methods of family planning that is provided or coordinated by the program. Topics must include all reversible methods of contraception, including natural methods, as well as sterilization. This must include experience in management of complications

---

[27] The ACGME program requirements also state that if institutional policies prevent residents from performing abortions within the home institution, the residency program "must not impede residents . . . who do not have religious or moral objections from receiving education and experience in performing abortions at another institution . . . " (IV-A-2-d, p. 15).

[28] In deference to institutional policies that do not permit performing induced abortions, residency programs are not required to provide this experience at the home institution.

as well as training in the performance of these procedures. This education can be provided outside the institution, in an appropriate facility, under the supervision of appropriately educated faculty. (IV-A-5-b-2, p.21)

Accordingly, current ACGME program requirements can justify denying residents' requests for conscience-based exemptions from family planning training.

Since assisted reproduction is contrary to some religious doctrines, it might occasion conscience-based objections. However, the ACGME list of program requirements includes "reproductive endocrinology and infertility" among the core competencies related to patient care (IV-A-5-a-2-b-vi, p.18). Therefore, those requirements justify denying conscience-based exemptions from training related to assisted reproduction.

Local core curricula

Established core educational requirements serve as general minimal standards. Accordingly, it generally is justified to deny conscience-based exemptions from satisfying core educational requirements. Schools and residency programs have limited discretion to grant exemptions from activities that are needed to *fully* satisfy core requirements. They also can *add* requirements to create a "local" core curriculum that is more extensive than the established core. Additional local requirements can be based on the judgment that certain areas not included within the established core should nevertheless be part of each student's or resident's medical education. For example, a curriculum committee might decide to require all students to complete an extensive scholarly research project. This decision might stem from a belief that, despite its exclusion from the established core, an ability to conduct scholarly research is properly part of a core curriculum. Alternatively, it might reflect only a commitment to a curricular profile for that school. For example, a particular school might aim to distinguish itself for its commitment to training clinician-scientists with an ability to conduct scholarly research. Decisions to add curricular requirements beyond established core requirements also can be based on a school's social mission. For example, a medical or nursing school in a mostly rural state might require all students to receive instruction oriented to practicing in rural areas. This requirement might be based on the goal of producing graduates who will have specialized training to enable them to better serve rural populations.

Requirements that students complete an extensive scholarly research project or receive instruction that will enable them to better serve rural populations are hardly controversial. As long as the school's particular profile is clearly communicated to prospective applicants, anyone who is not interested in the distinctive areas of a school's local core curriculum can apply to schools that do not have these additional core requirements. Conversely, schools with distinctive local core curricula are likely to attract applicants with corresponding interests. For example, a school with a local core requirement that all students complete an extensive scholarly research project is likely to attract applicants with corresponding interests.

It might be objected that since financial considerations can limit applicants to their own state's public professional school(s), a resident of a state in which all public professional schools of medicine, nursing, or pharmacy have curricular requirements beyond the established core would have no real options. However, even if some applicants are left little, if any, choice, as long as the curricular requirements are not arbitrary and are reasonably related to a legitimate objective, such as maintaining rural residents' access to important health services, generally it is ethically acceptable for professional schools to add local requirements to the established core.

Although students may want to opt out of research and rural training requirements for a variety of reasons, such requirements are unlikely to occasion requests for conscience-based exemptions. By contrast, a local family planning instruction requirement may well occasion conscience-based refusals by students and residents. As in the case of a research requirement, this requirement might derive from a local conception of a core education. Alternatively, it might derive from an institution's or a program's social mission. For example, the family planning instruction requirement might be based on the goal of sustaining patient access to family planning services.

May a medical or nursing school or an obstetrics and gynecology residency program with a family planning instruction requirement justifiably deny exemptions to students or residents with conscience-based objections to family planning? Recalling a distinction introduced earlier, there are two types of requirements in relation to family planning instruction: (1) a requirement to learn about the various options, their relative effectiveness, and their respective benefits and risks, and (2) a requirement to provide or assist in providing information and contraceptives to patients. Insofar as it is generally justified to refuse to exempt students from cognitive requirements, a school may justifiably refuse to grant conscience-based exemptions from the first set of requirements. However, it remains to consider whether a local requirement to *participate* in family planning activities can justify denying students an exemption from participating in those activities.

It might be argued that the reason for objecting to a local requirement does not matter. Suppose students and residents are unwilling to receive instruction in rural medicine or family planning because they have no interest in practicing in a field in which the corresponding skills would be relevant. If schools and residency programs may justifiably refuse to exempt such unwilling students and residents from a requirement to receive instruction in rural medicine or family planning, why may they not also justifiably refuse to exempt students and residents whose unwillingness is conscience-based?

One obvious answer is that, for the reasons previously identified, conscience-based refusals merit special consideration. But does this special consideration preclude justifiably denying conscience-based exemptions from local requirements that are reasonably related to a legitimate objective? Suppose school S_1 and residency program R_1 clearly communicate to applicants the expectation that all students/residents must satisfy a requirement to receive family planning instruction. S_1 and R_1 also explain the basis for this requirement: a commitment to provide instruction that will contribute to maintaining a sufficient supply of practitioners to meet the demand for this crucial health service. Ms. A wants to attend S_1 and Mr. B wants to attend R_1, but both are unwilling to receive family planning instruction due to their religious beliefs. There are two other schools, S_2 and S_3, comparable to S_1 that have admitted Ms. A and two other residency programs, R_2 and R_3, comparable to R_1 that have admitted Mr. B. Under these conditions, Ms. A and Mr. B would not be faced with a decision between pursuing a career in the health profession of their choice and the dictates of their consciences. Consequently, it could not be asserted that if S_1 and R_1 do not exempt Ms. A and Mr. B from their family planning requirements, Ms. A and Mr. B would be forced to choose between the dictates of their conscience and a career in their preferred professions. At most, it might be said that as a result of the policies of S_1 and R_1, Ms. A and Mr. B are presented with a choice between attending S_1/R_1 and violating their religious beliefs or attending S_2/R_2 or S_3/R_3 and not violating them.

In the real world, however, applicants' choices can be limited by financial and other factors, such as test scores, grades, recommendations, income, and family circumstances. Moreover, S_1 and R_1 may be able to satisfy their commitment to producing health professionals who can provide family planning services without requiring *all* students or residents to receive such instruction. Thus, some flexibility may be warranted. For example, S_1 and R_1 might communicate to applicants that exemptions to their family planning instruction requirement can be granted – but only at the school's/program's discretion and only in special circumstances. Applicants might be invited to submit in writing reasons why they should be granted an exemption, and some or all might be invited for a follow-up personal interview. Alternatively, applicants might be asked to present their reasons in person. No one has a right to attend medical, nursing, or pharmacy school, or to become an obstetrics and gynecology resident, let alone to be accepted by a particular school or residency program. Nevertheless, in view of the reasons for accommodating conscience-based objections, it would be regrettable if admissions committees did not at least make a reasonable effort to avoid placing otherwise qualified applicants in a situation of having to choose between the dictates of their conscience and a career in the health profession of their choice. Ultimately, however, it is within the discretion of S_I and R_I to decide on the basis of their missions to deny exemptions to their family planning instruction requirement.[29]

A school of medicine or nursing or an obstetrics and gynecology residency program that has as part of its mission producing professionals who will sustain women's access to abortion might cite that mission in an attempt to justify requiring all students or residents to receive abortion training.[30] However, there are several reasons to treat abortion as a special case and for all obstetrics and gynecology residency programs and schools of medicine and nursing, notwithstanding their specific missions, to grant

---

[29] This conclusion is consistent with the position of the AMA: "Medical schools should be free to develop their own policies related to what activities come under a 'conscience clause,' and how students should go about gaining an exemption from the specified activities" (CME Report 9 (I-98), "Conscience Clause: Final Report").

[30] Concern about access to abortion is not purely academic. One study reports a consistent decrease in the number of abortion facilities between 1992 and 2005. See (Jones *et al.* 2008: 6–16). In 2005 a total of 1,787 facilities provided abortions, a decline of 2% since 2000. Between 1996 and 2000, there was a decline of 11%, and between the years of 1992 and 1996, the decline was 14%. The study reported a dramatic disparity in the distribution of abortion facilities among counties. Whereas 31% of counties in metropolitan areas had at least one abortion facility, only 3% of non-metropolitan counties had at least one abortion facility. Twenty-four percent of women residing in metropolitan areas lacked an abortion facility in their county and 92% of women living in non-metropolitan areas lacked an abortion facility in their county. In 2002, New York City implemented a policy that requires all obstetrics and gynecology residents who receive training in any of the city's public hospitals to receive abortion training unless they have a moral or religious objection. A *Chicago Tribune* article describing the policy offered the following rationale:

The move comes as the number of physicians performing abortions is in a two-decade decline nationwide, due in large part to retirement and pressure from anti-abortion forces. "'Physicians are getting older, they are retiring, and new physicians coming in are not training in these procedures as much as they once did,' said Dr. Van Dunn, senior vice president for medical and professional affairs for New York City's 11 public hospitals. We identify a need to make sure that there continues to be doctors in the pipeline'." (Osnos, 2002: p. 1)

exemptions to residents and students with conscience-based objections to performing and/ or assisting in performing abortions.

Two reasons apply specifically to US obstetrics and gynecology residency programs. First, as indicated previously in the context of examining core educational requirements for obstetrics and gynecology residents, the ACGME accreditation standards explicitly prohibit requiring induced abortion training for residents with ethical or religious objections. Those standards also explicitly state that residency programs with ethical or religious objections may not be required to provide abortion training. Second, the Coats Amendment (42 U.S.C. § 238n) offers special legal abortion-related protections to residents and residency programs in the United States. Specifically, it prohibits the federal government as well as state and local governments that receive federal funds from discriminating against individuals who attend or attended a postgraduate physician training program that "does not (or did not) perform induced abortions or require, provide or refer for training in the performance of induced abortions, or make arrangements for the provision of such training" (42 U.S.C. § 238n(a)(3)). It also requires the federal government as well as states and local governments to treat as accredited any postgraduate physician training program that was denied accreditation solely because it failed to satisfy an accreditation standard that mandates providing abortions or requiring, providing, or facilitating access to abortion training. Although the Coats Amendment does not explicitly prohibit residency programs from requiring abortion training, it clearly establishes that refusing to receive or provide abortion training enjoys special legal protection under US federal law.

Another section of the Coats Amendment is not limited to postgraduate physician training programs. It prohibits the federal government as well as state and local governments that receive federal funds from discriminating against any "participant in a program of training in the health professions" who refuses abortion training (42 U.S.C. § 238n(c)(2)). Although this section of the Coats Amendment does not explicitly prohibit residency programs and schools of medicine and nursing from requiring abortion training, it clearly establishes that refusing abortion training receives special legal protection under US federal law.

A second US federal law, the Church Amendment (42 U.S.C. 300a-7), provides special legal protections to applicants to obstetrics and gynecology residency programs and schools of medicine and nursing who have conscience-based objections to participating in abortions. A section of the Church Amendment states that no "entity" that receives certain federal funds:

may deny admission or otherwise discriminate against any applicant . . . because of the applicant's reluctance, or willingness, to counsel, suggest, recommend, assist, or in any way participate in the performance of abortions or sterilizations contrary to or consistent with the applicant's religious beliefs or moral convictions. (42 U.S.C. 300a-7(e))

Schools of medicine and nursing as well as obstetrics and gynecology residency programs are included within the scope of this provision. It applies directly only to admissions policies and prohibits schools and residency programs from considering an applicant's willingness to participate in performing abortions. It does not directly prohibit schools and residency programs from requiring admitted students or residents to perform and/or participate in performing abortions.[31] Arguably, however, it does prohibit discouraging individuals who have conscience-based objections to abortion from applying. The primary means to achieve the goal of discouraging such applicants would be to communicate to them that all students or residents will be required to receive abortion training. Accordingly, to comply with the law and minimize the risk of legal challenges, schools and residency programs might not disclose their abortion training requirement to prospective applicants. However, applicants have a legitimate interest in receiving information that will enable them to select a school or residency program that will not confront them with a choice after enrollment between satisfying requirements and following the dictates of their conscience. Hence, even if a policy of not disclosing a requirement to receive abortion training to applicants were to satisfy the letter of the law, it would not satisfy its spirit and it would be unfair to applicants/residents who are conscientiously opposed to abortion.

There are two additional reasons to treat abortion as a special case and for all obstetrics and gynecology residency programs and schools of medicine and nursing, notwithstanding their specific missions, to grant exemptions to residents and students with conscience-based objections to performing and/or participating in performing abortions. First, as evidenced by the Coats and Church Amendments, of all legal and professionally accepted medical procedures, abortion is undoubtedly the most divisive and

---

[31] Some states directly prohibit such a requirement. For example, Massachusetts law includes the following provision:

Conscientious objection to abortion shall not be grounds for dismissal, suspension, demotion, failure to promote, discrimination in hiring, withholding of pay or refusal to grant financial assistance under any state aided project, or used in any way to the detriment of the individual in any hospital, clinic, medical, premedical, nursing, social work, or psychology school or state aided program or institution which is supported in whole or in part by the commonwealth. (M.G.L. ch.112 §121)

controversial. Moreover, disagreements about abortion reflect differences in core beliefs about moral standing, the value and meaning of human life, personhood, autonomy, and sex. Accordingly, it would seem especially important to make reasonable efforts to avoid confronting individuals with a choice between: (a) receiving education and training for a health profession, or (b) not violating their conscience-based objections to abortion.

Second, conscience-based exemptions in relation to abortion are firmly established and entrenched in law as well as practice. As a result, there may well be a legitimate expectation that exemptions will be granted for students and residents who cannot in good conscience participate in performing abortions. Since schools and residency programs routinely grant exemptions for students and residents with a conscience-based objection to participating in abortions, continuing to grant them is unlikely to increase significantly faculty and administrator burdens. Moreover, compared to less routinely granted exemptions, students and residents who do not seek to be excused from abortion-related activities are more likely to accept conscience-based exemptions for students and residents who do and also are less likely to experience associated additional work assignments as an excessive burden.

For all these reasons, then, and notwithstanding their special missions, it is appropriate for schools of medicine and nursing and obstetrics and gynecology training programs to treat conscience-based refusals to participate in abortions as a special case. However, the cumulative effect of granting conscience-based exemptions in relation to abortion training can be a legitimate overriding consideration. Accordingly, a school of medicine or nursing or obstetrics and gynecology residency program might justify denying such exemptions by citing evidence that the cumulative effect over time of granting them is likely to be an insufficient supply of practitioners to meet the demand for abortion.[32]

Non-discrimination

A prohibition of invidious discrimination is the basis of another justification for denying students' and residents' requests for conscience-based exemptions.[33] Insofar as it is wrong to discriminate on the basis of race, ethnicity,

---

[32] Unless it receives a waiver, an obstetrics and gynecology residency program with such a local requirement would run afoul of ACGME accreditation standards.

[33] See the discussion of "invidious discrimination" in Chapter 3.

national origin, age, religion, sex, sexual orientation, and gender identity, it is justified to deny students' and residents' requests for conscience-based exemptions if they have a discriminatory basis. Arguably, when requests for conscience-based exemptions are based on invidious discrimination, it is wrong to grant them.

The wrongness of invidious discrimination is recognized by accreditation standards. An LCME accreditation standard for medical schools (MS-32) specifically prohibits discrimination against medical school applicants. If applicants are protected against discrimination, it would be inconsistent to grant exemptions that enable admitted applicants to discriminate. Indeed, the LCME anti-discrimination requirement appears to apply to discrimination both against and by medical students. Standard MS-31 in Section C, "The Learning Environment," states: "In the admissions process and *throughout medical school*, there should be no discrimination on the basis of gender, sexual orientation, age, race, creed, or national origin" (emphasis added).[34] The next standard (MS-31-A), one that first took effect on July 1, 2008 states: "Medical schools must ensure that the learning environment for medical students promotes the development of explicit and appropriate professional attributes (attitudes, behaviors, and identity) in their medical students." Medical schools would fail to satisfy this standard if they were to grant conscience-based exemptions that enabled students to practice invidious discrimination. Since invidious discrimination is ethically unacceptable when physicians decide whom to accept as patients,[35] medical schools would be communicating the wrong message if they were to accommodate invidious discrimination by students.

"The Essentials of Baccalaureate Education for Professional Nursing Practice," the AACN's standards for nursing schools, also proscribes invidious discrimination. Essential VIII endorses several values. Invidious discrimination is incompatible with two of them, human dignity and social justice. The first is characterized as "respect for the inherent worth and uniqueness of individuals and populations. In professional practice, concern for human dignity is reflected when the nurse values and respects all patients and colleagues" (p. 27). Social justice is characterized as "acting in accordance with fair treatment regardless of economic status, race, ethnicity, age,

---

[34] The AMA recommended adding gender identity to the list of characteristics that constitute invidious discrimination in relation to admissions (H-295.969, "Nondiscrimination Toward Medical School and Residency Applicants").

[35] "Physicians cannot refuse to care for patients based on race, gender, sexual orientation, gender identity, or any other criteria that would constitute invidious discrimination ... " (AMA *Code of Ethics*, "Potential Patients," E-10.05 [2-b]).

citizenship, disability, or sexual orientation" (p. 28). Moreover, one of the sample content areas is "stereotypes and biases, such as gender, race, and age discrimination" (p. 29).

Similar to the LCME standards for medical schools, the Accreditation Council for Pharmacy Education includes a non-discrimination requirement in relation to the treatment of applicants and students. Guideline 16.5 states:

The college or school must establish and implement a policy on student services, including admissions and progression, that ensures nondiscrimination as defined by state and federal laws and regulations, such as on the basis of race, religion, gender, lifestyle, sexual orientation, national origin, or disability. (p. 28)

Again, if applicants and students are protected against discrimination, it would be inconsistent to grant exemptions that enable students to discriminate. Moreover, since the American Pharmacists Association *Code of Ethics for Pharmacists* explicitly prohibits discrimination,[36] pharmacy schools would be communicating the wrong message if they were to accommodate invidious discrimination by students.

The ACGME Program Requirements for Graduate Medical Education in Obstetrics and Gynecology also includes a proscription of discrimination. A competency listed in the category of "professionalism" is "sensitivity and responsiveness to a diverse patient population, including but not limited to diversity in gender, age, culture, race, religion, disabilities, and sexual orientation" (IV-A-5-e, p. 24). Clearly, invidious discrimination is incompatible with the required "sensitivity."

When attempting to determine whether invidious discrimination underlies students' and residents' conscience-based refusals to provide health care services to patients, a pertinent consideration is whether the student or resident would refuse to provide the service(s) to *any* patient in similar clinical circumstances. If the objection is only to providing the service(s) to patients with certain personal characteristics (e.g. Muslims or gays), it is warranted to suspect that the refusal is based on invidious discrimination. If objections to treating patients with infectious diseases (e.g. HIV, SARS, or Ebola) are based on an unwillingness to be exposed to health risks, the objection is not conscience-based. However, if the objection is based on the patient's actual or assumed behavior or personal characteristics (e.g. substance abuse or sexual orientation), it reflects invidious discrimination, and an exemption is unwarranted. Exemptions should also be denied if students

---

[36] Principle IV: "A pharmacist avoids discriminatory practices . . . "

or residents assert conscience-based objections to serving on teams with other students or residents, attendings, or nurses due to their race, sex, sexual orientation, and so forth.

Previously, I maintained that established curricular standards (e.g. LCME and AAMC Guidelines) can justify denying conscience-based exemptions to medical students who refuse to examine members of the opposite sex if students cannot satisfy those standards unless they perform examinations on males and females. Another possible reason for denying such an exemption to medical and nursing students is the constraint against accommodating invidious discrimination. However, a student's refusal to treat members of the opposite sex is not necessarily an instance of invidious discrimination. For example, if it is based on a general religious proscription against viewing uncovered bodies of members of the opposite sex, absent disdain, contempt, disrespect, and the like, the refusal cannot be characterized as an instance of invidious discrimination. By contrast there is invidious discrimination if a male medical student's objection to performing examinations on women is based on beliefs about the inherent inferiority and/or uncleanliness of women and/or their bodies. However, if there is a benign basis for the objection, the charge of invidious discrimination may be unwarranted. In such cases, the best response to requests for exemptions may be to attempt to strike a reasonable balance between tolerance of religious and cultural diversity and intolerance of invidious discrimination.

Impact on patients

Expected negative impact on patient well-being can provide another justification for denying students' and residents' requests for conscience-based exemptions from clinical and practice-related activities. Denying an exemption is justified if patient harm is a foreseeable result of granting it. For example, if an induced abortion is performed on an emergent basis, and a student's or resident's assistance is essential during or after the procedure, it is justified to deny a request for an exemption.[37] In non-emergent situations, it is justified to deny a student's or resident's request for an exemption if no substitute is available and it is expected that the patient will not receive standard of care if an exemption is granted.

---

[37] As noted previously, the ACGME requires all obstetrics and gynecology residents to receive "experience with management of complications of abortion" (IV-A-2-d, p. 15).

In both emergent and non-emergent situations, the timing of requests for conscience-based exemptions can be crucial. Granting unanticipated last-minute requests runs the highest risk of negatively impacting patients. By contrast, if requests for exemptions are made well in advance, more time is available to make arrangements for substitutes so that patients are not harmed if a student or resident is exempted from participating in a procedure or assisting in administering or dispensing a medication. Accordingly, a concern for patient well-being might justify denying last-minute requests for exemptions even if similar requests could have been granted without jeopardizing patient well-being if they had been presented earlier. However, when suitable substitutes are not available, an overriding concern for patient well-being can justify not granting even timely requests for conscience-based exemptions.[38]

When considering potential impact on patient care and well-being, it is appropriate to consider the cumulative impact of granting similar exemptions. For example, depending on the composition of the student body or residency program and the corresponding patient population, whereas exempting one medical or nursing student or resident from providing information about family planning may not have any negative impact on patient care, granting a similar conscience-based exemption to all students or residents might. When considering cumulative effects, unless there is reason to believe that all students or residents are likely to request a similar conscience-based exemption, it is not appropriate to ask in the abstract, "What if every student or resident were to ask for a similar exemption?"[39] Instead, a consideration of cumulative effects should be based on reasonable estimates of the actual frequency of similar requests. Requiring students and residents to present requests for exemptions when they first enter a school or program can help facilitate such estimates.[40]

Impact on substitutes and supervisors

Beyond the potential negative impact on patient well-being, conscience-based exemptions from clinical activities can have additional disruptive

---

[38] As noted above, an AMA Council on Medical Education Report explicitly endorses the priority of patient care. It includes the following statement: "Patient care should not be compromised in permitting students to be excused from participating in a given activity" (CME Report 9 (I-98) "Conscience Clause").

[39] This question can express concerns about fairness, an issue I consider in the following section.

[40] Training, clinical experience, exposure to human suffering, and the situational complexities of ethical decision-making can result in changes in a student's ethical beliefs. Accordingly, requests for exemptions made when students first enter a school or program should be treated as only preliminary indications of their future willingness to participate in educational activities.

effects that provide reasons for denying them. When medical or nursing students or residents are exempted from participating in clinical activities, other members of the health care team (e.g. students, interns, or residents) may have to fill in. Similarly, when pharmacy students are exempted from practice-related activities, others (e.g. students, interns, or employees) may be called on to act as substitutes. When replacements or substitutes are required, depending on the circumstances, there can be three reasons for not granting conscience-based exemptions from clinical and practice-related activities: (1) No suitable substitutes are available; (2) An undue burden will be placed on substitutes; and (3) The process of securing substitutes gives rise to excessive administrative burdens or inconvenience.

With respect to the first reason, and consistent with the analysis in the previous section, if providing standard of care requires substitutes, and no substitutes are available, requests for conscience-based exemptions justifiably may be denied. As the second reason suggests, when someone (e.g. another student or resident or a practitioner) has to take over the responsibilities of a student or resident who is granted a conscience-based exemption, the workload of the replacement may increase. To be sure, it may be possible to reassign responsibilities among exempted students and residents and their replacements in such a way that there are no significant changes in workloads. However, if an exemption results in a significantly decreased workload for an exempted student or resident and/or a significantly increased workload for someone else, the latter may be in a position to justifiably object that the reassignment is unfair. Although a willingness to accommodate students and residents with conscience-based objections is desirable, there are limits to what can be expected of others to facilitate such accommodations. There may be no clear line separating reasonable and excessive burdens, but wherever the line is drawn, conscience-based exemptions justifiably may be denied if granting them is expected to impose excessive burdens on other students or residents or practitioners.

To turn to the third reason, reassigning responsibilities in order to accommodate students or residents who request conscience-based exemptions from clinical or practice-related activities can increase the workload of supervisors (e.g. residents, faculty, or pharmacy managers). One means to minimize such additional burdens is to require students and residents who request conscience-based exemptions to find substitutes. However, even if students have to identify willing substitutes, supervisors still bear the ultimate responsibility for oversight and assuring that there will be no gaps in providing services to patients. Once again, there may be no clear line separating reasonable and excessive burdens, but wherever the line is drawn, conscience-based exemptions justifiably may be denied if granting them is expected to impose excessive burdens on supervisors.

When considering potential impact on substitutes and supervisors, it is appropriate to consider the cumulative impact of granting similar exemptions. Whereas granting a one-time exemption to one student or resident may not be unduly burdensome, depending on the composition of the student body or the residency program and the corresponding patient population, granting all students or residents with a conscience-based objection a standing exemption from participating in a clinical activity might be excessively burdensome.

POLICIES AND PROCEDURES

By enacting a conscience-based exemption policy and clearly communicating it to applicants as well as students or residents, schools of medicine, nursing, and pharmacy and residency programs can facilitate informed choices and consistency and minimize contention and disagreement due to ambiguity, confusion, and unrealistic expectations. In the case of medical schools, enacting such a policy also complies with AMA guidelines that state: "There should be formal written policies that govern the granting of an exemption, including the procedures to obtain an exemption and the mechanism to deal with matters of conscience that are not covered in formal policies."[41]

There are several possible options for conscience-based exemption policies. They can include a list of specific activities that qualify for conscience-based exemptions. For example, a policy might identify clinical activities related to abortion and sterilization as activities that qualify for conscience-based exemptions. Policies also might identify areas that do not qualify for exemptions, such as learning the relevant basic science and clinical facts and acquiring the knowledge needed to inform, counsel, and refer patients. Instead of listing specific activities, policies can present general substantive criteria that determine whether or not an exemption will be granted in specific cases. For example, a policy might provide a list of factors that will be considered, such as core educational requirements, non-discrimination, impact on patients, and impact on students, residents, and supervisors.

---

[41] H-295.896 Conscience Clause: Final Report. As noted previously, medical schools are allowed considerable discretion with respect to the content of conscience-based exemption policies. However, the AMA guidelines call for schools to attempt to identify activities that qualify for exemption and to describe the "mechanism by which an exemption can be obtained."

Policies can also combine both of the forgoing features, providing general guidelines as well as a non-inclusive list of activities that normally do and do not qualify for exemptions. Yet another option is to forgo both specific and general substantive criteria and provide instead a process for determining whether requests for conscience-based exemptions are granted or denied. Policies of this type might require students or residents to explain in writing requests for conscience-based exemptions and/or explain their views in person to a dean, director, or committee. The policy might also specify an appeals process. Finally, policies can provide specific and/or general substantive criteria as well as procedural rules.

It may well be impossible to anticipate all requests for conscience-based exemptions. This point is especially pertinent in a society such as the United States that is steadily becoming more and more multicultural. Hence, it may be short-sighted to formulate a policy that provides an inclusive list of activities for which conscience-based exemptions will be granted. However, a partial list may be appropriate if there are certain activities, such as assisting in performing abortions, for which exemptions will be more or less automatically granted. In the absence of any substantive guidelines, applicants who expect to request conscience-based exemptions are not given a basis for making informed choices about schools or residency programs. Disclosing data about the requests for conscience-based exemptions that a school or residency program has granted and denied in the past might provide some guidance. However, the usefulness of such data is limited in the absence of specific information about the students or residents whose requests were granted and denied. Moreover, there will be no record about conscience-based exemptions if none of a school's students or residency program's residents requested them.

Requiring students or residents to provide written and/or oral explanations provides an opportunity to determine the basis and sincerity of their objections. It also may discourage attempts to "game the system." If students or residents could automatically receive an exemption by checking a box on a form, some who do not have a conscience-based objection might be tempted to request an exemption to avoid onerous, higher risk, and/or unpleasant tasks. An in-person meeting with an opportunity to question students or residents who request conscience-based exemptions can enhance understanding of their reasons. An opportunity to engage in dialogue with students or residents also can help to determine if invidious discrimination is a factor. It is justified to deny requests for conscience-based exemptions on grounds of invidious discrimination or insincerity. However, to deny requests merely because they are deemed to be based on "unsound values" would thwart the goals of offering conscience-based exemptions.

Whether or not a policy provides specific and/or general substantive criteria, the full advantages of having a policy will be realized only if it includes procedural guidelines that describe the application and decision process. If appeals are allowed, the policy should also include a description of the appeals process. Whatever format is selected, a policy will be effective only if applicants and students or residents are familiar with it, or, at the very least, know how to access it. Optimally, the policy should be clearly posted on the school's or residency program's website.[42] It should also be available in written material (e.g. student or resident handbooks), and it should be one of the topics discussed during orientation sessions for new students and residents.

CONCLUSION

There are several reasons for granting conscience-based exemptions to students and residents. First, not granting exemptions may promote ethical insensitivity. Second, granting conscience-based exemptions can serve as a catalyst for improving the ethical environment within a school or residency program and possibly even within the profession. Third, refusing to grant conscience-based exemptions can undermine the goal of maintaining a diverse student or resident population and, thereby, present a barrier to achieving diversity in the corresponding professions. Fourth, denying students' or residents' requests for conscience-based exemptions fails to respect, and threatens to undermine, their moral autonomy and moral integrity.

There are, however, competing values and interests that need to be considered when determining whether or not to grant such exemptions. Relevant considerations include: (1) established core educational requirements, (2) local core curricula, (3) non-discrimination, (4) impact on patients, and (5) impact on students, residents, and supervisors.

---

[42] Despite the reported significance to prospective residents of information posted on obstetrics and gynecology residency program websites, a study found that few such websites provide information about abortion training. See (Foster, Jackson and Martin 2008: 99–105). The study reported that of 246 websites surveyed, only 17.5% provided any information about abortion training, and many fewer (6.9%) included information about their abortion training policies. Among the websites included in the study, abortion training was identified as "routine" (opt-out) at 14.6%, "elective" (opt-in) at 1.6%, and not offered at 1.2%.

By enacting a conscience-based exemption policy and clearly communicating it to applicants as well as students and residents, schools of medicine, nursing, and pharmacy and obstetrics and gynecology residency programs can facilitate informed choices and consistency and minimize contention and disagreement due to ambiguity, confusion, and unrealistic expectations.

CHAPTER 6

Conscience clauses: too much and too little protection

Legal rules and regulations that protect the exercise of conscience are referred to as "conscience clauses."[1] The first US federal health care conscience clause, the Church Amendment (42 U.S.C. § 300a-7(a–b)), was enacted in 1973. It protects conscience-based refusals related to abortion and sterilization. Subsequently, numerous federal and state laws and regulations have been enacted that protect the exercise of conscience by health care professionals. At the federal level, sections were added to the Church Amendment, significantly expanding its scope. One additional section (42 U.S.C. § 300a-7(c)) prohibits discrimination against a practitioner for refusing to perform or assist in the performance of "any lawful health service or research activity on the grounds that his performance or assistance in the performance of such service or activity would be contrary to his religious beliefs or moral convictions . . ."[2] Another added section (42 U.S.C. § 300a-7(d)) states:

No individual shall be required to perform or assist in the performance of any part of a health service program or research activity funded in whole or in part under a program administered by the Secretary of Health and Human Services if his performance or assistance in the performance of such part of such program or activity would be contrary to his religious beliefs or moral convictions.[3]

---

[1] As noted in Chapter 1, although conscience clauses protect the exercise of conscience, their protection generally is not limited to refusals based on core moral beliefs. Instead, they often are broader in scope and protect refusals that are based on ethical or religious beliefs.
[2] The prohibition against discrimination applies only to an "entity" that receives grants or contracts "for biomedical or behavioral research under any program administered by the Secretary of Health and Human Services." The original Church Amendment stated only that the receipt of certain government funds "does not authorize any court or any public official or other public authority" to require a practitioner to perform or assist in the performance of abortions or sterilizations. Another provision in the added section goes further by prohibiting "entities" that receive certain government funds from discriminating against providers who refuse to provide or assist in providing abortions or sterilizations.
[3] The last of the three added sections (42 U.S.C. § 300a-7(e)) states that no "entity" that receives funds under designated federal programs "may deny admission or otherwise discriminate against any applicant (including applicants for internships and residencies) for training or study . . ."

Additional federal legislation includes the Coats Amendment (42 U.S.C. §
238n) and the Weldon Amendment (121 Stat. 1844, 2209). The Coats
Amendment prohibits the federal government as well as state and local
governments that receive federal funds from discriminating against: (1)
postgraduate physician training programs that refuse to provide abortions
or require, provide, or facilitate access to abortion training, and (2) trainees
who refuse to acquire abortion training or provide abortions.[4] It also
requires the federal government as well as states and local governments to
treat as accredited any postgraduate physician training program that failed
to receive accreditation solely because it did not satisfy an accreditation
standard that mandates providing abortions or requiring, providing, or
facilitating access to abortion training.

The Weldon Amendment was first adopted as part of the 2005
Consolidated Appropriations Act, Public Law 108–447 (Dec. 8, 2004)
and has been adopted in some form each subsequent year through 2008.[5]
It places restrictions on the use of funds allocated in the Appropriations Act
in which it is included. Specifically, it states that none of the relevant funds:

> may be made available to a Federal agency or program, or to a State or local
> government, if such agency, program, or government subjects any institutional or
> individual health care entity to discrimination on the basis that the health care
> entity does not provide, pay for, provide coverage of, or refer for abortions.

In December 2008, the Department of Health and Human Services (HHS)
issued the Final Rule referred to in Chapter 2 entitled "Ensuring that
Department of Health and Human Services Funds Do Not Support
Coercive or Discriminatory Policies or Practices in Violation of Federal
Law" (45 CFR § 88).[6] As explained there, the HHS Final Rule provided
broad and comprehensive protection for practitioners and institutions that
refuse to provide a health service. HHS claimed that the Final Rule
systematized several previous statutory provisions, collectively designated

---

[4] The Coats Amendment was introduced after the Accreditation Council for Graduate Medical
Education (ACGME) adopted new accreditation rules for obstetrics-gynecology residency programs
that went into effect January 1, 1996. See (Foster, Van Dis and Steinauer 2003: 1777–8). The rules
required such programs to provide abortion training or access to it – either on-site or at another
facility. However, residents and training programs were permitted to opt out if they had moral or
religious objections.

[5] *Federal Register* 73, 245 (Friday, December 19, 2008), p. 78073. Available online at: http://edocket.
access.gpo.gov/2008/pdf/E8–30134.pdf; accessed July 11, 2010.

[6] Ibid., pp. 78072–101. As noted in Chapter 2, HHS rescinded the Final Rule shortly after President
Obama's inauguration.

the "federal health care conscience protection laws:" the original Church Amendment and subsequent additions to it (42 U.S.C. § 300a-7) as well as the Coats and Weldon Amendments.[7]

The US health care reform legislation enacted in March 2010, the Patient Protection and Affordable Care Act (Public Law No. III–148), includes provisions that protect refusals related to abortion.[8] One protects refusals based on ethical or religious beliefs. It prohibits discrimination by health plans against individual health care providers or health care facilities "because of a willingness or an unwillingness, if doing so is contrary to the religious or moral beliefs of the provider or facility, to provide, pay for, provide coverage of, or refer for abortions" (§ 1303(a)(3)). Another provision states that the legislation shall not be understood to require any health plan to provide coverage of abortions for which public funds are either prohibited or permitted. The act also prohibits discrimination based on a refusal to "provide any health care item or service furnished for the purpose of causing, or for the purpose of assisting in causing, the death of any individual, such as by assisted suicide, euthanasia, or mercy killing"

---

[7] Ibid., pp. 78072–3. None of the earlier federal conscience clause laws (the Church, Coats, and Weldon Amendments) offered a definition of "abortion." A draft of the HHS Final Rule that was never publicly released offered the following broad definition: "any of the various procedures – including the prescription, dispensing and administration of any drug or the performance of any procedure or any other action – that results in the termination of the life of a human being in utero between conception and natural birth, whether before or after implantation." See (Pear 2008a: sec. A, p. 17). This expansive definition of "abortion" might be understood to include some forms of contraceptives (e.g. EC, IUD, and oral contraceptives) and arguably would have significantly extended the scope of abortion-related protections in the earlier federal conscience clauses (Jeffrey Young, "Leavitt: 'Conscience' rule won't affect birth control," *The Hill* online: http://thehill.com/homenews/news/15988-leavitt-; accessed July 11, 2010). Michael Leavitt acknowledged the ambiguity in the Final Rule, which omitted any definition of "abortion." According to an article in the *Washington Post*:

[W]hen pressed about whether the regulation would protect health-care workers who consider birth control pills, Plan B and other forms of contraception to be equivalent to abortion, Leavitt said: "This regulation does not seek to resolve any ambiguity in that area. It focuses on abortion and focuses on physicians' conscience in relation to that." (Stein 2008a: sec. A, p. 1)

Since the Church Amendment and the HHS Final Rule provide blanket protection to individual health care professionals who have conscience-based objections to *any* procedure, including contraception, the primary practical significance of the meaning of "abortion" relates to institutions and organizations (e.g. hospitals, insurance companies, health plans, and pharmacies), whose refusals are protected only in relation to abortion and sterilization. Accordingly, if abortion is understood to include certain types of contraception, there would have been a conflict between the HHS Final Rule and state laws requiring insurance plans that provide coverage for prescription drugs to cover birth control. It also would have conflicted with state laws that require hospital emergency departments to offer EC to rape victims. See (Pear 2008b: sec. A, p. 14).

[8] The act is available online at: http://frwebgate.access.gpo.gov/cgi-bin/getdoc.cgi?dbname=III_cong_bills&docid=f:h3590enr.txt.pdf accessed July 11, 2010.

(§ 1553(a)).[9] Another provision states that the legislation will not have any effect on federal laws regarding "conscience protection; . . . willingness or refusal to provide abortion; and . . . discrimination on the basis of the willingness or refusal to provide, pay for, cover, or refer for abortion or to provide or participate in training to provide abortion" (§ 1303(b)(2)(A)). In addition, the legislation affirms that nothing in subsection § 1303(b) "shall alter the rights and obligations of employees and employers under title VII of the Civil Rights Act of 1964," which offers some protection for conscience-based refusals (§ 1303(b)(3)). Finally, the legislation also provides a narrow conscience-based exemption from the requirement to purchase insurance for members of a "recognized religious sect," such as the Amish, which opposes participation in private or public health insurance plans (§ 5000A(d)(2)(A)).[10]

Most states also have enacted conscience clause legislation. Forty-six allow individual health care providers, and 44 allow health care institutions to refuse to provide abortion services; 17 states permit individual health care providers, and 16 allow health care institutions to refuse to provide sterilization services; and 5 states explicitly permit pharmacists, and one (Mississippi) explicitly permits pharmacies, to refuse to dispense contraceptives.[11] Some states provide protections for refusals in relation to additional services (e.g. family planning, artificial insemination, human embryonic stem cell research, human embryonic cloning, physician-assisted suicide, and euthanasia).[12] Two states, Illinois (Ill Rev Stat ch 745, § 70 (1998)) and Mississippi (Miss Code § 41–107 (2004)), have broad conscience protection laws that provide blanket protection for conscience-based refusals of any health care procedure or service. Although the

---

[9] The Act explicitly states that this subsection shall *not* "be construed to apply to, or to affect, any limitation relating to" withholding or withdrawing medical treatment, including nutrition and hydration, abortion, or "the use of an item, good, benefit, or service furnished for the purpose of alleviating pain or discomfort, even if such use may increase the risk of death, so long as such item, good, benefit, or service is not also furnished for the purpose of causing, or the purpose of assisting in causing, death, for any reason" (P.L. 11–48 §1553(a)).

[10] The scope of the exemption is based on the following test included in the Internal Revenue Code: A person is exempt "if he is a member of a recognized religious sect or division thereof and is an adherent of established tenets or teachings of such sect or division by reason of which he is conscientiously opposed to acceptance of the benefits of any private or public insurance which . . . makes payments toward the cost of, or provides services for, medical care . . ."(§1402(g)(1)).

[11] Guttmacher Institute, "State Policies in Brief as of July 1, 2010: Refusing to Provide Health Services." Available online at: www.guttmacher.org/statecenter/spibs/spib_RPHS.pdf; accessed July 8, 2010. Broad legislation may protect refusals by pharmacists in 5 additional states, and refusals by pharmacies in 4 additional states.

[12] The Protection of Conscience Project: www.consciencelaws.org/Conscience-Laws-USA/Conscience-Laws-USA-01.html; accessed July 8, 2010.

protections of the Illinois statute may extend to pharmacists and pharmacies, only Mississippi's explicitly states that pharmacists and pharmacies are included within the scope of its protections.[13] In addition, state laws that authorize advance directives typically provide exemptions for health care professionals who have ethical or religious objections to implementing instruction directives and/or the decisions of designated surrogates (Meisel and Cerminara 2009).

As is to be expected given the controversial nature of the issue, some states have enacted legislation to restrict conscientious objection. For example, as of July 1, 2010, 16 states and the District of Columbia require emergency departments to provide information about emergency contraception; 12 states and the District of Columbia require emergency departments to dispense emergency contraception if requested by victims of sexual assault; 4 states require pharmacies to fill all valid EC prescriptions; and one state requires pharmacists to fill all valid EC prescriptions.[14]

The almost four decades that have elapsed since the Church Amendment's enactment in 1973 have produced a sometimes confusing patchwork of laws and regulations that, depending on the jurisdiction, offer varying degrees of protection for the exercise of conscience by health care professionals. Paradoxically, such conscience clauses can be faulted for offering both too much and, insofar as they apply only to conscience-based *refusals*, too little protection of conscience.

TOO MUCH PROTECTION OF CONSCIENCE

As noted in Chapter 1, in a news release accompanying the publication of the HHS Final Rule, Michael Leavitt, the Secretary of the Department at the time, stated: "Doctors and other health care providers should not be forced to choose between good professional standing and violating their conscience ... This rule protects the right of medical providers to care for their patients in accord with their conscience."[15] I argued in Chapter 1 that there are several reasons for respecting and protecting the exercise of conscience by health care professionals. However, it would be unwarranted

---

[13] Guttmacher Institute, "State Policies in Brief as of July 1, 2010: Emergency Contraception." Available online at: www.guttmacher.org/statecenter/spibs/spib_EC.pdf; accessed July 8, 2010.

[14] Ibid. Illinois law requires pharmacies that stock contraceptives to dispense emergency contraception (Ill. Adm. Code tit. 68 § 1330.91(j) (2008)).

[15] Department of Health and Human Services News Release, December 18, 2008. Available online at: www.hhs.gov/news/press/2008pres/12/20081218a.html; accessed July 11, 2010.

to avoid the choice that Leavitt deplored by inappropriately lowering the bar of "good professional standing" and allowing health care professionals to exercise their conscience at the expense of core professional obligations.

Conscience clauses and ethical constraints and requirements in relation to patients

I argued in Chapter 3 that core professional obligations set ethical limits to the exercise of conscience. Accordingly, a conscience clause provides too much protection if it can be understood to exempt physicians, nurses, and/ or pharmacists from fulfilling core professional obligations. I will not attempt to provide a comprehensive review of conscience clauses. Instead, I will identify examples of ways in which some fail to incorporate the constraints and requirements identified in Chapter 3 and thereby provide too much protection of conscience.[16] The five constraints and requirements in relation to patients identified in Chapter 3 are: (1) a constraint against invidious discrimination; (2) a constraint against excessive patient harms and burdens; (3) a qualified requirement to disclose options; (4) a qualified requirement to refer and/or facilitate a transfer; and (5) a qualified advance notification requirement.[17]

---

[16] The focus of this examination of conscience clauses will be on the scope of the protection they provide with the aim of determining whether they can be understood to exempt health care professionals from fulfilling their professional obligations. It is worth noting, however, that there are a variety of modes of protection, ranging from prohibiting and penalizing discrimination against health care professionals who refuse to provide a good or service to granting them immunity from disciplinary action, criminal liability, and/or civil liability.

[17] Nothing comparable to the flurry of conscience clause legislation in the United States has occurred in the United Kingdom. On a national level there are two conscience clauses. One is part of the Abortion Act 1967 and the other is in a section of the Human Fertilisation and Embryology Act 1990 (The Protection of Conscience Project). However, in 2007 the General Medical Council (GMC) issued draft guidelines, "Personal Beliefs and Medical Practice," with broad protections for conscientious objection. In response to criticisms, the GMC issued a revised set of guidelines the following year. Neither draft limits the scope of conscience-based refusals (i.e. restricts it to specific procedures as recommended by the British Medical Association). However, there are some significant differences between the two drafts, such as: (1) the final draft strengthens anti-discrimination provisions; (2) the explicit statement in the first draft that referral is not required was deleted from the final draft; (3) the final draft strengthens requirements to assure that patients are adequately informed; and (4) the final draft includes an explicit prohibition of obstruction. In addition, the final draft includes the following qualifications that were not in the first draft: (1) it states twice that "the care of your patient [is] your first concern;" (2) it refers to a need to "balance doctors' and patients' rights;" and (3) it states that physicians will be expected "to set aside their personal beliefs where this is necessary in order to provide care in line with the principles in *Good Medical Practice*." The final draft of "Personal Beliefs and Medical Practice" is available online at: www.gmc-uk.org/guidance/ethical_guidance/ personal_beliefs/personal_beliefs.asp; accessed July 11, 2010.

Invidious discrimination

Many conscience clauses allow health professionals to refuse to provide one or more specified goods or services, such as emergency contraception (EC) and abortion. If a refusal is based on the nature of the good or service rather than on characteristics of patients, it is not likely to involve invidious discrimination. Accordingly, conscience clauses that protect the exercise of conscience with respect to specified goods or services may not require a proscription against invidious discrimination, and none of the state conscience clauses of this type do.[18] However, the situation is different in relation to conscience clauses that provide blanket protection for the exercise of conscience. If conscience clauses do not specify the goods and services that health care professionals are permitted to refuse, absent an explicit statement to the contrary, such blanket permission might be understood to include (or not exclude) refusals that are based on invidious discrimination. Arguably, the stakes are too high to risk ambiguity with respect to invidious discrimination. Thus, in contrast to conscience clauses that protect only refusals to provide specified goods or services, conscience clauses that offer blanket protection offer too much protection of conscience if they do not include an explicit prohibition of invidious discrimination.

As noted, Mississippi and Illinois are the two states with broad conscience clauses that do not limit protected refusals to specified goods or services. Mississippi's states: "A health care provider has the right not to participate, and no health care provider shall be required to participate in a health care service that violates his or her conscience" (Miss Code § 41–107–5 (2004)). One might argue that the reference to "health care service" limits protected refusals to those that are based on an objection to *a type of service*. However, "health care service" is ambiguous, and it is not plausible to claim that the foregoing interpretation of the phrase is required by its plain meaning. Indeed, the statement of the right to refuse in the Mississippi statute is immediately followed by a prohibition of invidious discrimination: "However, this subsection does not allow a health care provider to refuse to participate in a health care service regarding a patient because of the patient's race, color, national origin, ethnicity, sex, religion, creed or sexual orientation" (Miss Code § 41–107–5 (2004)). If the plain meaning of "health care service" rules out refusals based on invidious discrimination, this sentence would be redundant. Its addition left no doubt that the

---

[18] The Protection of Conscience Project.

broad protection of conscience-based refusals does not include any that are based on invidious discrimination. Hence, to prevent ambiguity, broad conscience clauses that do not limit protected refusals to specified goods or services can and should include specific statements prohibiting invidious discrimination.

In contrast to Mississippi, the Illinois conscience clause does not include an explicit statement prohibiting invidious discrimination. The law states:

It is the public policy of the State of Illinois to respect and protect the right of conscience of all persons who refuse to obtain, receive or accept, or who are engaged in, the delivery of, arrangement for, or payment of health care services and medical care . . . No physician or health care personnel shall be civilly or criminally liable to any person, estate, public or private entity or public official by reason of his or her refusal to perform, assist, counsel, suggest, recommend, refer or participate in any way in any particular form of health care service which is contrary to the conscience of such physician or health care personnel. (Ill Rev Stat ch 745, § 70/2 (1998))

Absent an explicit prohibition of invidious discrimination, it remains unclear whether the law's protection of the exercise of conscience excludes invidious discrimination.

A similar point applies to the two sections of the federal Church Amendments (§ 300a–7(c-2)) and (§ 300a–7(d)) that provide blanket protection for refusals to "perform or assist in the performance of" any "health service or research activity" as well as corresponding sections in the HHS Final Rule. None explicitly excludes conscience-based refusals based on invidious discrimination; neither does the Patient Protection and Affordable Care Act. To be sure, various state and federal laws prohibit discrimination on the basis of specified characteristics (e.g. race, religion, and sex).[19] However, adding a nondiscrimination statement to conscience clauses would prevent potential conflicts and avoid any need to resolve them.

---

[19] When the HHS Final Rule was published in the *Federal Register*, it included the following reference to earlier critical comments:

Many Comments stated concern that the proposed regulation could serve as a pretext for health care workers to claim religious beliefs or moral objections under the protections of the fourth provision of the Church Amendments, 42 U.S.C. 300a–7(d), in order to discriminate against certain classes of patients, including illegal immigrants, drug and alcohol users, patients with disabilities or patients with HIV, or on the basis of race or sexual preference.

HHS provided the following response: "[H]ealth care conscience protection laws exist as one part of a number of federal laws that address discrimination on a variety of grounds, and . . . actions . . . that violate federal civil rights laws, continue to violate federal civil rights laws" *Federal Register* 73, 245 (December 19, 2008), p. 78080. The HHS Final Rule did not include any statement about discrimination.

Patient harms and burdens

I argued in Chapter 3 that an obligation to avoid exposing patients to excessive harms and/or burdens is an important ethical limitation on conscience-based refusals by health care professionals. However, few conscience clauses include any constraints that would protect patients from harms or burdens as a result of conscience-based refusals. The federal Church and Weldon Amendments, the HHS Final Rule, and the Patient Protection and Affordable Care Act include no consideration of the impact of conscience-based refusals on patients. Only eight states include exceptions for emergency situations, and with two exceptions (Illinois and Louisiana), the conscience clause is limited to abortion.[20] California specifies "spontaneous abortions" in addition to "medical emergency situations" as exceptions (Cal HSC Code § 123420 (d)).[21] Significantly, only one of the two states with broad conscience clauses that do not limit protected refusals to specified goods or services (Illinois) includes exceptions for emergency situations. As indicated in Chapter 4, failing to offer pregnancy termination in medical emergency situations can result in excessive harm. However, when conscience clauses extend to all procedures, the potential for harm is substantially increased. Accordingly, conscience clauses offer too much protection if they do not limit refusals in emergency situations to prevent excessive harm to patients (e.g. by permitting such refusals only when another provider is available to provide treatment without delay).

Louisiana's conscience clause has a constraint against compromising patient access to health care. However, other than the exceptions already identified, state conscience clauses do not include constraints that recognize health care professionals' obligation to prevent excessive harms and burdens. Indeed, one state (Mississippi) explicitly stipulates that preventing harm to patients does not justify requiring health care providers to act against their conscience: "It shall not be a defense to any claim arising out of the violation of this chapter that such violation was necessary to prevent additional burden or expense on any ... patient" (Miss Code § 41–107–11 (2004)).

---

[20] The Protection of Conscience Project. Oklahoma's exception is more specific: It does not permit conscience-based refusals for abortion aftercare "when the aftercare involves emergency medical procedures which are necessary to protect the life of the patient." The Oklahoma abortion conscience clause includes one additional exception: "medical procedures in which a woman is in the process of the spontaneous, inevitable abortion of an unborn child, the death of the child is imminent, and the procedures are necessary to prevent the death of the mother" (Okla Stat §63–1–741(B-C) (1978)).

[21] In addition to protecting individual practitioners with conscience-based objections to abortion, the California statute protects hospitals "organized or operated by a religious corporation or other religious organization" that refuse to perform abortions. The same two exceptions apply to hospitals as well as individual practitioners.

None of the four states with specific pharmacist conscience clauses (Arkansas, Georgia, Mississippi, and South Dakota) recognizes contextual factors that might affect patients. The broadest, the Georgia law, states: "It shall not be considered unprofessional conduct for any pharmacist to refuse to fill any prescription based on his/her professional judgment or ethical or moral beliefs" (Ga Code Ann § 480–5–.03(n) (2001)). Insofar as these pharmacist conscience clauses offer no protection to patients, they offer too much protection to pharmacists' exercise of conscience.

Disclosing options and referral and/or transfer

I argued in Chapter 3 that health care professionals have qualified (contextual) obligations to disclose options as well as to refer and facilitate a transfer. Typically, however, conscience clauses are either silent or exempt providers from a requirement to disclose, refer, or facilitate a transfer. Louisiana, Arkansas, and Illinois are among the states that provide such exemptions in their conscience clauses. In this respect, those conscience clauses provide too much protection of conscience.

Louisiana's conscience clause protects refusals related to abortion, abortifacient drugs, human embryonic stem cell research, human embryo cloning, euthanasia, and physician-assisted suicide. It includes the following provision in relation to abortion that can be understood to exempt health care professionals from any requirement to disclose options, refer, or facilitate a transfer:

> No physician, nurse, student or other person or corporation shall be held civilly or criminally liable, discriminated against, dismissed, demoted, or in any way prejudiced or damaged because of his refusal for any reason to *recommend, counsel,* perform, assist with or *accommodate* an abortion. (La. Rev. Stat. Ann. tit. 40, § 1299.31 (1973); emphasis added)

The Arkansas conscience clause pertaining to contraception appears to have similar exemptions related to disclosure. It states:

> No private institution or physician, nor any agent or employee of such institution or physician, nor any employee of a public institution acting under directions of a physician, shall be prohibited from refusing to provide contraceptive procedures, supplies, and *information* when the refusal is based upon religious or conscientious objection. No such institution, employee, agent, or physician shall be held liable for the refusal. (Ark Code Ann § x 20–16–304 (1973); emphasis added)

Finally, the following provision in the broad Illinois conscience clause explicitly exempts health care providers from any requirement to "counsel, suggest, recommend, or refer:"

No physician or health care personnel shall be civilly or criminally liable to any person, estate, public or private entity or public official by reason of his or her refusal to perform, assist, *counsel, suggest, recommend, refer* or participate in any way in any particular form of health care service which is contrary to the conscience of such physician or health care personnel. (Ill Rev Stat ch 745, § 70/1(4) (1998); emphasis added)

Maryland's conscience clause considers some contextual factors and is an exception. It states that the protections of the conscience clause do not apply to referral:

if the failure to refer a patient to a source for any medical procedure that results in sterilization or termination of pregnancy would reasonably be determined as: (1) The cause of death or serious physical injury or serious long-lasting injury to the patient; and (2) Otherwise contrary to the standards of medical care. (Md Code Ann § 20–214(d) (1991))

Similar to many state conscience clauses, the protections of the federal Church and Weldon Amendments apply to conscience-based refusals "to perform or assist in the performance of" (specified or unspecified) procedures or activities. Neither includes an explanation of what it means to "assist in the performance of." However, the HHS Final Rule provided an extremely broad definition: "to participate in any activity with a reasonable connection to a procedure, health service or health service program, or research activity, so long as the individual involved is a part of the workforce of a Department-funded entity" (45 CFR § 88.2).[22] On the basis of this broad definition, "assist in the performance of" is said to include "counseling, referral, training, and other arrangements for the procedure, health service, or research activity" (ibid.). This broad definition and the absence of a consideration of contextual factors warrant the conclusion that the HHS Final Rule offered too much protection of conscience.[23] Insofar as the Patient Protection and Affordable Care Act offers blanket protection of

---

[22] Arguably, the HHS Final Rule's expansive definition of "workforce" significantly broadens the scope of protected individuals compared to the Church and Weldon Amendments. The Final Rule offers the following definition: "employees, volunteers, trainees, contractors, and other persons whose conduct, in the performance of work for a Department-funded entity, is under the control or authority of such entity, whether or not they are paid by the Department funded entity, or health care providers holding privileges with the entity" (45 CFR § 88.2). The "Section-by-Section Description of the Final Rule" offers two examples of its broad scope: "[A]n operating room nurse would assist in the performance of surgical procedures; an employee whose task it is to clean the instruments used in a particular procedure would also be considered to assist in the performance of the particular procedure . . ." (*Federal Register*, 73, 245 (December 19, 2008), p. 78090).

[23] The expansive definition of "assist in the performance of" is one of the features of the HHS Final Rule that Julie Cantor characterizes as "conscientious objection gone awry." See (Cantor 2009: 1484–5).

refusals to provide abortion related referrals and fails to consider contextual factors, arguably it, too, offers too much protection.

Advance notification

I argued in Chapter 3 that, depending on the situation and circumstances, health care professionals may have an obligation to notify patients or prospective patients in advance of their conscience-based objections to providing goods or services that fall within the scope of their discipline or specialty. Typically, both state and federal conscience clauses are silent in relation to providing such advance notification. Michigan's conscience clause is unusual insofar as it even mentions informing patients. It limits its protection against liability for abortion-related conscience-based refusals to physicians who have informed patients: "A physician who informs a patient that he or she refuses to give advice concerning, or participate in, an abortion is not liable to the hospital, clinic, institution, teaching institution, health facility, or patient for the refusal" (Mich Comp Laws § 14.15(20183) (1978)). However, there is no requirement concerning the timing of patient notification. For example, an obstetrician-gynecologist would satisfy this requirement if he waited until a pregnant patient requests an abortion or needs emergency surgery for an ectopic pregnancy.

To be sure, no conscience clauses specifically offer protection to health care professionals who choose not to provide patients or prospective patients with advance notification. In this respect, then, it cannot be claimed that they offer too much protection of conscience. Nevertheless, in virtue of their silence, they fail to condition their protections of conscience on fulfilling core professional obligations. In this respect, it might be claimed that they offer too much protection of conscience.

Conscience clauses and ethical constraints in relation to employers and other health care professionals

In addition to ethical constraints derived from core professional obligations, I identified constraints in Chapter 3 to protect employers and other health care professionals. Typically, both state and federal conscience clauses limit the extent to which supervisors and managers may implement such constraints. Maine's abortion-related conscience clause is representative of such limitations:

No physician, nurse or other person, who refuses to perform or assist in the performance of an abortion, shall, because of that refusal, be dismissed, suspended, demoted or otherwise prejudiced or damaged by a hospital, health care facility, firm, association, professional association, corporation or educational institution with which he or she is affiliated or requests to be affiliated or by which he or she is employed . . . (Title 22 Me Rev Stat Ann § 1591 (1977))

Accordingly, even if accommodating a nurse who refuses to assist with abortions were to impose an excessive burden on the hospital (e.g. require hiring another nurse) or other nurses (e.g. require changing shifts when it is excessively burdensome), the conscience clause would prevent a supervisor from taking any action against the nurse for refusing to perform her assigned duties. As a result, the supervisor would be powerless to enforce a denial of the nurse's request for accommodation. In effect, then, the conscience clause requires the supervisor to grant an accommodation, no matter how great the burden to the hospital and other nurses.

Of all conscience clauses, Mississippi's provides the most comprehensive limitations on the ability of supervisors and managers to enforce justified constraints on the exercise of conscience by employees:

It shall be unlawful for any person, health care provider, health care institution, [or] public or private institution . . . to discriminate against any health care provider in any manner based on his or her declining to participate in a health care service that violates his or her conscience. For purposes of this chapter, discrimination includes, but is not limited to: termination, transfer, refusal of staff privileges, refusal of board certification, adverse administrative action, demotion, loss of career specialty, reassignment to a different shift, reduction of wages or benefits . . ., or any other penalty, disciplinary or retaliatory action. (Miss Code § 41–107–5(3) (2004))

This provision appears to require pharmacy and nurse managers to accommodate employees, no matter how burdensome it might be. Indeed, the Mississippi conscience clause explicitly states that preventing burdens to any other health care provider or health care institution does not justify a failure to comply with the legal requirement to accommodate the exercise of conscience: "It shall not be a defense to any claim arising out of the violation of this chapter that such violation was necessary to prevent additional burden or expense on any other health care provider . . . [or] health care institution . . ." (Miss Code § 41–107–11 (2004)).

Consider once again the case of Neil Noesen, which was presented in Chapter 3. Noesen, a Wisconsin pharmacist, refused for reasons of conscience to have any contact with customers who might want contraceptives or information about them. The only accommodation acceptable to him was for another pharmacy employee to pre-screen all calls and on-site customers. Under the Mississippi conscience clause, no matter how burdensome the accommodation would have been, the pharmacy manager would not have been able to dismiss Noesen if he refused to answer the phone or have contact with unscreened customers. Surely this is too much protection of conscience. Generally, conscience clauses that include explicit or implicit prohibitions against enforcing justified limits on conscience-based refusals offer too much protection of conscience.[24]

In contrast to the Mississippi conscience clause, a California law allows a consideration of relevant contextual factors. It states:

A licentiate [licensed pharmacist] may decline to dispense a prescription drug or device ... only if the licentiate has previously notified his or her employer, in writing, of the drug or class of drugs to which he or she objects, and the licentiate's employer can, without creating undue hardship, provide a reasonable accommo-dation of the licentiate's objection. The licentiate's employer shall establish proto-cols that ensure that the patient has timely access to the prescribed drug or device despite the licentiate's refusal to dispense the prescription or order. (Cal Business and Professions Code § 733 (2009))

Conscience clauses, pharmacies, and health care institutions

I maintained in Chapter 4 that since a pharmacy licensee has an obligation to promote the public health, safety, and welfare, a pharmacy may justifi-ably refuse to stock and dispense a medication for reasons of conscience only if members of the population in its service area have timely and convenient access to the medication at other pharmacies. Four states (Arkansas, Colorado, Maine, and Tennessee) have broad conscience clauses that can be understood to include pharmacies within the scope of protections of institutional refusals; and one state (Mississippi) explicitly includes phar-macies within the following provision of its conscience clause:[25] "A health care institution has the right not to participate, and no health care institu-tion shall be required to participate in a health care service that violates its conscience" (Miss Code § 41–107–7 (2004)). Insofar as the other four states offer similar protections to pharmacies, all five conscience clauses fail to consider the impact on patient access to prescription and limited distribu-tion medications. Such blanket protection of conscience can also prevent state pharmacy boards from enacting regulations designed to ensure that

---

[24] Cantor suggests that that the HHS Final Rule may be inconsistent with Title VII of the 1964 Civil Rights Act. Ibid.
[25] Guttmacher Institute, "State Policies in Brief as of July 1, 2010: Refusing to Provide Health Services."

conscience-based refusals by pharmacy licensees are not incompatible with a reasonable specification of the obligation to promote the public health, safety, and welfare. In these respects, the five conscience clauses offer too much protection of conscience.

I also argued in Chapter 4 that there are situations in which hospitals can be obligated to offer a service that compromises its identity and integrity. However, several conscience clauses provide unqualified protection to hospitals and in this respect provide too much protection of conscience. Typically, abortion-related conscience clauses protect hospitals as well as individual practitioners, and in most cases, exceptions are not made for emergency medical conditions. The federal Church Amendment, the HHS Final Rule, and the Patient Protection and Affordable Care Act protect hospitals from being required to facilitate abortions, and no exception is made for emergency situations.

A Kansas statute is illustrative of state conscience clauses. It includes the following provision: "No hospital, hospital administrator or governing board shall be required to permit the termination of human pregnancies within its institution and the refusal to permit such procedures shall not be grounds for civil liability to any person" (Kan Stat Ann § 65–444 (1970)). The statute provides no exception for pregnant patients in emergency medical situations.

The broad Mississippi conscience clause applies to health care institutions as well as individual practitioners. "A health care institution has the right not to participate, and no health care institution shall be required to participate in a health care service that violates its conscience" (Miss Code § 41–107–7(1) (2004)). No exception is made for emergency medical conditions. The only qualification is a patient consent requirement:

A health care institution that declines to provide or participate in a health care service that violates its conscience shall not be civilly, criminally or administratively liable if the institution provides a consent form to be signed by a patient before admission to the institution stating that it reserves the right to decline to provide or participate in a health care service that violates its conscience. (Miss Code § 41–107–7(2) (2004))

Arguably, if an unforeseen emergency condition were to develop during hospitalization, a hospital would be obligated to offer standard of care to prevent death or other serious harms despite a previously signed consent form. Accordingly, the Mississippi statute is another example of a conscience clause that provides too much protection of conscience to hospitals and other health care institutions.

Are the protections of conscience clauses limited to conscience-based refusals?

Strictly speaking, not all laws and regulations that protect refusals by practitioners and institutions and are commonly classified as "conscience clauses" warrant that characterization. To be correctly classified as a *conscience* clause, a legal rule or regulation at least would have to specify that the refusal is *conscience*-based. However, several laws and regulations that are commonly classified as "conscience clauses" do not require refusals to be based on ethical or religious beliefs, let alone conscience. On a federal level, the protections afforded by the Weldon and Coats Amendments are not limited to refusals based on ethical or religious beliefs.[26] Neither are some of the protections provided by the Patient Protection and Affordable Care Act.

Similarly, many state statutes that protect refusals related to abortion are not limited to those based on ethical or religious beliefs. An Ohio statute is representative of these laws. It states: "No person is required to perform or participate in medical procedures which result in abortion, and refusal to perform or participate in the medical procedures is not grounds for civil liability nor a basis for disciplinary or other recriminatory action" (Ohio Rev Code Ann § 47–4731.91 (1974)). A Minnesota statute explicitly states that the reason for abortion-related refusals is not relevant: "No person and no hospital or institution shall be coerced, held liable or discriminated against in any manner because of a refusal to perform, accommodate, assist or submit to an abortion *for any reason*" (Minn Stat § 145.414 (1995); emphasis added).

A South Dakota statute protects pharmacist refusals without requiring an ethical or religious basis:

> No pharmacist may be required to dispense medication if there is reason to believe that the medication would be used to: cause an abortion; or destroy an unborn child . . .; or cause the death of any person by means of an assisted suicide, euthanasia, or mercy killing.[27] (S. D. Codified Laws § 36–11–70 (2005))

The absence of a limitation to refusals that are based on ethical or religious beliefs, let alone conscience, invites speculation that an unstated intent of such legislation may be to reduce the frequency of certain procedures, such as abortion. Speculation aside, such laws provide too much protection for

---

[26] Daniel Coats, the primary sponsor of the amendment that bears his name, stated during the US Senate debate that reasons for refusing could include "practical" and "economic" considerations (*Congressional Record*, March 19, 1996, p. S2264).

[27] "Unborn child" is defined as: "an individual organism of the species homo sapiens from fertilization until live birth" (S. D. Codified Laws § 22–1–2(50A) (2005)).

refusals to provide or participate in providing legal and professionally accepted health care goods and services.

TOO LITTLE PROTECTION OF CONSCIENCE

Discussions of appeals to conscience by health care professionals typically focus on situations in which they object to providing a legal and professionally permitted service, such as abortion, sterilization, prescribing or dispensing emergency contraception, and organ retrieval pursuant to donation after cardiac death (DCD). "Negative appeals to conscience" will designate such appeals to conscience. When health care professionals advance negative appeals to conscience, they do so to secure permission to refuse to provide or participate in providing a legal and professionally accepted good or service within the scope of their competence.

Consistent with this focus on negative appeals to conscience, when conscientious objection is legally recognized in conscience clauses, they typically function to exempt health care professionals from penalties for refusing to provide or participate in providing goods or services when doing so would be contrary to their ethical or religious beliefs. All of the previously examined conscience clauses protect negative appeals to conscience and conscience-based *refusals*.

Positive appeals to conscience

Significantly, conscience clauses typically offer no protection for health care professionals who claim to have a conscience-based obligation to *provide* professionally permitted goods or services (e.g. medications and procedures) when doing so is prohibited by law, institutional rules, employer policies, and so forth. That is, health care provider conscience clauses typically do not protect what I will refer to as "*positive* appeals to conscience."

A Pennsylvania law pertaining to health care decision-making, referred to as "Act 169" (20 Pa Cons Stat Ann § 54 (2006)), illustrates the failure to recognize positive appeals to conscience. With a few exceptions, Act 169 does not permit physicians to honor the advance directives of pregnant women who lack decision-making capacity if doing so would require forgoing life-sustaining treatment:[28]

---

[28] Over 30 states limit, or do not permit, implementing advance directives of pregnant women if it would require forgoing life-sustaining treatment. See (Meisel and Cerminara 2009: at 7–91).

Notwithstanding the existence of a living will, a health care decision by a health care representative or health care agent or any other direction to the contrary, life-sustaining treatment, nutrition and hydration shall be provided to a pregnant woman who is incompetent and has an end-stage medical condition or who is permanently unconscious unless, to a reasonable degree of medical certainty as certified on the pregnant woman's medical record by the pregnant woman's attending physician and an obstetrician who has examined the pregnant woman, life-sustaining treatment, nutrition and hydration: (1) will not maintain the pregnant woman in such a way as to permit the continuing development and live birth of the unborn child; (2) will be physically harmful to the pregnant woman; or (3) will cause pain to the pregnant woman that cannot be alleviated by medication. (20 Pa Cons Stat Ann § 5429 (a) (2006))

Significantly there is no exemption for a physician who believes, as a matter of conscience, that she has an obligation to respect a patient's documented wishes to forgo life-sustaining treatment. To be sure, Act 169 does permit a physician with a conscience-based objection to "opt out" by facilitating a transfer to another physician. In this respect, Act 169 protects a negative appeal to conscience by permitting a physician to refuse to provide life-sustaining treatment. However, the opt-out provision does not protect a positive appeal to conscience by a physician who claims to have an ethical duty to order and supervise the process of forgoing life-sustaining treatment in accordance with a patient's advance directive. Act 169 provides no exemption to enable such a physician to fulfill her perceived ethical obligation to her patient.

The following are a few additional illustrations of contexts in which health care professionals might advance positive appeals to conscience that are not legally recognized:

- The South Dakota Women's Health and Human Life Protection Act (HB 1215), signed into law in March 2006 and later repealed by voters, included the following provision:

  No person may knowingly administer to, prescribe for, or procure for, or sell to any pregnant woman any medicine, drug, or other substance with the specific intent of causing or abetting the termination of the life of an unborn human being. No person may knowingly use or employ any instrument or procedure upon a pregnant woman with the specific intent of causing or abetting the termination of the life of an unborn human being.[29]

---

[29] South Dakota HB 1215 added sections 17–7 through 17–12 to SD Cod Laws § 22–17 and repealed sections 23-A-2 to 23-A-5 of SD Cod Laws § 34–23. These changes were rejected by a November 7, 2006, referendum. HB 1215 defined "unborn human being" as "an individual living member of the species, homo sapiens, throughout the entire embryonic and fetal ages of the unborn child from fertilization to full gestation and childbirth."

The Act included an exception for abortions performed to prevent the death of the pregnant woman but no exemption for health care professionals who believe that there are other circumstances in which they have an ethical obligation to terminate pregnancies.

- Section 202 of the Border Protection, Antiterrorism, and Illegal Immigration Control Act of 2005 (HB 4437), which passed in the US House but not in the Senate, included provisions that, according to some commentators, would have prohibited health professionals from providing services to "illegal aliens."[30] The Act included no exemption for health care professionals who believe that they have an obligation to provide services to anyone who needs them, regardless of immigration status.
- So called "gag rules" prohibit health care professionals from informing patients about specified family planning options, such as abortion. For example, the so-called "global gag rule," reinstated by President George W. Bush on January 22, 2001 and rescinded by President Obama a few days after his inauguration, prohibited foreign non-governmental organizations (NGOs) who receive US Agency for International Development (USAID) family planning funds from providing information to pregnant women about the option of legal abortion or where they can obtain abortion services (P. Baker 2009; Cohen 2001).[31] As is typical of gag rules, the global gag rule provided no exemption for health care professionals who believe that they have an ethical obligation to inform patients about all legal and professionally accepted family planning options.
- As indicated in Chapter 4, some hospitals, especially those affiliated with the Catholic Church, have policies that prohibit terminating pregnancies or providing emergency contraception (EC); and some pharmacies have policies against dispensing EC. Although some conscience clauses may permit hospitals and pharmacies to refuse to provide those goods and services, individuals who practice within them and who believe that they have an ethical obligation to provide the prohibited goods and services typically do not have an opportunity to follow the dictates of their conscience. For example, Sister Margaret McBride, a senior administrator and ethics committee member at St. Joseph's Hospital in Phoenix, Arizona reportedly was pressured to resign from her administrative position and was excommunicated after following her conscience and approving a first trimester pregnancy termination for a patient with life-threatening pulmonary hypertension (Kristof 2010).

---

[30] The proposed bill is available online at: www.govtrack.us/congress/billtext.xpd?bill=h109–4437; accessed July 11, 2010.

[31] The former article is available online at: www.guttmacher.org/pubs/tgr/04/3/gr040301.pdf; accessed July 11, 2010.

There are a few exceptions to the general failure to recognize and protect positive appeals to conscience. For example, Native Americans have been exempted from some drug laws to enable them to practice rituals that require drugs; and employers have been required to allow exemptions from dress codes to permit employees to fulfill their religious obligations. However, exceptions generally are not made for health care professionals' positive appeals to conscience.

Is the selective protection of negative appeals to conscience justified?

If one considers the ethical basis of protecting health care professionals' conscience-based objections, selectively protecting *negative* appeals to conscience does not appear to be justified. The primary reason for recognizing and safeguarding appeals to conscience is to protect moral integrity. This rationale applies equally to negative and positive appeals to conscience. One's moral integrity can be damaged by either performing an action that is contrary to one's core ethical beliefs or by failing to perform an action that is required by those beliefs. Consider the following two cases: (1) Physician A believes that it is seriously wrong ethically to discontinue life support in accordance with the documented wishes of a male patient who currently lacks decision-making capacity. (2) Physician B believes that it is seriously wrong ethically to fail to discontinue life support in accordance with the documented wishes of a pregnant woman who currently lacks decision-making capacity. Just as a failure to respect Physician A's negative appeal to conscience can be injurious to her moral integrity; so, too, a failure to respect Physician B's positive appeal to conscience can be injurious to his moral integrity. Accordingly, positive appeals to conscience can have moral weight and can merit protection for the same reasons as negative appeals to conscience.

Although I have no evidence for claiming that the selective recognition of negative appeals to conscience is in part politically motivated, it is worth noting that in the current US social and political context, the exclusive protection of negative appeals to conscience has tended to privilege positions that are generally associated with "social conservatives" who oppose legally permitted practices such as participating in abortions and dispensing EC. The result has been to disregard positive appeals to conscience that might be more consistent with positions of "social liberals," such as honoring the living wills of pregnant women, providing unrestricted access to EC, performing abortions, providing counseling concerning reproductive options, and providing health care services to people irrespective of their immigration status.

Negative and positive duties and moral asymmetry

Political ideology aside, what might be said to justify selectively protecting negative appeals to conscience? A promising strategy may appear to be to argue that the duties that correspond to negative and positive appeals to conscience are *morally asymmetrical*. Advocates of moral asymmetry might invoke the familiar distinction between "negative" and "positive" duties.

Unfortunately, there is little agreement about how to define each type of duty. Some definitions focus on a distinction between *omissions* and *acts*. For example, according to Marcus Singer, "A negative duty is a duty not to do something, a duty of omission. A positive duty is a duty to do something and cannot be fulfilled by inaction" (Singer 1965: 98–9). Jan Narveson offers a similar account: "A positive duty is a duty to do something, whereas a negative duty is a duty ('merely') to refrain from doing something" (Narveson 1985: 51). Other definitions include a reference to *harm* and *harm prevention*. For example, according to H. M. Malm, negative duties are "duties not to cause harm," and positive duties are "duties to prevent harm" (Malm 1991: 187). Similarly, Raymond Belliotti defines negative duties as duties to "refrain from harming or injuring others" and positive duties as duties to "render assistance to those in distress" (Belliotti 1981: 82). By contrast, Nancy Davis limits negative duties to duties to refrain from harmful acts of commission and understands positive duties as duties to perform beneficial acts of commission. Negative duties are said to be "duties not to *actively* harm," and positive duties are said to be "duties to *actively* benefit" (N. Davis 1980: 179).

N-duties and P-duties and the moral asymmetry thesis

To avoid being drawn into a distracting conceptual controversy, I will refer to the duties that correspond to negative appeals to conscience as "N-duties" and the duties that correspond to positive appeals to conscience as "P-duties." The *"Moral Asymmetry Thesis"* (MAT) advances claims with respect to N-duties and P-duties corresponding to familiar claims about negative and positive duties.

MAT

At least one of the following claims is true:[32]

(1) Violations of N-duties are morally worse or more serious than violations of P-duties.

(2) Agents who violate N-duties are more culpable or blameworthy than agents who violate P-duties.

---

[32] Proponents of moral asymmetry accept at least one, but not necessarily all, of the three claims.

(3) N-duties are stricter or stronger than P-duties.

There are several strategies for attempting to establish moral asymmetry between negative and positive duties, and similar strategies, such as the following, might be used to defend MAT: (1) A common strategy is to compare cases involving one kind of duty with cases involving the other kind of duty and evaluate them in relation to considered moral judgments or moral intuitions.[33] (2) A second strategy is to identify characteristics or features that are said to distinguish the two kinds of duties and establish or ground their moral asymmetry. Alleged bases for distinguishing between negative and positive duties, such as the following, might be invoked to support MAT: (*a*) whereas duties of one type require *omissions*, duties of the other type require *acts*;[34] (*b*) whereas duties of one type prohibit *causing harm*, duties of the other type require *preventing harm* or *benefiting*;[35] (*c*) only one of the two types of duties is *rights-based*;[36] (*d*) whereas duties of one type can be *discharged completely*, duties of the other type cannot;[37] (*e*) duties of one type are *less burdensome* and *less restrictive of liberty* than duties of the other type;[38] (*f*) responsibility for background conditions is greater in relation to one of the two types of duty.[39] (3) A third strategy is to ground moral asymmetry in ethical theory (e.g. contractarian or rights-based theories).[40]

Regardless of which strategy is used to defend MAT, that thesis clearly is unacceptable. Consider Case 1 and Case 2.

CASE 1

Marvin witnesses a boating accident. He is unable to rescue the survivors himself, but he could call the Coast Guard on his cell phone. Had he done so, the Coast Guard would have been able to rescue the survivors. Marvin had a P-duty to call the Coast Guard, but he decided not to because he would have incurred a roaming charge of $1.50. The survivors died.

CASE 2

On her way home, carrying a bag of tomatoes, Marjorie walks by a protest. She disagrees with the politics of the protestors and violates an N-duty by throwing tomatoes at them.

---

[33] See, e.g. (Malm 1991: 187–210).   [34] See, e.g. (Abelson 1982: 219–28).
[35] See, e.g. (Gorr 1985: 93–100) and (Green 1980: 195–204).
[36] See, e.g. (Wreen 1984: 395–402).   [37] See, e.g. (Trammell 1975: 131–7).
[38] See, e.g. (Fitzgerald 1967: 133–9) and (Trammell 1985: 75–81).
[39] See, e.g. (Trammell 1975).   [40] Narveson offers a contractarian account: (Narveson 1985: 51–65).

Contrary to MAT: (1) Marvin's violation of his P-duty is morally worse than Marjorie's violation of her N-duty. (2) Marvin is more culpable or blameworthy for violating his P-duty than Marjorie is for violating her N-duty. (3) Marvin's P-duty is stricter than Marjorie's N-duty. That is, Marvin requires a stronger reason to justify violating his P-duty than Marjorie requires for violating her N-duty.

In response, it might be suggested that MAT should be revised to compare *corresponding* N-duties and P-duties. For example, an N-duty corresponding to the P-duty in Case 1 might be a duty *not to kill*.[41] Consider Case 3.

CASE 3

Frank violates an N-duty by deliberately killing the survivors of a boating accident.

Unlike Case 1 and Case 2, Case 1 and Case 3 appear to be consistent with MAT, which suggests revising it to contrast *corresponding* N-duties and P-duties. MAT* is the result of a revision along these lines.

MAT*
At least one of the following claims is true:
(1) Violations of N-duties are morally worse or more serious than violations of *corresponding* P-duties.
(2) Agents who violate N-duties are more culpable or blameworthy than agents who violate *corresponding* P-duties.
(3) N-duties are stricter or stronger than *corresponding* P-duties.

But consider Cases 4 and 5.

CASE 4

Ethan violates an N-duty by unintentionally but negligently killing the survivors of a boating accident.

CASE 5

Stephanie violates a P-duty by deliberately failing to throw a life preserver to Jacob, her husband, after their sailboat capsized due to a sudden violent

---

[41] For the purpose of considering whether the selective protection of negative appeals to conscience is justified, it is not necessary to specify criteria for identifying N-duties that correspond to P-duties. Moreover, nothing relevant to this issue turns on whether the N-duties and P-duties that are cited as examples of corresponding duties satisfy the appropriate criteria.

wind burst. She wants him to die because he has had extramarital affairs with both of her sisters.

It is not implausible to claim that: (1) Stephanie's violation of her P-duty is morally worse than Ethan's violation of his N-duty. (2) Stephanie is more culpable or blameworthy for violating her P-duty than Ethan is for violating his N-duty. (3) Stephanie's P-duty is stricter than Ethan's N-duty.

Cases 4 and 5 suggest that if the moral asymmetry thesis is not to be rejected outright, a much more nuanced formulation of it is required. In particular, an "all other things being equal" qualifier appears to be needed to account for possible morally significant differences in motive, intention, burdensomeness, and so forth. MAT** is a revised moral asymmetry thesis that incorporates this condition.

MAT**

All other things being equal, at least one of the following claims is true:
(1) Violations of N-duties are morally worse or more serious than violations of corresponding P-duties.
(2) Agents who violate N-duties are more culpable or blameworthy than agents who violate corresponding P-duties.
(3) N-duties are stricter or stronger than corresponding P-duties.

The moral asymmetry thesis and selectively protecting negative claims of conscience

MAT** requires that duties be considered *in pairs*: a particular P-duty and a corresponding N-duty. For the sake of argument, let us accept MAT** and assume that, all other things being equal, for each P-duty and corresponding N-duty, a violation of the latter is morally worse or more serious than a violation of the former. It still would not follow that no appeals to conscience that are based on P-duties warrant protection. It would follow only that:

(C_1): For each appeal to conscience that is based on a P-duty, if there is a corresponding N-duty, its violation would be morally worse or more serious.[42]

Suppose, for example, a Pennsylvania physician has a pregnant patient who lacks decision-making capacity and who has an advance directive. Honoring the advance directive in the clinical circumstances would require withdrawing life-sustaining treatment, which is prohibited by Act 169. The physician has a conscience-based objection to that law because she believes that she

---

[42] Strictly speaking, C_1 should refer to *perceived* P- and N-duties. However, for the sake of simplicity, I will omit the qualifier "perceived."

has an ethical obligation to honor her patient's advance directive. C_1 does not support the inference that the physician's conscience-based objection lacks sufficient moral weight to warrant protection. If it is assumed that a violation of a duty that is morally worse or more serious provides a basis for an appeal to conscience with more moral weight, at most C_1 implies that a conscience-based objection to withdrawing life-support from a pregnant patient would have *more* moral weight. A similar analysis and conclusion are supported if we accept MAT** and assume that, all other things being equal, agents who violate N-duties are more culpable or blameworthy than agents who violate corresponding P-duties.[43]

If we accept MAT** and assume that, all other things being equal, for each P-duty and corresponding N-duty, a stronger reason is required to justify a violation of the latter than the former, it would follow that:

(C_2): For each appeal to conscience that is based on a P-duty, if there is a corresponding N-duty, it requires a stronger reason to justify its violation.

Consider a pharmacist who is employed by a pharmacy that has a strict policy against dispensing EC. The pharmacist has a conscience-based objection to that policy because he believes that unless there is a clear clinical counter-indication in a particular case, he has a duty to provide EC to all women seventeen and older who request it and to younger women who present a valid prescription for it. At first sight, it does not appear that C_2 is even relevant because the pharmacist is not seeking to justify *violating* a P-duty. Instead, he seeks an exemption from the pharmacy policy to enable him to *fulfill* a P-duty. However, suppose it is assumed that an obligation that requires a stronger reason to warrant its violation provides a basis for an appeal to conscience with more moral weight. Then C_2 would support the conclusion that a conscience-based objection to dispensing EC by a second pharmacist, one who works in a pharmacy that dispenses EC and believes that she has an ethical obligation *not to dispense* it, would have *more* moral weight than the conscience-based objection of the first pharmacist. However, C_2 still would not support the inference that the first pharmacist's conscience-based objection lacks sufficient moral weight to warrant protection. Accordingly, neither C_1 nor C_2 justifies selectively protecting negative appeals to conscience.[44]

---

[43] That conclusion requires the additional assumption that a violation of a duty for which an agent is more culpable or blameworthy provides a basis for an appeal to conscience with more moral weight.

[44] I am not claiming that if the second pharmacist's conscience-based refusal is accommodated, it is not ethically justified to refuse to accommodate the first pharmacist's positive appeal to conscience. Contextual differences can justify different responses. I am claiming only that the fact that the first pharmacist appealed to a P-duty and the second pharmacist appealed to an N-duty does not justify accommodating the second pharmacist but not the first pharmacist.

There is one additional reason for questioning whether MAT** can justify selectively protecting negative appeals to conscience. MAT** is a moral principle, and it might be rejected by health care professionals who advance positive appeals to conscience. If a health care professional rejects MAT**, its use to justify failing to protect a positive appeal to conscience might undermine the agent's moral integrity, the safeguarding of which is an important objective of the practice of recognizing and protecting appeals to conscience.

Additional reasons for selectively protecting negative claims of conscience
There are two additional arguments that might be advanced to justify selectively protecting negative appeals to conscience.

Permission to violate the law
One argument is based on the claim that whereas health care professionals who advance positive appeals to conscience seek permission to *violate* the law, health care professionals who advance negative appeals to conscience only seek protection from being required to provide legally permissible goods and services and do not seek permission to break the law. For example, a physician who has a conscience-based objection to Pennsylvania Act 169 seeks permission to violate the law. By contrast, a pharmacist who has a conscience-based objection to dispensing EC only seeks permission to refrain from engaging in a legally permissible activity. Hence, it is argued, insofar as it is inappropriate to endorse or condone law-breaking, it is warranted to selectively protect negative appeals to conscience.

Putting aside the issue of when it is or is not appropriate to endorse or condone law-breaking, there are two problems with this line of reasoning. First, it does not apply to all positive appeals to conscience. It applies only when health care professionals advance positive appeals to conscience in relation to laws that prohibit them from fulfilling a (perceived) ethical obligation. However, as the example of the pharmacist employed by a pharmacy with a policy against dispensing EC illustrates, health care professionals who advance positive appeals to conscience need not seek permission to break a law. The pharmacist who believes he has a duty to dispense EC merely seeks permission to engage in lawful and professionally permitted behavior.

Second, the foregoing line of reasoning begs the question because the issue is precisely whether legal and institutional rules should recognize and protect conscience-based objections. If Pennsylvania Act 169 were to recognize conscience-based exemptions, it would not be unlawful for physicians to honor the refusal directives of pregnant women. Conversely, if pharmacists were legally required to dispense EC to all patients with valid prescriptions unless there is a clinical counter indication in a particular case, then pharmacists with conscience-based objections to dispensing EC would seek permission to violate the law (or a legal exemption from the law).

Patient rights

A second argument alleges that protecting positive appeals to conscience will result in the infringement of important patient rights. This reason applies in some, but not all cases. For example, it applies in relation to physicians who are conscientiously opposed to forgoing medically provided nutrition and hydration (MPNH) in compliance with advance directives because they believe that they have an ethical obligation to provide it. To recognize such positive appeals to conscience would authorize physicians to provide treatment against the explicit wishes of patients.[45] However, this objection does not apply to a positive appeal to conscience in relation to Pennsylvania Act 169. Arguably protecting a physician's positive claim of conscience in this context would enable a physician to *respect* the rights of pregnant women. Generally, when advanced by providers who practice in an institutional environment with policies that prohibit forgoing MPNH or providing a legal and professionally accepted good or service, such as EC, abortion, or sterilization, protecting positive appeals to conscience can *safeguard* important patient rights.

CONCLUSION

Since the enactment of the Church Amendment in 1973, numerous conscience clauses have been enacted at both the federal and state levels in the United States. Although the aim of protecting the exercise of conscience by health care professionals is admirable, their obligations set limits to justified protections. Limits derived from core professional obligations include (1) a constraint against invidious discrimination; (2) a constraint against excessive patient harms and burdens; (3) a qualified requirement to disclose options; (4) a qualified requirement to refer and/or facilitate a transfer;

---

[45] Permission to withdraw from the case and transfer the patient's care to another physician who will honor the advance directive exempts a physician from an obligation to forgo MPNH in compliance with a patient's advance directive and protects a *negative* appeal to conscience. However, withdrawing from the case without fulfilling a perceived obligation to provide MPNH would not satisfy a *positive* appeal to conscience.

and (5) a qualified advance notification requirement. Other limits derive from obligations to employers, colleagues, and other professionals. Some conscience clauses exceed these limits and provide too much protection of conscience.

Typically, conscience clauses protect *negative* appeals to conscience and conscience-based *refusals* and offer no protection to *positive* appeals to conscience, which are advanced by health care professionals who claim to have a conscience-based obligation to *provide* professionally permitted goods or services. From the perspective of respecting moral integrity, the primary reason for protecting the exercise of conscience, there is no basis for selectively safeguarding negative appeals to conscience. Since a health care professional's moral integrity is at stake in either case, insofar as it is a value worth safeguarding in relation to negative appeals to conscience, it is also worth protecting in relation to positive appeals to conscience.

A consideration of a distinction between types of duties that underlie the two types of appeals to conscience fails to justify selectively protecting negative appeals to conscience. Arguments that appeal to the law and patient rights also fail to support selectively protecting negative appeals to conscience. Accordingly, it is not justified to safeguard negative appeals to conscience while summarily dismissing positive appeals to conscience.

References

Abbott, Jean (2005), 'Emergency Contraception: What Should Our Patients Expect?' *Annals of Emergency Medicine*, 46 (2), 111–13.

Abelson, Raziel (1982), 'To Do or Let Happen', *American Philosophical Quarterly*, 19 (3), 219–28.

Abelson, Reed and Singer, Natasha (2010), 'In Health Shift, More Patients Get Pharmacist's Appointment', *New York Times*, August 14, sec. A, p. 1, 11.

Alexander, John K. (2005), 'Promising, Professional Obligations, and the Refusal to Provide Service', *HEC Forum*, 17 (3), 178–95.

Allen, Rebecca H. and Goldberg, Alisa B. (2007), 'Emergency Contraception: A Clinical Review', *Clinical Obstetrics and Gynecology*, 50 (4), 927–36.

Allmark, Peter (1995), 'Can There be an Ethics of Care?' *Journal of Medical Ethics*, 21, 19–24.

Almeling, Rene, Tews, Laureen and Dudley, Susan (2000), 'Abortion Training in U.S. Obstetrics and Gynecology Residency Programs, 1998', *Family Planning Perspectives*, 32, 268–71, 320.

American College of Obstetricians and Gynecologists Committee on Ethics (2007), 'The Limits of Conscientious Refusal in Reproductive Medicine: ACOG Committee Opinion: No. 385', *Obstetrics and Gynecology*, 110 (5), 1203–8.

American Medical Association Council on Ethical and Judicial Affairs (2010), *Code of Medical Ethics: Current Opinions with Annotations 2010–11* (Chicago, IL: American Medical Association).

American Nurses Association (2003), *Nursing's Social Policy Statement* (2nd edn; Silver Spring, MD: American Nurses Association).

American Society of Health-System Pharmacists (1999), 'ASHP Statement on Pharmacist Decision-making on Assisted Suicide', *American Journal of Health-System Pharmacy*, 56 (16), 1661–4.

American Thoracic Society (1991), 'Withholding and Withdrawing Life-Sustaining Therapy', *Annals of Internal Medicine*, 115 (6), 478–85.

Amey, Annette L. and Bishai, David (2002), 'Measuring the Quality of Medical Care for Women Who Experience Sexual Assault With Data From the National Hospital Ambulatory Medical Care Survey', *Annals of Emergency Medicine*, 39 (6), 631–8.

Annas, George J. (1987), 'Transferring the Ethical Hot Potato', *The Hastings Center Report*, 17 (1), 20–1.

Anonymous (1987), *Guidelines on the Termination of Life-Sustaining Treatment and the Care of the Dying* (Briarcliff Manor, NY: The Hastings Center).

(1993), 'University of Pittsburgh Medical Center Policy and Procedure Manual: Management of Terminally Ill Patients Who May Become Organ Donors after Death', *Kennedy Institute of Ethics Journal*, 3 (2), A1–15.

(1996), 'The Goals of Medicine: Setting New Priorities', *The Hastings Center Report*, 25, S1–27.

(2002), 'ACOG Practice Bulletin Emergency Oral Contraception', *International Journal of Gynecology & Obstetrics*, 78, 191–8.

(2005), 'Moralists at the Pharmacy', *New York Times*, April 3, p. 12.

Arnold, Robert M. and Youngner, Stuart J. (1993), 'Back to the Future: Obtaining Organs from Non-Heart-Beating Cadavers', *Kennedy Institute of Ethics Journal*, 3 (2), 103–11.

Arras, John D. (1988), 'The Fragile Web of Responsibility: AIDS and the Duty to Treat', *The Hastings Center Report*, 18 (2), 10–20.

Baier, Annette (1986), 'Trust and Antitrust', *Ethics*, 96 (2), 231–60.

Baker, Peter (2009), 'Obama Reverses Rule On U.S. Abortion Aid', *New York Times*, January 24, sec. A, p. 13.

Baker, Robert (1995), 'Introduction', in Robert Baker (ed.), *The Codification of Medical Morality: Historical and Philosophical Studies of the Formalization of Western Medical Morality in the Eighteenth and Nineteenth Centuries* (vol. II; Dordrecht: Kluwer Academic Publishers), 1–22.

(2006), 'Medical Ethics and Epidemics: A Historical Perspective', in John Balint et al. (eds.), *Ethics and Epidemics* (Advances in Bioethics; Oxford, UK: Elsevier Ltd.), 93–133.

Baker, Robert B. *et al.* (1999), *The American Medical Ethics Revolution: How the AMA's Code of Ethics Has Transformed Physicians' Relationships to Patients, Professionals, and Society* (Baltimore, MD: Johns Hopkins University Press).

Bastianelli, Carlo, Farris, Manuela and Benagiano, G. (2008), 'Emergency Contraception: A Review', *The European Journal of Contraception and Reproductive Health Care*, 13 (1), 9–16.

Bayles, Michael D. (1979), 'A Problem of Clean Hands: Refusal to Provide Professional Services', *Social Theory and Practice*, 5 (2), 165–81.

Beauchamp, Tom L. and Childress, James F. (2009), *Principles of Biomedical Ethics* (6th edn; New York, NY: Oxford University Press).

Bell, John (1995), 'Introduction to the Code of Medical Ethics', in Baker (ed.), *The Codification of Medical Morality*, 65–72.

Belliotti, Raymond A. (1981), 'Negative and Positive Duties', *Theoria*, 47, 82–92.

Benfield, G. D. *et al.* (1991), 'Teaching Intubation Skills Using Newly Deceased Infants', *Journal of the American Medical Association*, 265 (18), 2360–3.

Benjamin, Martin (1990), *Splitting the Difference: Compromise and Integrity in Ethics and Politics* (University of Kansas Press).

(2004), 'Conscience', in Stephen G. Post (ed.), *Encyclopedia of Bioethics* (3rd edn, vol. I; New York: Macmillan Reference), 513–17.

Blum, Lawrence A. (1988), 'Gilligan and Kohlberg: Implications for Moral Theory', *Ethics*, 98, 472–91.

Blustein, Jeffrey (1993), 'Doing What the Patient Orders: Maintaining Integrity in the Doctor–Patient Relationship', *Bioethics*, 7 (4), 289–314.

Borrego, Matthew E. *et al.* (2006), 'New Mexico Pharmacists' Knowledge, Attitudes, and Beliefs Toward Prescribing Oral Emergency Contraception', *Journal of the American Pharmacists Association*, 46 (1), 33–43.

Bowman, Tom and Fishlock, Diana (2006), 'Rape Victim Denied Morning-After Pill', *Patriot News*, July 25, p. A-1.

British Medical Association (1999), *Withholding and Withdrawing Life-prolonging Medical Treatment: Guidance for decision making* (London: BMJ Books).

—— (2007), *Withholding and Withdrawing Life-prolonging Medical Treatment: Guidance for decision making* (3rd edn; Hoboken, NJ: John Wiley & Sons, Inc.).

Brock, Dan (2008), 'Conscientious Refusal by Physicians and Pharmacists: Who is Obligated to do What, and Why?' *Theoretical Medicine and Bioethics*, 29, 187–200.

Brock, Peter (2006), *Against the Draft: Essays on Conscientious Objection from the Radical Reformation to the Second World War* (University of Toronto Press).

Brodie, D. C., Parish, P. A. and Poston, J. W. (1980), 'Societal Needs for Drugs and Drug Related Services', *American Journal of Pharmaceutical Education*, 44, 276–8.

Brody, Howard (1994), 'The Physician's Role in Determining Futility', *Journal of the American Geriatrics Society*, 42 (8), 875–8.

—— and Miller, Franklin G. (1998), 'The Internal Morality of Medicine: Explication and Application to Managed Care', *Journal of Medicine and Philosophy*, 23 (4), 384–410.

Buchanan, Wyatt (2005), 'Doctor and Patient Both Say Their Liberty Was Violated', *San Francisco Chronicle*, July 29, sec. A.

Butler, Joseph (1827), *Sermons* (Cambridge, MA: Hilliard and Brown).

Canedy, Dana (1999), 'Wal-Mart Decides Against Selling a Contraceptive', *New York Times*, May 14, sec. C, p. 1.

Cantor, Julie (2009), 'Conscientious Objection Gone Awry – Restoring Selfless Professionalism in Medicine', *New England Journal of Medicine*, 360 (15), 1484–5.

—— and Baum, Ken (2004), 'The Limits of Conscientious Objection – May Pharmacists Refuse to Fill Prescriptions for Emergency Contraception?' *New England Journal of Medicine*, 351 (19), 2008–12.

Card, Robert F. (2007), 'Conscientious Objection and Emergency Contraception', *The American Journal of Bioethics*, 7 (6), 8–14.

Chervenak, Frank A. and McCullough, Laurence B. (2008), 'The Ethics of Direct and Indirect Referral for Termination of Pregnancy', *American Journal of Obstetrics and Gynecology*, 199, 232.e1–3.

Childress, James F. (1979), 'Appeals to Conscience', *Ethics*, 89 (4), 315–35.

(1985), 'Civil Disobedience, Conscientious Objection, and Evasive Noncompliance: A Framework for the Analysis and Assessment of Illegal Actions in Health Care', *Journal of Medicine and Philosophy*, 10, 63–83.

Cohen, Susan A. (2001), 'Global Gag Rule: Exporting Antiabortion Ideology at the Expense of American Values', *Guttmacher Report on Public Policy*, 1–3.

Cooper, Mary Carolyn (1988), 'Covenantal Relationships: Grounding for the Nursing Ethic', *Advances in Nursing Science*, 10 (4), 48–59.

Corley, Mary C. (2002), 'Nurse Moral Distress: A Proposed Theory and Research Agenda', *Nursing Ethics*, 9 (6), 636–50.

et al. (2001), 'Development and Evaluation of a Moral Distress Scale', *Journal of Advanced Nursing*, 33 (2), 250–6.

Council on Ethical and Judicial Affairs of the American Medical Association (2002), 'Performing Procedures on the Newly Deceased', *Academic Medicine*, 77 (12), 212–16.

Curlin, Farr A. *et al.* (2007), 'Religion, Conscience, and Controversial Clinical Practices', *New England Journal of Medicine*, 356 (6), 593–600.

Curtin, Leah L. (1979), 'The Nurse as Patient Advocate: a Philosophical Foundation for Nursing', *Advances in Nursing Science*, 1 (3), 1–10.

D'Arcy, Eric (1977), 'Conscience', *Journal of Medical Ethics*, 3, 98–9.

Daar, J. F. (1993), 'A Clash at the Bedside: Patient Autonomy v. A Physician's Professional Conscience', *Hastings Law Journal*, 44, 1241–89.

Daniels, Norman (1991), 'Duty to Treat or Right to Refuse?' *The Hastings Center Report*, 21 (2), 36–46.

(2008), *Just Health: Meeting Health Needs Fairly* (Cambridge University Press).

Davidoff, Frank and Trussell, James (2006), 'Plan B and the Politics of Doubt', *Journal of the American Medical Association*, 296 (14), 1775–8.

Davis, Bruce G. (1986), 'Defining the Employment Rights of Medical Personnel within the Parameters of Personal Conscience', *Detroit College Law Review*, 3, 847–78.

Davis, Nancy (1980), 'The Priority of Avoiding Harm', in Bonnie Steinbock (ed.), *Killing and Letting Die* (Englewood Cliffs, NJ: Prentice-Hall), 172–214.

Denny, Christopher J. and Kollek, Daniel (1999), 'Practicing Procedures on the Recently Dead', *Journal of Emergency Medicine*, 17 (6), 949–52.

Diekema, Douglas S. and Botkin, Jeffrey R. (2009), 'Clinical Report – Forgoing Medically Provided Nutrition and Hydration in Children', *Pediatrics*, 124 (2), 813–22.

Dodge, Susan (1989), 'Under Pressure from Students, Medical Schools Offer Alternatives to Use of Live Animals in Experiments', *The Chronicle of Higher Education*, A41, A43.

Dresser, Rebecca (2005), 'Professionals, Conformity, and Conscience', *The Hastings Center Report*, 35 (6), 9–10.

Durbach, Nadja (2005), *Bodily Matters: The Anti-Vaccination Movement in England, 1853–1907* (Durham, NC: Duke University Press).

Dworkin, Ronald (1978), *Taking Rights Seriously* (Cambridge, MA: Harvard University Press).

Eastwood, Katherine L. *et al.* (2006), 'U.S. Abortion Training', *Obstetrics and Gynecology*, 108 (2), 303–8.

Engelhardt, H. Tristram, Jr. (1986), *The Foundations of Bioethics* (New York, NY: Oxford University Press).

(2001), 'The DeChristianization of Christian Health Care Institutions, or, How the Pursuit of Social Justice and Excellence can Obscure the Pursuit of Holiness', *Christian Bioethics*, 7 (1), 151–61.

Evans, Emily, Patel, Mallika and Stranton, Derek (2007), 'Student Pharmacist Knowledge and Attitudes Regarding Oral Emergency Contraception', *Journal of the American Pharmacists Association*, 47, 711–16.

Feudtner, Chris, Christakis, Dimitri A. and Christakis, Nicholas A. (1994), 'Do Clinical Clerks Suffer Ethical Erosion? Students' Perceptions of their Ethical Environment and Personal Development', *Academic Medicine*, 69 (8), 670–9.

Fine, Paul *et al.* (2010), 'Ulipristal Acetate Taken 48–120 Hours After Intercourse for Emergency Contraception', *Obstetrics and Gynecology*, 115 (2), 257–63.

Fitzgerald, P. J. (1967), 'Acting and Refraining', *Analysis*, 27 (4), 133–9.

Foster, Angel M., van Dis, Jane and Steinauer, Jody (2003), 'Educational and Legislative Initiatives Affecting Residency Training in Abortion', *Journal of the American Medical Association*, 290 (13), 1777–8.

Foster, Angel M., Jackson, Courtney B. and Martin, Sarah B. (2008), 'Reproductive Health and Cyber (Mis)representations: A Content Analysis of Obstetrics and Gynecology Residency Program Websites', *Contraception*, 78, 99–105.

Foster, Diana G. *et al.* (2004), 'Knowledge of Emergency Contraception Among Women Aged 18 to 44 in California', *American Journal of Obstetrics and Gynecology*, 191, 150–6.

Fourre, Mark W. (2002), 'The Performance of Procedures on the Recently Deceased', *Academic Emergency Medicine*, 9 (6), 595–8.

Fowler, Marsha Diane Mary (2008), *Guide to the Code of Ethics for Nurses: Interpretation and Application* (Silver Spring, MD: American Nurses Association).

Frader, Joel and Bosk, Charles L. (2009), 'The Personal is Political, the Professional is Not: Conscientious Objection to Obtaining/Providing/Acting on Genetic Information', *American Journal of Medical Genetics Part C Seminars in Medical Genetics* 151C, 62–7.

Freedman, Lori R., Landy, Uta and Steinauer, Jody (2008), 'When There's a Heartbeat: Miscarriage Management in Catholic-Owned Hospitals', *American Journal of Public Health*, 98 (10), 1774–8.

Fry, Sara T. (1989), 'Toward a Theory of Nursing Ethics', *Advances in Nursing Science*, 11, 9–22.

(2008), 'Philosophical and Theoretical Issues in Nursing Ethics', in Winifred J. Ellenchild Pinch and Amy M. Haddad (eds.), *Nursing and Health Care Ethics: A Legacy and a Vision* (Silver Spring, MD: American Nurses Association), 45–55.

and Johnstone, Megan-Jane (2008), *Ethics in Nursing Practice: A Guide to Ethical Decision Making* (3rd edn; Oxford, UK: Wiley-Blackwell).

Fuss, Peter (1964), 'Conscience', *Ethics*, 74 (2), 111–20.

Gadow, Sally (1988), 'Covenant without Cure: Letting Go and Holding on to Chronic Illness', in Jean Watson and Marilyn A. Ray (eds.), *The Ethics of Care and the Ethics of Cure: Synthesis in Chronicity* (New York, NY: National League for Nursing), 5–14.

—— (1990), 'Existential Advocacy: Philosophical Foundations of Nursing', in T. Pence and J. Cantrall (eds), *Ethics in Nursing: An Anthology* (New York, NY: National League for Nursing), 40–51.

Gadow, Sally A. (1985), 'Nurse and Patient: The Caring Relationship', in Anne H. Bishop and John R. Scudder, Jr. (eds.), *Caring, Curing, Coping: Nurse Physician Patient Relationships* (University of Alabama Press), 31–43.

Gastmans, Chris (1999), 'Care as a Moral Attitude in Nursing', *Nursing Ethics*, 6 (3), 214–23.

Gease, Heidi Bell (2007), 'Pharmacist's Beliefs to Limit Birth-control Access: Next Closest Pharmacy 80 Miles Away', *Rapid City Journal*, December 17.

Gorr, Michael (1985), 'Some Reflections on the Difference Between Positive and Negative Duties', *Tulane Studies in Philosophy*, XXXIII, 93–100.

Grace, Pamela J. (2001), 'Professional Advocacy: Widening the Scope of Accountability', *Nursing Philosophy*, 2, 151–62.

Green, O. H. (1980), 'Killing and Letting Die', *American Philosophical Quarterly*, 17, 195–204.

Hamric, Ann B. (2000), 'Moral Distress in Everyday Ethics', *Nursing Outlook*, 48, 199–201.

—— and Blackhall, Leslie J. (2007), 'Nurse–Physician Perspectives on the Care of Dying Patients in Intensive Care Units: Collaboration, Moral Distress, and Ethical Climate', *Critical Care Medicine*, 35 (2), 422–9.

Hansen, Laura B., Saseen, Joseph J. and Teal, Stephanie B. (2007), 'Levonorgestrel-Only Dosing Strategies for Emergency Contraception', *Pharmacotherapy*, 27 (2), 278–84.

Harman, Gilbert (1996), 'Moral Relativism', in Gilbert Harman and Judith Jarvis Thomson (eds.), *Moral Relativism and Moral Objectivity* (Cambridge, MA: Blackwell Publishers), 3–19.

Harris, Gardiner (2010), 'U. S. Approves a Second Pill for After Sex', *New York Times*, August 14, sec. A, p. 1, 3.

Harrison, Teresa (2005), 'Availability of Emergency Contraception: A Survey of Hospital Emergency Department Staff', *Annals of Emergency Medicine*, 46 (2), 105–10.

Hart, L. Gary, Norris, Thomas E. and Lishner, Denise M. (2003), 'Attitudes of Family Physicians in Washington State Toward Physician-Assisted Suicide', *The Journal of Rural Health*, 19 (4), 461–9.

Hays, Issac (1995), 'Code of Ethics', in Baker (ed.), *The Codification of Medical Morality*, 75–87.

Hepler, Charles D. (1979), 'Professions in Modern Society: Contract vs. Covenant', *Pharmacy Management*, 151 (3), 102–4.

(1985), 'Pharmacy as a Clinical Profession', *American Journal of Hospital Pharmacy*, 42, 1298–306.

(1987), 'The Third Wave in Pharmaceutical Education: The Clinical Movement', *American Journal of Pharmaceutical Education*, 51 (4), 369–85.

(1996), 'Philosophical Issues Raised by Pharmaceutical Care', in Amy Marie Haddad and Robert A. Buerki (eds.), *Ethical Dimensions of Pharmaceutical Care* (Binghamton, NY: Pharmaceutical Products Press), 19–47.

(2005), 'Balancing Pharmacists' Conscientious Objections with Their Duty to Serve', *Journal of the American Pharmacists Association*, 45 (4), 434–6.

and Strand, Linda M. (1990), 'Opportunities and Responsibilities in Pharmaceutical Care', *American Journal of Hospital Pharmacy*, 47, 533–43.

Herbe, Donald W. (2002), 'The Right to Refuse: A Call for Adequate Protection of a Pharmacist's Right to Refuse Facilitation of Abortion and Emergency Contraception', *Journal of Law and Health*, 17 (1), 77–102.

Hicks, Lisa K. *et al.* (2001), 'Understanding the Clinical Dilemmas that Shape Medical Students' Ethical Development: Questionnaire Survey and Focus Group Study', *British Medical Journal*, 322 (24), 709–10.

Ho, P. C. and Kwan, M. S. W. (1993), 'A Prospective Randomized Comparison of Levonorgestrel with the Yuzpe Regimen in Post-Coital Contraception', *Human Reproduction*, 8 (3), 389–92.

Hook, Sidney (1971), 'Social Protest and Civil Obedience', in Jeffrie G. Murphy (ed.), *Civil Disobedience and Violence* (Belmont, CA: Wadsworth Publishing Company, Inc.), 53–63.

Jameton, Andrew (1984), *Nursing Practice: The Ethical Issues* (Englewood Cliffs, NJ: Prentice Hall).

(1993), 'Dilemmas of Moral Distress: Moral Responsibility and Nursing Practice', *AWHONNS Clinical Issues in Perinatal and Women's Health Nursing*, 4 (4), 542–51.

Jansen, Lynn A. (2004), 'No Safe Harbor: The Principle of Complicity and the Practice of Voluntarily Stopping of Eating and Drinking', *Journal of Medicine and Philosophy*, 29 (1), 61–74.

Jones, Rachel K. *et al.* (2008), 'Abortion in the United States: Incidence and Access to Services, 2005', *Perspectives on Sexual and Reproductive Health*, 40 (1), 6–16.

Kadish, Sanford H. (1985), 'Complicity, Cause and Blame: A Study in the Interpretation of Doctrine', *California Law Review*, 73 (2), 323–410.

(1997), 'Reckless Complicity', *The Journal of Criminal Law and Criminology*, 87 (2), 369–94.

Kagan, Shelly (1998), *Normative Ethics* (Boulder, CO: Westview Press).

Kaldjian, L. C. *et al.* (2004a), 'Internists' Attitudes Towards Terminal Sedation in End of Life', *Journal of Medical Ethics*, 30, 499–503.

Kaldjian, Lauris C. *et al.* (2004b), 'Medical House Officers' Attitudes Toward Vigorous Analgesia, Terminal Sedation, and Physician-assisted Suicide', *American Journal of Hospice & Palliative Medicine* (5), 381–7.

Kälvemark, S. *et al.* (2004), 'Living with Conflicts – Ethical Dilemmas and Moral Distress in the Health Care System', *Social Science & Medicine*, 58, 1075–84.

Kälvemark, Sporrong S., Höglund, A. and Arnetz, B. (2006), 'Measuring Moral Distress in Pharmacy and Clinical Practice', *Nursing Ethics*, 13, 416–27.

Knowlton, Brian (2010), 'U.S. Job Site Bans Bias Over Gender Identity', *New York Times*, January 6, sec. A, p. 15.

Kristof, Nicholas D. (2010), 'Sister Margaret's Choice', *New York Times*, May 27, sec. A, p. 35.

Kroeger-Mappes, Joy (2001), 'Ethical Dilemmas for Nurses: Physicians' Orders versus Patients' Rights', in Thomas A. Mappes and David DeGrazia (eds.), *Biomedical Ethics* (5th edn; Boston: McGraw-Hill), 161–8.

LaFollette, Eva and LaFollette, Hugh (2007), 'Private Conscience, Public Acts', *Journal of Medical Ethics*, 33, 249–54.

Lawrence, Ryan E. and Curlin, Farr A. (2007), 'Clash of Definitions: Controversies About Conscience in Medicine', *The American Journal of Bioethics*, 7 (12), 10–14.

Liptak, Adam (2010), 'Justices, 5–4, Reject Corporate Spending Limit', *New York Times*, January 22, sec. A, p. 1.

Lumalcuri, James and Hale, Ralph W. (2010), 'Medical Liability: An Ongoing Nemesis', *Obstetrics & Gynecology*, 115 (2, Part 1), 223–8.

Lynch, Holly Fernandez (2008), *Conflicts of Conscience in Health Care: An Institutional Compromise* (Cambridge, MA: The MIT Press).

Macklin, Ruth (1998), 'Ethical Relativism in a Multicultural Society', *Kennedy Institute of Ethics Journal*, 8 (1), 1–22.

Malm, H. M. (1991), 'Between the Horns of the Negative–Positive Duty Debate', *Philosophical Studies*, 61, 187–210.

Malpass, Susie (1976), 'Hospitals – a Current Analysis of the Right to Abortions and Sterilizations in the Fourth Circuit: State Action and the Church Amendment', *North Carolina Law Review*, 54 (6), 1307–16.

May, William F. (1975), 'Code, Covenant, Contract, or Philanthropy', *The Hastings Center Report*, 5 (6), 29–38.

(1983), *The Physician's Covenant: Images of the Healer in Medical Ethics* (Philadelphia, PA: Westminster Press).

McLeod, Carolyn (2008), 'Referral in the Wake of Conscientious Objection to Abortion', *Hypatia*, 23 (4).

Medical School Objectives Project (1998), 'Report I: Learning Objectives for Medical Student Education: Guidelines for Medical Schools' (Washington, DC: American Association of Medical Colleges), 1–13.

Meisel, Alan and Cerminara, Kathy L. (2009), *The Right to Die: The Law of End-of-Life Decisionmaking* (3rd edn, 2009 Supplement edn; Austin: Wolters Kluwer).

Merchant, Roland C. *et al.* (2007), 'Patients' Emergency Contraception Comprehension, Usage, and View of the Emergency Department Role for Emergency Contraception', *The Journal of Emergency Medicine*, 33 (4), 367–75.

Miller, Franklin G. and Brody, Howard (1995), 'Professional Integrity and Physician-Assisted Death', *The Hastings Center Report*, 25 (3), 8–16.

(2001), 'The Internal Morality of Medicine: An Evolutionary Perspective', *Journal of Medicine and Philosophy*, 26 (6), 581–99.

and Chung, Kevin C. (2000), 'Cosmetic Surgery and the Internal Morality of Medicine', *Cambridge Quarterly of Healthcare Ethics*, 9 (3), 353–64.

Mohl, Bruce (2006), 'State Orders Wal-Mart to Sell Morning-After Pill', *Boston Globe*, February 15, p. F1.

Moran, Greg (2005), 'Maternal Wish, Doctors' Faith at Odds in Court', *The San Diego Union-Tribune*, August 7, sec. News, p. A-1.

Mullan, Kenneth, Allen, William L. and Brushwood, David B. (1996), 'Conscientious Objection to Assisted Death: Can Pharmacy Address this in a Systematic Fashion?' *Annals of Pharmacology*, 30, 1185–91.

Narveson, Jan (1985), 'Positive/Negative: Why Bother?' *Tulane Studies in Philosophy*, XXXIII, 51–65.

Noddings, Nel (1984), *Caring: A Feminine Approach to Ethics & Moral Education.* (Berkeley, CA: University of California Press).

Nunn, Amy *et al.* (2003), 'Contraceptive Emergency: Catholic Hospitals Overwhelmingly Refuse to Provide EC', *Conscience*, 38–41.

Nussbaum, Martha C. (2008), *Liberty of Conscience: In Defense of America's Tradition of Religious Equality* (New York, NY: Basic Books).

O'Rourke, Kevin (2001), 'Catholic Hospitals and Catholic Identity', *Christian Bioethics*, 7 (1), 15–28.

Osnos, Evan (2002), 'NYC Leads New Effort to Train MDs in Abortions', *Chicago Tribune*, July 4, p. 1.

Pauly, Bernadette *et al.* (2009), 'Registered Nurses' Perceptions of Moral Distress and Ethical Climate', *Nursing Ethics*, 16 (5), 561–73.

Pear, Robert (2008a), 'Abortion Proposal Sets Condition on Aid', *New York Times*, July 15, sec. A, p. 17.

(2008b), 'Protests Over a Rule to Protect Health Providers', *New York Times*, November 18, sec. A, p. 14.

Pellegrino, Edmund D. (1993), *The Virtues in Medical Practice* (New York: Oxford University Press).

(1994), 'Patient and Physician Autonomy: Conflicting Rights and Obligations in the Physician–Patient Relationship', *Journal of Contemporary Health Law and Policy*, 10, 47–68.

(2001), 'The Internal Morality of Clinical Medicine: A Paradigm for the Ethics of the Helping and Healing Professions', *Journal of Medicine and Philosophy*, 26 (6), 559–79.

(2002a), 'Professionalism, Profession and the Virtues of the Good Physician', *Mount Sinai Journal of Medicine*, 69 (6), 378–84.

(2002b), 'The Physician's Conscience, Conscience Clauses, and Religious Beliefs: A Catholic Perspective', *Fordham Urban Law Journal*, 30, 221–44.

(2006), 'Toward a Reconstruction of Medical Morality', *American Journal of Bioethics*, 6 (2), 65–71.

and Thomasma, David C. (1981), *A Philosophical Basis of Medical Practice: Toward a Philosophy and Ethic of the Healing Professions* (New York: Oxford University Press).

Pence, Gregory E. (2004), *Classic Cases in Medical Ethics: Accounts of Cases that Have Shaped Medical Ethics, with Philosophical, Legal, and Historical Backgrounds* (Boston: McGraw-Hill).

Phaneuf, Maria C. (1972), *The Nursing Audit: Self-regulation in Nursing Practice* (New York, NY: Appleton-Century-Crofts).

Pitts, Leonard, Jr. (2005), 'Find Another Job; Pharmacists Who Refuse to Sell Contraceptives Should Take a Hike', *Pittsburgh Post-Gazette*, April 22, sec. A, p. 13.

Polis, Chelsea, Schaffer, Kate and Harrison, Teresa (2005), 'Accessibility of Emergency Contraception in California's Catholic Hospitals', *Women's Health Issues*, 15, 174–8.

President's Commission for the Study of Ethical Problems in Medicine and Biomedical and Behavioral Research (1983), *Deciding to Forego Life-Sustaining Treatment: Ethical, Medical, and Legal Issues in Treatment Decisions* (Washington, DC: US Government Printing Office).

Prine, Linda (2007), 'Emergency Contraception, Myths and Facts', *Obstetrics and Gynecology Clinics of North America*, 34, 127–36.

Ragland, Denise and West, Donna (2009), 'Pharmacy Students' Knowledge, Attitudes, and Behaviors Regarding Emergency Contraception', *American Journal of Pharmaceutical Education*, 73 (2), 1–4.

Repenshek, Mark and Slosar, John Paul (2004), 'Medically Assisted Nutrition and Hydration: A Contribution to the Dialogue', *The Hastings Center Report*, 34 (6), 13–16.

Rhodes, Rosamond (2006), 'The Ethical Standard of Care', *American Journal of Bioethics*, 6 (2), 76–8.

Rietjens, Judith A. C. *et al.* (2007), 'Having a Difficult Time Leaving: Experiences and Attitudes of Nurses with Palliative Sedation', *Palliative Medicine*, 21, 643–9.

Ritter, Jim (2005), 'Planned Parenthood Protests Over Morning-After Pill; Downtown Pharmacist Wouldn't Sell Emergency Contraceptive', *Chicago Sun-Times*, March 23, sec. News, p. 10.

Savulescu, Julian (2006), 'Conscientious Objection in Medicine', *British Medical Journal*, 332, 294–7.

Schlissel, Lillian (1968), *Conscience in America: A Documentary History of Conscientious Objection in America, 1757–1967* (New York: E.P. Dutton & Co., Inc.).

Schneider, Jason S. and Levin, Saul (1999), 'Uneasy Partners: The Lesbian and Gay Health Care Community and the AMA', *Journal of the American Medical Society*, 282 (13), 1287–8.

Scolaro, Kelly L. (2007), 'OTC Product: Plan B Emergency Contraception', *Journal of the American Pharmacists Association*, 47 (2), e2–e3.

Shannon, Thomas A. (2001), 'Living the Vision: Health Care, Social Justice and Institutional Identity', *Christian Bioethics* 7(1), 49–65.

(2005), 'Nutrition and Hydration (letter)', *The Hastings Center Report*, 35 (3), 4.

and Walter, James J. (2004), 'Implications of the Papal Allocution on Feeding Tubes', *Hastings Center Report*, 34 (4), 18–20.

Sibley, Muford Q. and Jacob, Philip E. (1952), *Conscription of Conscience: The American State and the Conscientious Objector, 1940–1947* (Ithaca, NY: Cornell University Press).

Singer, Marcus G. (1965), 'Negative and Positive Duties', *The Philosophical Quarterly*, 15 (59), 97–103.

Smith Iltis, Ana (2001), 'Institutional Integrity in Roman Catholic Health Care Institutions', *Christian Bioethics*, 7 (1), 95–103.

Smugar, Steven S., Spina, Bernadette J. and Merz, Jon F. (2000), 'Informed Consent for Emergency Contraception: Variability in Hospital Care of Rape Victims', *American Journal of Public Health*, 90 (9), 1372–6.

Stein, Rob (2005), 'Pharmacists' Rights at Front of New Debate: Because of Beliefs, Some Refuse to Fill Birth Control Prescriptions', *Washington Post*, March 28, sec. A, p. 1.

—— (2006), 'FDA Approves Plan B's Over-the-Counter Sale: No Prescription Will Be Required for Women 18 or Older', *Washington Post*, August 25, sec. A.

—— (2008a), 'Protections Set for Antiabortion Health Workers', *Washington Post*, August 21, sec. A, p. 1.

—— (2008b), '"Pro-Life" Drugstores Market Beliefs: No Contraceptives For Chantilly Shop', *Washington Post*, June 16, sec. A, p. 1.

—— (2009a), '17-Year-Olds to Gain Access to Plan B Pill', *Washington Post*, April 23, sec. A, p. 3.

—— (2009b), 'Government Approves Study Using Human Embryonic Stem Cells', *Washington Post*, January 24, p. A06.

Stempsey, William E. (2001), 'Institutional Identity and Roman Catholic Hospitals', *Christian Bioethics*, 7 (1), 3–14.

Stenberg, Marjorie J. (1979), 'The Search for a Conceptual Framework as a Philosophic Basis for Nursing Ethics: An Examination of Code, Contract, Context, and Covenant', *Military Medicine*, 144 (1), 9–22.

Sulmasy, Daniel P. (2007), 'Preserving Life? The Vatican & PVS', *Commonweal*, CXXXIV (21), 16–18.

—— (2008), 'What is Conscience and Why is Respect for it so Important?' *Theoretical Medicine and Bioethics*, 29, 135–49.

Tanne, Janice Hopkins (2005), 'Emergency Contraception is Under Attack by US Pharmacists', *British Medical Journal*, 330, 983.

—— (2008), 'US Health Groups Protest Against Proposed Government "Conscience Rule"', *British Medical Journal*, 2008 (337), 7673.

Task Force on Postovulatory Methods of Fertility Regulation (1998), 'Randomised Controlled Trial of Levonorgestrel Versus the Yuzpe Regimen of Combined Oral Contraceptives for Emergency Contraception', *Lancet*, 352, 428–33.

Task Force to Develop the Care of Terminally-Ill Oregonians (1998), *The Oregon Death With Dignity Act: A Guidebook for Health Care Providers* (Portland, OR: Center for Ethics in Health Care).

Temin, Elizabeth *et al.* (2005), 'Availability of Emergency Contraception in Massachusetts Emergency Departments', *Academic Emergency Medicine*, 12 (10).

Trammell, Richard L. (1975), 'Saving Life and Taking Life', *The Journal of Philosophy*, 72 (5), 131–7.

Trammell, Richard Louis (1985), 'A Criterion for Determining Negativity and Positivity', *Tulane Studies in Philosophy*, XXXIII, 75–81.

United States Conference of Catholic Bishops (2009), *Ethical and Religious Directives for Catholic Health Care Services*, 5th edn (Washington, DC: USCCB Publishing).

Uustal, Diann B. (1987), 'Values: The Cornerstone of Nursing's Moral Art', in Marsha D. M. Fowler and June Levine-Ariff (eds.), *Ethics at the Bedside: A Source Book for the Critical Care Nurse* (Philadelphia, PA: J. B. Lippincott Company), 136–53.

Van Riper, Kristi K. and Hellerstedt, Wendy L. (2005), 'Emergency Contraceptive Pills: Dispensing Practices, Knowledge and Attitudes of South Dakota Pharmacists', *Perspectives on Sexual and Reproductive Health*, 37 (1), 19–24.

Veatch, Robert M. (1981), *A Theory of Medical Ethics* (New York, NY: Basic Books, Inc.).

Wallace, Jennifer L. *et al.* (2004), 'Emergency Contraception: Knowledge and Attitudes of Family Medicine Providers', *Family Medicine*, 36 (6), 417–21.

Wardle, Lynn D. (1993), 'Protecting the Rights of Conscience of Health Care Providers', *The Journal of Legal Medicine*, 14, 177–230.

Wear, Stephen (1991), 'The Moral Significance of Institutional Integrity', *The Journal of Medicine and Philosophy*, 16, 225–30.

LaGaipa, Susan and Logue, Gerald (1994), 'Toleration of Moral Diversity and the Conscientious Refusal by Physicians to Withdraw Life-Sustaining Treatments', *Journal of Medicine and Philosophy*, 19 (2), 147–59.

Weier, Anita (2004), 'Patient, Pharmacist Collide: Birth Control Pill Conflict Shows Dilemma', *Capital Times*, March 16, sec. Front, p. A-1.

Wicclair, Mark R. (2000), 'Conscientious Objection in Medicine', *Bioethics*, 14 (3), 205–27.

(2006), 'Pharmacies, Pharmacists, and Conscientious Objection', *Kennedy Institute of Ethics Journal*, 16 (3), 225–50.

(2007), 'Reasons and Healthcare Professionals' Claims of Conscience', *American Journal of Bioethics*, 7 (6), 21–2.

(2008), 'Is Conscientious Objection Incompatible with a Physician's Professional Obligations?' *Theoretical Medicine and Bioethics*, 29 (3), 171–85.

(2009), 'Negative and Positive Claims of Conscience', *Cambridge Quarterly of Healthcare Ethics*, 18 (1), 14–22.

(2010), 'Conscience-Based Exemptions for Medical Students', *Cambridge Quarterly of Healthcare Ethics*, 19 (1), 38–50.

Wildes, Kevin Wm. (1997), 'Institutional Identity, Integrity, and Conscience', *Kennedy Institute of Ethics Journal*, 7 (4), 413–19.

Wilson, Durr (2009), 'Patching a Wound: Working to End Conflicts at Harvard Medical', *New York Times*, March 3, sec. Business Day, p. B1, B6.

Winckler, Susan C. and Gans, John A. (2006), 'Conscientious Objection and Collaborative Practice: Conflicting or Complementary Initiatives?' *Journal of the American Pharmacists Association*, 46 (1), 12–13.

Wreen, Michael (1984), 'Breathing a Little Life into a Distinction', *Philosophical Studies*, 46, 395–402.

Index